Interactive Multimedia Instruction

INTERACTIVE MULTIMEDIA INSTRUCTION

RICHARD A. SCHWIER
EARL R. MISANCHUK

THE UNIVERSITY OF SASKATCHEWAN

EDUCATIONAL TECHNOLOGY PUBLICATIONS
ENGLEWOOD CLIFFS, NEW JERSEY 07632

Camera-ready copy was prepared for this book by Earl R. Misanchuk and Richard A. Schwier on Macintoshes, and output to a Laser-Writer IIg. The primary software used was Microsoft Word 5.0 and Canvas 3.0.

Comments and corrections should be sent to the authors at:

Richard A. Schwier
College of Education

Earl R. Misanchuk
Extension Division

The University of Saskatchewan
Saskatoon, SK S7N 0W0

(306) 966-7641
(306) 966-8719 (Fax)

(306) 966-5555
(306) 966-5567 (Fax)

SCHWIER@SASK.USASK.CA

MISANCHUK@SASK.USASK.CA

Library of Congress Cataloging-in-Publication Data

Schwier, Richard
    Interactive multimedia instruction / Richard A. Schwier, Earl R. Misanchuk.
        p. cm.
    Includes bibliographical references and index.
    ISBN 0-87778-251-2
    1. Educational technology. 2. Interactive media. 3. Teaching—Aids and devices. I. Misanchuk, Earl R. II. Title.
LB1028.3.S378 1993
371.3'078—dc20   92-29627
                                                         CIP

Printed in the United States of America.

Library of Congress Catalog Card Number: 92-29627.

International Standard Book Number: 0-87778-251-2.

First Printing: January, 1993.
Second Printing: June, 1994.

Acknowledgments

Many people helped shape our thinking on this subject; our list of references reflects that fact. In addition to written works, we learned much through other means of communication: Larry Katz inspired us with fine examples of his work during a visit to our campus, and Milt Petruk was one of our most influential "teachers." We would also particularly like to acknowledge Len Proctor, Barry Brown, Robert Powell, Karin Melberg Schwier, and Linda Misanchuk, who provided us with valuable advice, information, and encouragement. Michael Misanchuk, Robert Kavanagh, and Kate Hardy helped clarify and illustrate some concepts.

Others contributed in other ways: Dave Snell did the original artwork for several illustrations, Guy Poncelet kindly allowed us to use some screens from a HyperCard stack he created, and Elizabeth Porat and Shannon Cossette did some word processing.

The editorial assistance of Lawrence Lipsitz and the Educational Technology Publications staff is much appreciated. Thanks are also due the Extension Division and the College of Education at the University of Saskatchewan for facilities and support for this project.

This book is dedicated to

Momo and Bobo
(RAS)

and to

Linda, Melanie, and Michael
(ERM)

Preface

This book is about interactive multimedia instruction (IMI). It includes some of the production and design material from *Interactive Video*, published in 1987. Soon after that book was released, the world of interactive media exploded. Hence, this book is very different from its parent. It considers, by necessity, a wider range of media and ways in which media can be combined to create powerful learning systems.

Perhaps the most dramatic change we have witnessed in the progression of instructional technology is the convergence of media. Multimedia used to imply a cardboard box (typically a large one) containing a host of different media (slides, audio tapes, models, simulation-games, videotapes, realia, and supporting print materials) which required the instructor or learner to use an array of equipment. Multimedia still implies a box—a computer—which manages (and in many cases houses internally) all of the components formerly contained in the cardboard box. It transparently combines text, audio, full-motion and still-frame video, digital graphics, and animation. The various source media blend into a single delivery medium. Authoring tools provide ease of use, impressive (yet still improving) flexibility, and the capability to track a multitude of learner performance variables during instruction. Also, in recent years, a great deal has been written about, and research conducted on, the design of interactive media. Despite changes in media comprising a multimedia system, the design principles underlying successful instructional designs survive. This book attempts to pull together much of that knowledge, and derive a reasoned examination of IMI which will help instructional designers exploit this hybrid medium fully.

This book is divided into four main sections:

- Interactive Multimedia Instruction Systems

- Components of Interactive Multimedia Instruction

- Designing Interactive Multimedia Instruction

- Interactive Multimedia Resources

Section I, *Interactive Multimedia Instruction Systems*, defines the parameters of IMI and examines the instructional settings in which IMI operates. The section also describes conventional levels of interactivity and proposes a new taxonomy of interaction based on three qualitative levels of interactivity.

Section II, *Components of Interactive Multimedia Instruction*, describes IMI environments, discusses the various components which comprise multimedia environments and their strengths and limitations, and describes learner interfaces. It also sets out production specifications and procedures for videodisc, CD-ROM, and computer authoring systems.

Section III, *Designing Interactive Multimedia Instruction*, looks at analyzing, designing, and evaluating interactive multimedia projects. What are some of the unique considerations for developing this type of instruction? What instructional design issues impact the development process? What does research tell us about the design of interactive multimedia instruction?

Section IV, *Interactive Multimedia Resources*, offers a collection of references for anyone designing interactive multimedia instruction. It includes a glossary of terms, lists of software distributors and producers, recommended readings, and an assortment of helpful materials.

This book is only about multimedia systems which are interactive and instructional. Some marvelous applications of multimedia are largely passive—you watch them, and you are usually impressed by them, but you are not invited to interact with them. Other applications are primarily commercial or entertaining, but not instructional. This book will not concern itself with those environments. We will, instead, focus on environments where learning is the principal outcome, superordinate to sales or pleasure. Certainly there is some overlap, and different purposes can be served by the same systems. But where a choice is to be made between what looks good and what facilitates learning, we will opt for the latter in these pages. For example, some research has demonstrated that for novice learners, simple line representations are more effective than realistic, complex, highly saturated illustrations (Dwyer, 1978; Fleming and Levie, 1978). The critical attributes of a visual are more apparent in a simple representation. So if instruction to novice learners is the primary purpose to which a particular visual will be put, then an instructional designer should opt for a simple drawing of a heart, even though a motion video treatment of an actual human heart might be more visually appealing. At the same time, there is some evidence that realistic cues may be more effective than less realistic cues in stimulating recall, and this may be attributed to encoding processes. Realistic cues may present a more complete representation of the learner's schemata, resulting in easier and more complete encoding (Jesky and Berry, 1991). This may suggest that more sophisticated learners can benefit from more realistic, and therefore complex, visuals.

As much as possible, any recommendations we make are based on research, and attributed to the source. Beyond conventional professional and academic reasons for this, we feel there is a need to highlight some of the outstanding thinking and inquiry which is converging on this technology from direct and indirect quarters. This area of study and development owes a great deal to individuals such as Michael Hannafin, David Jonassen, David Merrill, Scott Grabinger, Jane Azbel, Brock Allen, Diane Gayeski, Larry Katz, Chris Dede, Mariela Tovar, and Ed Schwartz, to name but a very few who have pioneered (no product endorsement intended) research and development efforts. We believe in the importance of research, and have attempted to use it to inform our recommendations in this work.

In this book, we use a book icon to direct you to additional or related information that we feel is especially noteworthy.

 A particularly significant book or article is recommended for additional reading.

Some technical terms are used in passing early in the book, before they are defined or explained. If you feel the need for a definition or explanation of the terms, you can refer to the Glossary. Commercial products and trademarked names are identified with the appropriate ™ or ® symbols the first time they are used; thereafter the symbols do not appear. If we inadvertently used a trademarked name without the appropriate credit, we would appreciate being informed so that we might correct our error in subsequent editions.

This book was laid out according to the principles presented in *Preparing Instructional Text: Document Design Using Desktop Publishing* (Educational Technology Publications, Inc., 1992).

Contents

Section I: Interactive Multimedia Instruction Systems

Section II: Components of Interactive Multimedia Instruction

Section III: Designing Interactive Multimedia Instruction

Section IV: Resources for Interactive Multimedia Instruction

Figures

Section I

Interactive Multimedia Instruction Systems

Chapter 1

Definition of Interactive Multimedia Instruction

It is not a simple matter to offer a concise working definition of interactive multimedia instruction. By its very nature, IMI is invertebrate. You poke it, and it slithers away. It can be constructed from an array of media, each of which has particular strengths and limitations. IMI systems can be quite modest, restricted to some computer-assisted instruction (CAI) and print materials, or extremely elaborate, including videodisc, CD-ROM, hypermedia, and virtual reality interfacing. And, of course, as every instructional designer knows, the power of an instructional approach lies in the science and art of instruction—not in the technological components which comprise a hardware system. Discussing this very problem, Rockley Miller (1990) articulated the challenge.

> ...imagine [an orchestra in which] each musician not only plays a different instrument, but also speaks a different language. Such is the case with interactive video, where the assembled team includes instructional designers who speak of authoring, pedagogics and remediation; graphic artists who talk of drop shadows, GUI's, and animated sprites; video producers who think in terms of wipes, fades, pictures, plots, scenes, and storylines; and computer specialists who deal in bits and bytes, images and data, icons, picons, micons, and programming languages all their own.

> Add a systems person who wants to integrate LDs and CD-ROMs with DVI and Windows via SCSI or RS232 ports, and then telecommunicate the whole mess to a host; an accountant who wants to estimate the cost per instructional seat-minute or unit of customer interaction; and of course, don't forget the subject matter expert who may know nothing about anything but hydraulic engineering (p. xvii).

Another problem in finding a useful definition is the rapid and seemingly endless changes occurring in the technology and language of IMI. Several definitions of the term exist (Galbreath, 1992). As we reviewed the precursor to this book, published in 1987, it was very apparent how quickly and dramatically the field has changed—and how vulnerable such a book is to the ravages of time.

So what are the stable characteristics of interactive multimedia instruction? Can a definition capture the essence of the medium and be sufficiently flexible to accommodate changes yet unknown? We will attempt to provide just such a definition by concentrating on the instructional features of IMI, in preference to the technical and systems features.

IMI is:

- instructional,
- multiply-sourced (i.e., multiple media sources are involved),
- segmented,
- intentionally designed, and
- coherent.

A prerequisite characteristic of IMI is that it is instructional. Many engaging uses of multimedia are possible. Point-of-purchase displays use touch screen video, computer programs, and other input devices for sales. Public information stations in several urban locations provide information about local attractions, restaurants, and the like. The entertainment industry is replete with extremely complex and powerful multimedia attractions. For example, the Back to the Future and Star Tours attractions at Universal Studios and Disneyland combine video, special effects and lighting, animatronics, and motion in a simulator. While good instruction may share some of the technology and characteristics of these other uses, the primary focus of IMI is always learning.

Interactive multimedia instruction brings mediated instruction from more than one source to bear on an instructional problem which the learner experiences as an integrated (although sometimes complex) medium. We can think of it in terms of many single inputs, with one multi-channel output. The instruction may contain motion images from a video disc, computer animation, text screens, and sound from a compact disc, for example, but the instruction is a tapestry woven from these sources. The learner experiences the tapestry, not the individual threads. What is the instructional effect of experiencing several channels of information proximately or simultaneously? Studies suggest that it is the nature of the instruction that matters. Content-relevant illustrations, coupled with text can provide significant gains, perhaps because each source provides unique and complementary information; perceptual capacity seems to increase where two modalities are used. On the other hand, purely redundant channels or unrelated cues in two channels can produce no gain, or even interfere with learning. There is also evidence that this relationship may also hold for sound-visual pairings (Fleming, 1987; Grimes, 1990; Mann, 1992). Also, if a presentation is too rapid, a learner must choose from among the sources competing for attention (Fleming and Levie, 1978, pp. 60–64). The upshot of this is that the effectiveness of multimedia instruction depends on the relationships built among its component parts, and the instructional designer must be on the lookout for complementary and antagonistic interactions.

Commonly, interactive multimedia instruction is broken into segments, rather than presented in a linear fashion. These "pieces" may be made up of motion sequences, still frames, questions, menus, audio, or combinations of these, and they define an array of paths the viewer may follow through the presentation. To facilitate "navigation," IMI incorporates periodic and structured input from the learner. In most cases, the input received from the learner will determine the number and sequence of instructional segments encountered, and therefore influence the shape or nature of the instruction received. In other words, interactivity relinquishes some control of the instructional presentation, and places it in the hands of the learner.

Another feature of IMI is its intentional design. Other media, singly or in combinations, may be susceptible to viewer intervention, and be confused with interactive multimedia. For instance, anyone watching a videotape can watch segments, rewind and watch segments again, or fast-forward to later sections. Thus, there are several hundred potential "paths" through the instruction, and they are learner controlled. Still, this is not an example of interactive multimedia, because the interactivity was not planned by the producer, and thus the program is not intentionally interactive.

Another feature of interactive multimedia instruction is the relationship among the various elements combined at any given time. Text, illustrations, animation, and full-motion video comprising a multimedia presentation are integrally related. For example, in our home town, many holiday fireworks displays are touted as multimedia extravaganzas by a local radio station. Supposedly, the fireworks are choreographed to music. To our ears, the choreography has involved playing loud music during the display. Any relationship between the two, beyond decibels, seems coincidental. IMI is the result of carefully integrating channels of information, not randomly slapping media together.

Thus, our definition follows:

> Interactive multimedia instruction (IMI) is an instructional program which includes a variety of integrated sources in the instruction with a computer at the heart of the system. The program is intentionally designed in segments, and viewer responses to structured opportunities (e.g., menus, problems, simulated crises, questions, virtual environments) influence the sequence, size, content, and shape of the program.

This definition attempts to place the emphasis on the program instead of on the hardware. For example, Johnston (1990) defines multimedia as "the capability to process various types of 'media'—i.e., text, data, graphics, still images, animation, video, audio, and special effects—on the same computer at the same time" (p. 47). We argue that whether multimedia programs happen on one screen, two screens, a video wall, or in virtual reality matters very little. The resonance and interactivity of the program lends it its identity.

A Taxonomy of Multimedia Interaction

Much ado is made about levels of interactivity possible in multimedia development, recognizing that the instructional potential of any medium is only realized in a highly interactive mode. Still, the levels of interactivity defined in the literature are largely medium-specific (videodisc), somewhat arbitrary, and not very descriptive. Following a brief review of conventional definitions, we offer a taxonomy of interaction based on the nature of the interaction rather than the capabilities of hardware or any specific medium.

Levels of Interactivity

Commonly accepted labels for levels of interactivity are Level I, II, III, and sometimes IV, depending on your reference (Iuppa, 1984; Katz, 1992; Katz and Keet, 1990; Schwartz, 1987; Schwier, 1987). These are largely drawn from the literature on interactive videodisc, and so are understandably medium-specific. For each level, videodisc is assumed to be the central instructional delivery medium.

Level I

Level I programs exhibit the most meager amount of interactivity. The user can control the player from the remote control unit, but a Level I videodisc player has no on-board memory and assumes no program control from an external source such as a microcomputer.

Programs are largely restricted to linear play, although a Level I videodisc can be programmed to stop at pre-designated frames. At that point the user can manually search to any chapter on the disc (up to 70 are possible) or search to any frame.

Level II

In videodisc programs, Level II treatments are determined by control codes permanently recorded on disc in audio track 2. As the disc is played, the control program is "dumped" into a microprocessor which is built into the player, and the disc is then played according to these instructions. This, of course, means that accurate program code must be written and encoded during mastering, and a more expensive videodisc player with a built-in microprocessor is needed to use the encoded program.

The encoded program must be compatible with the playback unit used. Currently, manufacturers consider their codes proprietary, and they are not standardized. Still, it is possible to include as many different programs as necessary (there are only two major ones— Pioneer and Sony) and the player will recognize and execute only its own code. This only requires a small amount of extra disc real estate from audio channel 2.

Under Level II control, the user can make choices at designated spots in the program manually (through the keypad) while the program runs automatically. The viewer makes choices and answers questions through keypad entries, and the program branches to predetermined locations and executes predetermined instructions. Simple counters can be programmed to keep track of user responses and to alter instructional paths based on user performance. This permits a much higher degree of interactivity than possible with Level I, but also greatly increases the potential complexity of development. Usually, manufacturers will allow producers to submit algorithms, flowcharts, or mnemonic descriptions of desired functions, and will assign programmers to create the necessary code—for a fee, of course.

Level II videodisc is best suited for programs which are not likely to change over time. Level II systems are relatively inexpensive, requiring only a player and a keypad. They are, by definition, limited to videodisc productions, and would not easily accommodate a multimedia approach to instruction. Any introduction of additional media to the system must occur during the production of the master tape from which videodiscs are pressed, with all media compressed into the videodisc format.

Level III

Level III interactivity includes an external device which is interfaced with a videodisc player; at this point we have a multimedia system. Any of an array of external devices may be used, but commonly a microcomputer is used. The computer provides the control program which "drives" the treatment, and the videodisc player acts as a peripheral device. Until recently, Level III systems have included two monitors—one for computer output and one for video—but increasingly, single displays combine multiple sources.

The power and flexibility of the computer allows a greater range of participant responses, and enhances interactivity. Instead of being limited to single keypad entries (Levels I and II), the user may respond to open-ended questions, for example. Level III interactivity combines the power, patience, and versatility of a computer with the quality, realism, and aesthetic appeal of the videodisc.

A Level III system is particularly attractive for those applications in which the treatment may change, content may require updating, or several versions of the same material are required. The computer is at the heart of this, and any other multimedia system, and it can take on different personalities when combined with videodisc:

- Computer as pathfinder—Video is dominant, with the videodisc carrying most of the instruction, and using the computer to provide only the programming necessary to allow the user to access the instruction provided on disc. Usually, this can be accomplished with a simple program, avoiding the expense and trappings of an authoring language or system. In this approach, the microcomputer is used to mimic the operation of a Level II program, housed externally rather than on the videodisc.

- Computer as partner—Instruction is divided between video and computer-assisted instruction. Some instruction is provided by CAI text and graphics, and some by video. This requires an authoring system or language which accommodates video.

- Computer as pedagogue—CAI is dominant, with the computer used as the primary source of instruction, and the videodisc used as an adjunct peripheral device. This combination is most prevalent when instruction is designed around existing video materials—commonly referred to as *repurposing*. This is an imposing task, and the developer must be particularly sensitive to constructing interaction, remedial segments, and effective feedback into the CAI, because the video will likely not be constructed interactively. If this caution is ignored, you run the risk of developing segmented, linear video attached to a page-turning device.

Level IV

In some cases, writers discriminate between the types of display and peripheral devices which comprise the instructional system, resulting in a fourth level of interactivity. In theory, Level IV includes any future innovations for development. Level IV systems, in effect, describe the hardware capabilities of multimedia systems. All sources are merged onto a single monitor. User interfaces are sophisticated devices such as touch screens, speech recognition, and virtual reality peripherals.

The four levels of interactivity are summarized in Figure 1-1.

Figure 1-1. Summary of characteristics at each level of interactivity.

Level I
- Least amount of interactivity.
- CAV or CLV discs can be used.
- Program largely linear—not controlled by software.
- Picture stops may be encoded on videodisc.
- Chapter and frame search enabled.

Level II
- Intermediate degree of interactivity possible.
- Control program permanently recorded on disc.
- Program code must be compatible with playback system.
- Manual (keypad) control possible by ignoring program.
- Single keypad-entry user input only.
- Requires that program be submitted with edit master tape.
- Ideal for unchanging content.

Level III
- System combines external computer and videodisc.
- Ideal for volatile content or treatments.
- Higher degree of interactivity possible.
- Various hardware configurations possible.
- Computer can perform as pathfinder, partner, or pedagogue when combined with videodisc.

Level IV
- All visual/audio/computer sources on single monitor.
- Sophisticated user interfaces such as touch screen.
- Theoretical domain for future interactive innovations.

A Revised Taxonomy of Interaction

At the risk of adding silt to already murky water, we suggest that "levels of interactivity" for multimedia environments should not be tied to hardware. Rather, it is more productive to characterize interaction according to the sophistication and quality of interactivity available to a learner in a particular program. For example, given the above categories, a learner responding through a touch screen is experiencing the highest level of interactivity. But most touch screen interactions we have seen or designed merely ask the learner to point at and touch a target on the screen—a very modest form of interaction. By contrast, the above definition suggests that a learner using a remote control unit to explore the contents of a videodisc is operating at the lowest level of interactivity. In fact, this may be a highly active, stimulating, and instructionally engaging type of interaction. The actual quality of the interaction may be much more significant than the corresponding touch screen experience. Which is the higher *level* in this case?

In order to construct a descriptive taxonomy of interaction for multimedia instruction, we will establish levels of interaction, examine functions played by interaction within these levels, and enumerate types of transactions at each functional level of interaction (Figure 1-2).

Figure 1-2.   A revised taxonomy of interaction.

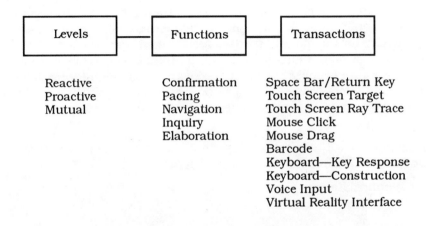

We suggest at least three levels of interaction based on the instructional quality of the interaction. Revealing the first two levels, interaction can be reactive or proactive in its orientation (Lucas, 1992; Thompson and Jorgensen, 1989). A reactive interaction is a response to presented stimuli, or an answer to a given question. Such approaches may offer a coaching, tutorial, or Socratic emphasis in designs; the learner and computer are engaged in a responsive, albeit preordained, discussion. Thompson and Jorgensen (1989) place tutorial/Socratic approaches into a separate category, labeled "interactive," but we regard this type of interaction as reactive, because learners still respond to presented stimuli. Proactive interaction emphasizes learner construction and generative activity. The learner goes beyond selecting or responding to existing structures and begins to generate unique constructions and elaborations beyond designer-imposed limits.

We would add one more level to these orientations: mutual interactivity. Mutual interactivity would be characterized by artificial intelligence or virtual reality designs, where the learner becomes a fully franchised citizen in the instructional environment. In such programs, the learner and system are mutually adaptive, that is, capable of changing in reaction to encounters with the other. Mutual interactivity is still in its infancy, but we suspect this is an area into which interactive multimedia will expand rapidly, given current research and development efforts.

The categories are not necessarily exclusive. Interactive multimedia programs may incorporate a combination of reactive and proactive approaches (few currently incorporate mutual approaches). The levels are hierarchical. The quality of interaction is higher at a mutual level than at a proactive level and higher at a proactive level than reactive. The quality of interaction is higher because there is greater opportunity for meaningful mental engagement and learner investment at higher levels of interaction than lower. We believe this categorization improves upon the hardware-based definitions used earlier, and offers a useful framework for thinking about the nature of interactivity, and the functions served by interaction during multimedia instruction.

Within each level, interaction can serve several functions. Hannafin (1989) identified five functions of interaction:

- confirmation,
- pacing,
- inquiry,
- navigation, and
- elaboration.

Confirmation serves to verify whether intended learning has occurred, say, through learner responses to embedded questions. Pacing relinquishes program time control to the learner; that is, the learner determines how quickly instructional content is encountered. Inquiry allows learners to ask questions or construct individual pathways through instruction (e.g., through access to supplementary material). Navigation manages learner access to instruction by facilitating access to some material and restricting access to other material. Elaboration involves the learner in combining existing knowledge with new instructional content, creating transitions and contexts for moving from known to unknown information.

Each function is expressed differently during instruction, depending upon the level of interaction. For example, reactive navigation is typified by menus or prescribed branching options presented to learners. Proactive navigation would permit the learner to initiate searches or participate in open-architecture movement throughout material. Mutual navigation might happen when a program anticipates navigation routes of the learner based on previous movement, and advises the learner about the nature of choices made. In mutual navigation, the learner could follow or ignore the advice, and also advise the system about the nature of navigation opportunities desired. Figure 1-3 describes examples of interaction obtained at each functional level of the taxonomy.

In order to fully describe a taxonomy of interactivity, we must also consider the transactions used to interact with a program. Transactions are the physical actions carried out by a learner during interaction. Certainly the level of interaction can be influenced by the type of interaction permitted by hardware configurations and instructional designs. Several reactive events cannot be easily adapted to higher levels of interaction. For example, the range of possible interactions is confined if the spacebar is the only method of interaction available to the learner; in this case, reaction would be the only possible interaction. Devices such as touch screens, and instructional design strategies such as menus, will not permit the learner to ask unique questions or construct unrestricted paths through instruction, thereby working in a proactive or mutual orientation. For example, a learner can use a touch screen or use a single keyboard entry to make menu selections or answer questions— a reactive level of interaction. Touch screens and single-key entries are too restrictive, however, to be used for generative interactions such as on-line note taking—a proactive level of interaction. Conversely, however, transactional methods available for proactive or mutual interaction can also perform reactive functions. For example a keyboard synthesizer can be used by a learner to compose a new song as input into a program (proactive), while the same keyboard synthesizer can be used to have learners play a score displayed by a program (reactive). In this way, transactional events can be adapted to lower levels of interaction, but not necessarily higher levels of interaction.

Figure 1-3. Types of interactive events at each functional level of interaction.

	Confirmation	Pacing	Navigation	Inquiry	Elaboration
Reactive	Answer matching	Page turning Replay segment	Prescribed branching (e.g., menu)	Prescribed help Supplementary info	Metaphor presented to learner Review concept map
Proactive	Learner asks system to check input Learner requests test	Request abbreviated or expanded version Replay learner-defined segments Learner defines speed of visual presentation	Open architecture searching Hypertext searching	Learner extracts information, keeps notebook Keyword searching	Learner modifies instruction to include learner experiences Learner creates metaphor for new information Learner generates concept of new material
Mutual	System adapts to learner progress and learner may challenge assessment	System responds to pace of learner in instruction—system adapts to learner	System advises about patterns of choices resulting in informed movement	Learner's patterns of choices leads system to suggest ways to ask productive questions	System constructs environment based on learner input—refines environment as learner discloses additional information

Figures 1-4, 1-5, and 1-6 categorize several transactional events which can be employed at reactive, proactive, and mutual levels of interaction. While the list of transactions is not exhaustive, it represents a cross-section of interactive strategies employed in IMI programs. The figures illustrate the notion that as interaction reaches for higher levels of engagement with learners, generative transactions are required.

Figure 1-4. Examples of transactions available to conduct functions at a reactive level of interaction.

	Confirm-ation	Pacing	Navig-ation	Inquiry	Elabor-ation
Space Bar/Return		•			
Touch Target	•	•	•	•	
Touch Trace	•				
Mouse Click	•	•	•	•	
Mouse Drag	•				
Barcode Scan	•	•	•	•	
Single Key	•	•	•	•	
Keyboard Construction	•	•	•	•	
Voice Input	•	•	•	•	
Virtual Reality Interface	•	•	•	•	

Note: At a reactive level of interaction, elaboration would be restricted to covert responses to stimuli, such as, "Think about this image." Therefore, physical transactions are not required for elaboration.

Figure 1-5. Examples of transactions available to conduct functions at a proactive level of interaction.

	Confirm-ation	Pacing	Navig-ation	Inquiry	Elabor-ation
Space Bar/Return					
Touch Target					
Touch Trace					
Mouse Click					
Mouse Drag					
Barcode Scan					
Single Key					
Keyboard Construction	•	•	•	•	•
Voice Input	•	•	•	•	•
Virtual Reality Interface	•	•	•	•	•

Note: Because the learner must generate original input to be truly proactive, only transactions which permit generation of complex information were identified. In some cases, individuals might argue that modest forms of proactivity can be accomplished with other types of transactions.

Figure 1-6.   Examples of transactions available to conduct functions at a mutual level
of interactivity.

	Confirm-ation	Pacing	Navig-ation	Inquiry	Elabor-ation
Space Bar/Return					
Touch Target					
Touch Trace					
Mouse Click					
Mouse Drag					
Barcode Scan					
Single Key					
Keyboard Construction	•	•	•	•	•
Voice Input	•	•	•	•	•
Virtual Reality Interface	•	•	•	•	•

Note: Mutuality implies sharing complex information between user and system. While
systems may be able to adapt programs based on a series of simple interactions, truly
mutual instruction requires complex dialogue.

References for Chapter 1

DeBloois, M. L. (1982). *Videodisc/microcomputer courseware design.*
Englewood Cliffs, NJ: Educational Technology Publications.

Dwyer, F. M. (1978). *Strategies for improving visual learning.* State College,
PA: Learning Services.

Fleming, M. L. (1987). Displays and communication. In R. M. Gagné (Ed.),
Instructional technology: Foundations (pp. 223–260). Hillsdale, NJ:
Lawrence Erlbaum Associates.

Fleming, M., and Levie, W. H. (1978). *Instructional message design.*
Englewood Cliffs, NJ: Educational Technology Publications.

Galbreath, J. (1992a). The educational buzzword of the 1990's: Multimedia,
or is it hypermedia, or interactive multimedia, or ...? *Educational
Technology, 32*(4), 15–19.

Gayeski, D. (1992). Making sense of multimedia: Introduction to special
issue. *Educational Technology, 32*(5), 9–13.

Grimes, T. (1990). Audio-video correspondence and its role in attention and
memory. *Educational Technology Research and Development, 38*(3),
15–26.

Hannafin, M. J. (1989). Interaction strategies and emerging instructional technologies: Psychological perspectives. *Canadian Journal of Educational Communication, 18*(3), 167–179.

Iuppa, N. V. (1984). *A practical guide to interactive video design.* White Plains, NY: Knowledge Industry Publications, Inc.

Jesky, R. R., and Berry, L. H. (1991). The effects of pictorial complexity and cognitive style on visual recall memory. In M. R. Simonson and C. Hargrave (Eds.), *Proceedings of the 1991 convention of the Association for Educational Communications and Technology* (pp. 290–296). Orlando, FL: Association for Educational Communications and Technology.

Johnston, S. J. (1990). Multimedia. *Info World, 12*(8), 47–52.

Katz, L. (1992). Essentially multimedia: An explanation of interactive laserdisc and optical technology. *The Canadian Multi Media Magazine, 1*(1), 18-20.

Katz, L., and Keet, C. (1990). *Innovations in laser and optical disc technology.* Calgary, Alberta: Alberta Laserdisc Committee.

Lucas, L. (1992). Interactivity: What is it and how do you use it? *Journal of Educational Multimedia and Hypermedia, 1*(1), 7–10.

Mann, B. L. (1992). The SSF model: Structuring the functions of the sound attribute. *Canadian Journal of Educational Communication, 21*(1), 45–65.

Miller, R. (1990). Introduction. In R. E. Bergman and T. M. Moore, *Managing interactive video/multimedia projects* (pp. xvii). Englewood Cliffs, NJ: Educational Technology Publications.

Schwartz, E. (1987). *The educators' handbook to interactive videodisc* (2nd ed.). Washington: Association for Educational Communications and Technology.

Schwier, R. (1987). *Interactive video.* Englewood Cliffs, NJ: Educational Technology Publications.

Thompson, J. G., and Jorgensen, S. (1989). How interactive is instructional technology? Alternative models for looking at interactions between learners and media. *Educational Technology, 29*(2), 24–26.

Chapter 2

Multimedia Instruction Environments

The nature of the learning task influences the nature of the instruction. There is no precision or advantage in thinking about IMI as an entity—a specific type of instruction which has meaning for the developer, educator, or learner. Given the earlier definition, the medium may provide specific opportunities, advantages, and limitations to the designer and learner. But ultimately, the nature of what is to be learned will also intervene, resulting in a variety of multimedia instruction environments. Romiszowski (1986), discussing the function of control in self-instructional media, organizes a schemata of systems for individualizing instruction. He identifies three characteristic positions: prescriptive, democratic, and cybernetic. We will extend the implications of these positions to multimedia instruction, but choose to use the term *environments* to describe the positions because they are, by nature, organic and malleable. They represent systems within which learning can happen. Instructional environments are influenced by external forces such as instructor preferences and learner characteristics, and they impose structure on instructional decisions, either by definition or convention. Multimedia instruction, in each environment, can contribute to creating a richer, more robust learning environment.

Prescriptive Environments

A prescriptive multimedia environment does just what the name implies: it prescribes what the learner is to learn. Instruction is concocted and delivered to the learner; the instructional system is used as a primary delivery medium. In many—if not most—cases, the instructional content and boundaries are decided by the designer/ producer, and the learner's role is to receive and gain facility with the content. There are usually specific objectives the learner is expected to achieve, and in most cases learning is evaluated in accordance with the specified objectives. Access to content is structured; an instructional analysis is usually performed to determine the sequence of presentation or at least identify the relationships among instructional elements. An attempt is usually made to match the individual differences of learners to instruction. Learners are either granted or denied access to areas of instruction based on their progress in the instruction, or they are advised which paths would be most profitable. The instructional methodology employed may range from a simple tutorial to an elaborate simulation, but the focus of this environment is the achievement of specified, externally defined goals. Prescriptive instruction may be characterized by several different designs. A popular breakdown of prescriptive instruction designs includes drill and practice, tutorials, most games, and some simulations (e.g., Alessi and Trollip, 1985; Hannafin and Peck, 1988; Heinich, Molenda, and Russell, 1989; Romiszowski, 1986). These may be offered to the learner in programmed instruction, computer-assisted instruction, and various systematic instruction formats, including multimedia instruction.

Drill and Practice

Drill and practice usually takes the form of a string of question-answer-feedback sequences. The purpose is usually to review previously learned material in a test-like environment rather than learn new material. In traditional media, you might think of drill and practice as a series of mathematics problems or a geography quiz in which the learner names the capital cities of countries.

For drill-and-practice, multimedia instruction can be used to increase the types, amounts, and layers of stimuli and feedback presented. For example, instead of using a map for the capital cities exercise mentioned above, the learner could be presented with a satellite photo, zooming into the target city. If the learner requires a clue, the national anthem of the country could be played, or additional data presented. A correct response could be greeted with a video or audio clip containing hearty congratulations from the actual head-of-state.

Tutorial

Tutorial instruction is what we most often associate with routine computer-assisted instruction or classroom instruction. Tutorials are used to teach new information. Information is usually presented, learners are given opportunities to practice using the information, and learning is reinforced. For example, a typical tutorial environment will have an introduction (including motivational set), organizing material (e.g., advance organizers, objectives, topics), novel content, embedded practice and interaction (e.g., adjunct questions, exercises, activities), feedback, review, and evaluation. The role of the delivery system is to mimic the best characteristics of a personal tutor. A well designed tutorial will motivate the learner to enter the instruction enthusiastically, guide or coax the learner to complete the instruction, provide ample opportunities for meaningful interaction, correct errors or misinterpretations, and applaud successes. This is particularly challenging in most mediated environments, because unless the materials are very skillfully designed, the intervention of the "tutor" can seem hollow and artificial. How many learners will warm to repetitive feedback like the following?:

- Sorry, try again, *or*
- Very good. Take an M & M from petty cash, *or*
- No. The correct response is _____, *or*
- Yes. You're doing very well.

Indeed, a human tutor could express similar sentiments and sound just as remote to the learner. But the danger is even more prevalent in mediated instruction, where insincere remarks are accentuated by the technology, and where there are no opportunities to adjust the instruction in reaction to a glassy stare. In mediated tutorial instruction, our challenge is often to provide a rich vicarious experience which approximates genuine human interaction.

Significant resources can be brought to bear on this challenge with IMI. Among the media which can be used singly or in combination are:

- print,
- still video,
- full-motion video,
- CD-quality audio,
- computer-generated graphics,

- animation, and
- textual overlays.

The art and science of instructional design will determine which media are appropriate to deliver instructional components. This is discussed in greater detail in "Section III: Designing Interactive Multimedia Instruction," but, for example, if the instruction requires the learner to compare the compositional styles of George Gershwin and Muddy Waters (try—we dare you), then at one level of instruction, printed scores might be sufficient. For greater depth of understanding, however, it might be useful to compare performances of sections of their work, demanding an audio treatment. Even greater depth might be accomplished by using a scrolling analysis of the score superimposed over a full motion and audio performances by Gershwin and Waters.

As has been established through decades of comparative media research, no medium is globally "better" than another. The power of any particular medium is realized through its proper application to an appropriate problem.

A tutorial approach has inherent instructional limitations. For one thing, tutorials constrict learner control over instruction. This is desirable in many instructional settings, but highly undesirable in others.

Games/Simulations

Games are usually directed at a specific goal and involve some measure of competition. Simulations provide an abstraction or simplification of reality—some level of mimicry, in which the learner encounters circumstances and tries to respond to them. Instructional games are rule-based, focused on specific goals or outcomes, usually divorced from reality and based on competition among players or against the system. Instructional simulations, by contrast, typically use rules to define the parameters of interaction within a model of reality, and play ultimately results in one of several available conclusions. Which conclusion is reached by a player is determined by choices and decisions made during instruction. Close approximation of the dynamics of reality is desired, and the learner becomes a part of the system rather than a competitor against it.

In multimedia instruction, features of games and simulations are often combined, as both approaches offer highly motivational, and potentially relevant environments. One caution must be underscored, however. Many simulations and games may not emphasize prescriptive instruction; the primary purpose of many games and simulations is entertainment or vicarious experience, with learning as a convenient by-product. Prescriptive instruction requires learning to be at the heart of the product, with the goals and parameters clearly defined.

Multimedia systems are ideally suited for gaming and simulation. In order to provide an interesting, robust environment, huge amounts of information must be available to the learner in realistic represent- ations of reality. For example, if you want to simulate life in a small German village during the Reformation, the learner must be able to encounter a range of social, political, and interpersonal variables in order to establish even a modest fidelity with actual life during those times. Computers and CD-ROM are capable of housing massive amounts of information in a number of useful formats (from print to compressed video), and videodisc offers the realism and immediacy of full motion video. The more these capabilities are exploited, the greater the potential for dynamic and realistic instructional environments.

Simulation-games have limitations. Perhaps the most significant limitation is related to efficiency. In many cases, the learner must invest a significant amount of time to extract modest cognitive learning gains which can be delivered in expository instruction very quickly. Conversely, some argue that simulations (or perhaps the inductive approach inherent in most simulations) promote learning which is not reflected in traditional achievement scores (e.g., a heightened appreciation of the plight of peasants in Germany during the Reformation).

Democratic Environments

Democratic environments shift the control of instruction to the user, thereby offering a very different environment from prescriptive instruction: structured learning strategies are not imposed on the learner. Democratic environments permit the learner to influence what is learned, or how it is learned, or at least the order in which it is learned. That is, the fundamental difference between a prescriptive environment and a democratic environment is really a question of learner control. Shifting the control of instruction to the user offers a very different environment from prescriptive instruction. Instructors or instructional designers do not impose structured instruction.

The democratic environment either supports prescribed instruction or it exists without reference to prescribed instruction. Depending on its function, an educational resource may or may not have the level of structure assumed in prescribed instruction. If the function is to provide additional instruction which is consistent with prescribed primary instruction, then the resource may take on a tutorial, drill and practice, or simulation-gaming strategy, and be cosmetically identical to prescribed instruction. The difference is in intent and control. Learner-controlled instruction would supplement prescribed instruction in this case, not substitute for it. The learner chooses to use it or reject it. For other democratic resources, the emphasis shifts from constructing and controlling instructional events to providing easy access to instructional support. These types of multimedia learning resources emphasize navigation, motivation, and access, and would likely downplay objectives and evaluation.

Supplementary Instruction

This type of educational resource assumes primary instruction exists elsewhere. Supplementary instruction either reinforces what has already been taught, or it attaches new instruction to what has been taught. While it may be prescribed by an instructor or program, or voluntarily selected by a learner, the intent is to either re-teach or enhance existing instruction. This type of instruction may exist in any of the forms described for prescriptive instruction, and will contain similar advantages and disadvantages. In other words, supplementary instruction may be indistinguishable from primary instruction in form. The difference is that supplementary instruction is voluntarily undertaken; the locus of decision-making rests with the learner. Some might argue that instructors could assign supplementary instruction too. In that case, according to our definition, the instructional material would be prescriptive rather than democratic.

Learning Resource

A learning resource is an organized data base of multimedia materials. For example, it might include a videodisc collection of sounds and still images for teaching biology. In this example, organization may merely include grouping images and sounds under headings. This means that organizational structuring is left largely in the hands of the user. While this has the advantage of flexibility, it also carries the liability of relatively difficult access. If an individual, say a learner in a laboratory, wants to review several of the images in a particular sequence, then the material must be searched for appropriate segments, which must be sequenced; then routines for accessing the chosen segments must be developed. Perhaps a remote control unit is used or barcodes are printed and pasted in a desired sequence, but nevertheless, manipulation must occur, and this places a burden on the user.

We are deliberately labeling this strategy a *learning* resource rather than an *instructional* resource. The two are quite different. If a teacher goes into a learning resource with the intention of abstracting information for use in her instruction, the resource isn't any different from if a student or researcher goes into it to find information. The fact that browsing through a learning resource can be educational (in the sense that you can "accidentally" learn things) does not make the resource instructional. To us, instuctionality is defined by intentionality, and simply allowing a learner to "graze" informational resources (databases) does not necessarily lead to instruction.

Organization can be imposed on learning resources. Perhaps segments can be grouped and sequenced by a designer. The user then accesses small collections of material. Of course, this sacrifices some flexibility, and assumes that the choices made by the designer are consistent with the user's instructional wishes.

Most well-designed learning resources provide multiple avenues of access to material. Completely open-architecture browsing is included as an option to those who want unrestricted and unstructured access to any portion of the materials. Groupings of material may provide a modest level of organization for those who have defined interests in portions of material. Highly organized instructional sets may also be included, providing learning resources which are very convenient to use. Multiple access materials require additional development time and they are more expensive to produce. Nevertheless, they preserve the flexibility cherished by some, while providing the convenience treasured by others. *The Visual Almanac*™ [1]

---

[1] *The Visual Almanac: An Interactive Multimedia Kit.* San Francisco: Apple Multimedia Lab, 1989.

provides an excellent example of multiple access. It is broken into Collections, Compositions, and Activities. These sections provide access to groups of material by topic, sample lessons constructed from some of the materials, and authoring tools needed to construct unique instructional configurations.

Nelsonian Hypermedia

Computing visionary Ted Nelson, who coined both the name and the concept of hypertext, envisioned a number of different kinds of hypermedia, including discrete hypertext, performing hypergrams, Stretchtext™, hypermap, queriable illustrations, and hyper-comics (Nelson, 1987). It is only the first of these kinds of hypertext, discrete, that is widely available commercially at this writing. In discrete hypertext, special indicators (e.g., asterisks, or boldface type) are used to indicate the existence of related additional information. The learner activates the indicators (say, by clicking on them with a mouse) and is presented with the additional information. The learner can then continue to explore the additional information (perhaps traversing the database yet again by clicking on another indicator), or return to the point of departure to continue the original path.

Some hypertext programs afford an opportunity to provide other forms of communication besides text—sound, animation, etc.—by "jumping out" to other application programs or by incorporating those features within the learning package itself. By and large, however, the dominant form of presentation is text. Macintosh's HyperCard is a good example of discrete hypertext, and its popularity and widespread availability has caused many to equate the term *hypertext* with discrete hypertext.

We will continue to use the word *hypertext* for its commonly-understood meaning—discrete hypertext. To provide a term that refers to all the various forms of hypertext that Nelson conceived of, including his storage and distribution system Xanadu™, we suggest the term *Nelsonian hypermedia*. We should stress that not all of the various forms of Nelsonian hypermedia are yet commercially available, but developments in this field are rapid and striking.

The major difference between the two classes of hypermedia (hypertext as the term is commonly used—i.e., discrete hypertext— and Nelsonian hypermedia) is the amount of control exercised by the program author as opposed to by the learner. The author effectively circumscribes the learner's actions by providing (or not providing) alternative paths through the content. (While it is true that hypertext provides much more flexibility and opportunity to the learner than, say, conventional computer-based instruction (CBI), the range available is still limited by the designer of the information structure.) In Nelsonian hypermedia, on the other hand, the learner is provided with a set of extremely powerful tools and connections to huge amounts of information (some of which may be structured and some of which may not), and allowed to roam freely within it. Thus there is a natural progression of learner control: from linear CBI to branching CBI to hypertext to Nelsonian hypermedia.

•   •   •

One final point about democratic environments needs to be made. Although it is labeled *democratic* to maintain fidelity with Romiszowski's categories, we could also call this *user-controlled* to more accurately describe the functions served in multimedia instruction. The user could as easily be an instructor gathering resources for teaching, as a learner choosing to be taught.

Cybernetic Environments

Some writers and producers question the limited approaches employed in computer-based designs (e.g., see Merrill, 1985; Dear, 1986). They suggest we are creatively confined by a "book metaphor." In other words, we think of interactive treatments in terms of chapters, tables of contents, pages, headings, and subheadings. The criticism is well-founded, and easily generalized from simple computer-assisted instruction to interactive multimedia treatments. Just leaf through this book, for example, and count the references to chapters, menus, and topics in reference to non-print media.

By contrast, human thought is a robust metaphor for interactive treatments. Conceptual environments, cognitive mapping, and logic structures may gain high status in the metaphoric pecking order. Approaches drawn from the field of artificial intelligence exploit the thought metaphor and have implications for interactive multimedia development. The research in this field is embryonic, yet it suggests new ways of thinking about interactive multimedia production which will likely influence future generations of software.

Presently, artificial intelligence (AI) is an exciting field of research and development in computer-assisted instruction. Be cautioned that the notions presented here are largely speculative, but they represent fertile ground for design, development, and research in interactive systems. On the other hand, some argue that AI may have little long-term significance for IMI.

The ultimate goal of artificial intelligence is to create systems that "think." By simulating human thought processes, computers will be able to respond to novel situations, create and implement strategies for solving problems, and learn from experience and introspection. The challenge is, we do not really know how people think and learn, so the metaphor is speculative at present, and application approaches fall into different camps which, for the sake of discussion, we call rule-based and semantic.

The first camp is founded on rule-based logic and is evidenced in program structures which exhibit IF-THEN rules. For example:

- IF   I am Belgian; and
- IF   I type answers to questions in French;
- THEN   I would prefer encountering training materials written or spoken in French.

In this simple example, a computer would analyze keyboard input and perform the logical functions based on the rule set imposed. The program would shift into French narration to accommodate the conclusion that I am a French-speaking Belgian. Underlying this approach to artificial intelligence environments is the notion that human thought can be faithfully reconstructed through a series of logical, sequenced, and predicted responses to rule sets. As you can imagine, in order to perform even rudimentary functions, such rule sets can become quite complex. Imagine the complexity involved if voice input is used instead of keyboard input. The program must be capable of identifying the language and idiomatic constructions while filtering individual quirks in usage.

The competition to rule-based inference is the semantic school of thought, which is predicated on the assumption that computers must be able to derive "meaning" from natural language. Rather than dealing with axioms and logic formulas, semantic approaches apply "knowledge structures" which are sufficiently complex to deal with the normal ambiguities of human language and experience. These structures allow a computer to impose an organized storehouse of knowledge on situations to clear up ambiguities and develop appropriate response strategies.

The debate is interesting, and indeed raging at the present time. Currently, artificial intelligence systems are most often highly specialized, custom designed, mainframe-dependent, and expensive. Still, like other innovations, the costs are falling, the number of users is increasing, and generic software is being designed for microcomputer environments. Let's peek into the near future, and speculate about what "intelligent" interactive multimedia environments may look like.

"Intelligent" interactive multimedia would use a computer to provide the intelligence. The information on videodisc and CD-ROM cannot be changed, so the most they can do is appear intelligent. Since learning is the key to intelligence, and we can only see change as evidence of learning, any "intelligence" must be provided by the computer. The other media can only house the artifacts of intelligence.

Using the human thought metaphor, we might think of a videodisc or CD-ROM as housing fixed thought, such as vivid memories, conclusions drawn from experience, or stable components of knowledge. As the storage capacity of archival media increases dramatically, so does the potential warehouse of thoughts. The computer (uneasily at present) adopts the functions of flexible thought, including mental activities such as comparison, inference, deduction, analysis, and insight.

From the perspective of rule-based inference, the microcomputer could be used to deal effectively with a collection of IF statements and relationships drawn from a user. The THEN execution might include exposure to selected information or instructional outcomes which reside on optical media. For example, let's examine two specific AI environments which may apply to intelligent interactive multimedia.

Expert Systems

Expert systems are only applications of rule-based (IF-THEN) inference approaches. In such an environment, a computer is given a knowledge-base which is equivalent to that of an expert, usually in a technical area. The user is able to answer questions posed by the program and ask questions of the computer in a relatively free-form structure, using natural language. Once queries and answers are analyzed, the computer is able to apply its expert knowledge base to the unique variables in the problem. The solution (or opinion) is tailored to the individual and sometimes is unique. Several such expert systems are presently giving advice in such areas as banking, investments, natural resource exploration, and medical diagnosis.

Where would interactive multimedia fit into such a system? It is quite possible that even highly complex areas of expertise can result in a finite number of fixed potential outcomes. For instance, within a certain range of medical symptoms, only several dozen diagnoses are possible. A computer could be used to conduct the medical interview portion of a diagnostic session, to compile, to analyze, and to diagnose a particular case. At that point, optical storage media could be used to present the outcome of the "expert" investigation, and the patient could consult with a doctor appearing on screen regarding the conclusions, implications, and treatment for the case.

Similar expert systems could combine the ability of the computer to generate graphics based upon information gained from the user, and superimpose the novel computer graphics over existing video on disc. For example, if an archaeologist were looking for the most likely location of the ancient lost city of Atlantis, the expert system could interact with the user, extract relevant information, and generate graphics over existing footage of world maps to hypothesize about likely locations of that site.

Heuristic Systems

Any of a number of heuristic systems could be adapted to intelligent interactive multimedia. The idea of heuristic models is that they use "best guess" approaches to make judgments about how students should progress through material, and how responses should be handled. In "intelligent" systems, the program is often also capable of expanding its knowledge base from the types of user responses encountered, and adapt its performance (i.e., it can "learn from experience").

This expands the potential for learner analysis commonly employed in instructional design. It could move from an activity which occurs prior to instruction for selection, placement, or treatment purposes to include a continuous monitor of user progress during instruction. A pattern of learner responses could result in a heuristic judgment concerning the most effective style of presentation for the learner, and impose that judgment on the learning situation. A variety of "paths" could be made available on disc to accommodate the various heuristic decisions which could be made.

For example, consider a sophisticated flight-training simulator. A series of minor navigational errors could mount to serious difficulties if left to compound. The program driving the simulator could detect a pattern in which navigational errors were consistently introduced when a strong tail wind was present. The videodisc, providing visual images and data, could be directed by the program to test the assumption by subjecting the simulator navigator to a variety of wind conditions. The computer could "interview" the pilot about decisions made. The pilot could consult with navigational experts on the multimedia system. A final judgment, based upon the test, could be to provide a series of tail wind experiences to the user.

To extend the discussion, we should consider the application of virtual reality interfaces within a heuristic environment. The learner could enter, and indeed become a participant in, a constructed environment which is visually and aurally saturated and dynamic. For example, the learner could wear an interface which allows the learning environment to be projected within the learner's changing field of vision. Projected elements would change to adapt to the learner's perspective, and respond to the actions of the learner. In fact, the learner could physically (virtually) manipulate items in the constructed environment; items could be picked up, carried and moved to another location, or massaged into a new shape. This is not a description of the future. Versions employing sophisticated computer graphics are currently available commercially. But multimedia can serve to enrich the virtual environments, and ultimately may serve to alter the nature of this type of learning experience completely:

> The scene is Ford's Theatre, Good Friday, April 14, 1865. You enter the theatre and sit through the first act of *Our American Cousin* starring Laura Keene. At the beginning of the second act you turn to the President's box above the stage, and witness the assassination of Abraham Lincoln. You smell gunpowder, watch John Wilkes Booth leap out of the box to the stage, hear Mrs. Lincoln scream, "They have killed the President" and you pursue him as he limps away during the confusion. Then it occurs to you: Perhaps you could have prevented the assassination.
>
> You start over, enter the theatre just before Act II. Instead of going to your seat, this time you stalk the hallways, looking for anyone who might help. You encounter President

Lincoln's guard standing outside Lincoln's theater box and attempt to warn him. The guard argues with you. You give him a description of Booth, but the guard finds your arguments and actions suspicious. He arrests you, and as you are being dragged into a holding room, you turn and see Booth slink into the President's box...

Far-fetched? Perhaps at the moment. Unattainable? No, of course not. As we mentioned earlier, the technology already exists, but such an environment presents an array of design, production, and technical challenges well beyond our current capabilities. Nevertheless, this type of exaggeration serves not only to illustrate some future possibilities, but also introduces some of the problems presented by this type of environment. For example, in this case, what are the implications of empowering learners to change historical events, in effect, distorting reality? We don't know what the actual disposition of the guard would have been, or in fact, understand the interplay of a number of other variables. The virtual reality environment is still, in this case, a construction—at least partially the invention of the designer. By permitting learners to tamper with history in this manner, and indeed helping construct outcomes based on their actions, we are perhaps contributing to the misinterpretation of the event. Indeed, this reveals a sobering caution for educators, regardless of the content presented. As our ability to represent "reality" increases, so does our responsibility to represent it fairly, accurately, and ethically. The concern extends beyond the historical example above. Similar difficulties arise in other professional, social science, natural science, and humanities arenas as well. Our ability to create rich environments is beginning to exceed our ability to deal with the resultant design and learning outcomes, and the implications are significant.

There are many other types of applications which may become possible through the development of intelligent interactive multimedia. The above discussion is meant only as a sample of possibilities which may soon appear on the horizon. Cybernetic applications are just gaining a foothold for microcomputer systems, but it is likely that when cybernetic applications are more commonplace, interactive multimedia will be at the forefront of training applications. Multimedia will serve to offer more dynamic and realistic artificial environments for learning.

For the time being, if you are interested in pursuing the topic further, you may want to start with a few of the references listed below.

References for Chapter 2

Alessi, S. M., and Trollip, S. R. (1985). *Computer-based instruction: Methods and development.* Englewood Cliffs, NJ: Prentice-Hall.

Alexander, T. (1985). Artificial intelligence. *Popular Computing, May,* 66–69, 142–145.

Amsterdam, J. (1985). Expert systems. *Popular Computing, May,* 70–72, 150, 153.

Davis, D. B. (1986). Artificial intelligence enters the mainstream. *High Technology, July,* 16–23.

Dear, B. L. (1986). Artificial intelligence techniques: Applications for courseware development. *Educational Technology, July,* 7–15.

Hannafin, M. J., and Peck, K. L. (1988). *The design, development, and evaluation of instructional software.* New York: Macmillan.

Hannafin, M. J., and Rieber, L. P. (1989). Psychological foundations of instructional design for emerging computer-based instructional technologies: Part I. *Educational Technology Research and Development, 37*(2), 91–101.

Heinich R., Molenda, M., and Russell, J. (1989). *Instructional media and the new technologies of instruction* (3rd ed.). New York: Macmillan.

Holden, C. (1986). Artificial intelligence techniques: Applications for courseware development. *Educational Technology, July,* 7–15.

Jonassen, D. H. (1988). *Instructional designs for microcomputer courseware.* Hillsdale, NJ: Erlbaum and Associates.

Merrill, M. D. (1985). Where is the authoring in authoring systems? *Journal of Computer-Based Instruction, 12*(4), 90–96.

Nelson, T. (1987). *Computer lib/Dream machines.* Redmond, WA: Microsoft.

Park, O., and Seidel, R. J. (1989). A multidisciplinary model for development of intelligent computer-assisted instruction. *Educational Technology Research and Development, 37*(3), 72–80.

Romizowski, A. J. (1986). *Developing auto-instructional materials.* New York: Nichols Publishing.

Wilson, B. G., and Welsh, J. R. (1986). Small knowledge-based systems in education and training: Something new under the sun. *Educational Technology, November,* 7–13.

Winne, P. H. (1989). Theories of instruction and of intelligence for designing artificially intelligent tutoring systems. *Educational Psychologist, 24*(3), 229–259.

Section II

Components of Interactive Multimedia Instruction

Chapter 3

Video

When we talk about video segments, we are really discussing a videodisc or the digitized video part of a multimedia system. As multimedia systems evolve, so do the technologies associated with each component. The most popular multimedia format for video until now has been videodisc, but other formats such as digital video interactive (DVI) are coming to the party in larger and larger numbers. While digital video will ultimately predominate, and is a preferred development medium, analog video will coexist with digital video for some time. We will address the development of various formats in this chapter.

Videodisc

No longer the "new kid" on the technological block, videodisc systems exhibit a plethora of characteristics which make videodisc highly attractive to trainers and educators. However, on the surface it does the same old thing as videotape—it shows television programs. The reason videodisc technology provides an exciting, innovative opportunity for educational, industrial, and consumer markets is that it offers important advantages in format, capacity, quality, and flexibility.

Videodisc units are simply devices capable of retrieving information from a 12 (or 8) inch disc which looks like a long-play record, and playing back the information on a television receiver. There is nothing startling about this; videotape players have been performing a similar service for several years. The nature of the format and the variety of media types which can be utilized make this type of system remarkable. Videodiscs combine the power of television with the flexibility of the computer.

Software (What Is a Videodisc?)

A videodisc is much like a standard long-playing (LP) record, covered by a clear coating of durable, mar-resistant plastic. Because information is embedded within the disc and protected by plastic, the product is extremely rugged. Unlike videotape, which can be torn, stretched, or crumpled by inept users, a videodisc can suffer considerable abuse and still reproduce an undamaged image. Some manufacturers claim you can use a videodisc as a meat platter to serve the Christmas turkey, wash it with the dishes, and then use it to watch a movie that evening. Although this is an outrageous exaggeration, it illustrates the impressive durability of videodisc software and the enthusiasm surrounding the innovation.

The record-like disc stores frames of information located in microscopic pits. Pits are made in the surface of the disc, and then covered with a protective transparent coating. A series of pits, read in sequence, yield a frame. Each frame can be thought of as a single frame of a motion picture which can be retrieved by most videodisc systems, either individually to produce still pictures, or in sequence to produce motion pictures. Each disc (12″, CAV format) contains 54,000 such frames per side, or 108,000 frames in total. This represents sufficient storage capacity to produce approximately one hour of continuous replay time in the motion format, or 108,000 still pictures. This is indeed impressive. For example, most of the great works of art available for study could be reproduced and stored on the same disc, and an art history teacher could house a complete collection of teaching materials on the office shelf in a space equivalent to that of one Frank Sinatra album. It should be noted that when single frame reproduction is utilized, a redundancy factor is often introduced when the disc is produced. Each frame is usually reproduced on the disc at least twice, thus halving the effective storage capacity of the disc, but also ensuring that a complete error-free frame is achieved.

Software Cost and Availability

Although videodisc recording units are available, most units currently being marketed only allow playback of pre-recorded material. This begs the question, "How much does educational software cost?"

Manufacturing costs for large quantities of videodiscs are low, but manufacturing figures alone are deceptive. As with any type of media development, front-end and production costs are extremely high, with

manufacturing and distribution of the final product accounting for
only a small portion of the overall costs. Commercial film producers
have already amortized front-end and production costs, and are able
to mass-market discs at a much lower unit cost than educational
producers, who must also recover production costs from a much
smaller market base. Taking this into account, it is unlikely that
videodiscs for training and education will be significantly less
expensive than competing media formats. Videodisc proponents using
lower cost as a purchase justification should probably look elsewhere.
It is most likely that commercially available videodiscs for training
and education will cost roughly the same amount as other media. *The
Videodisc Compendium* is an excellent source of information about
available educational videodisc and CD-ROM software.

 The Videodisc Compendium, Emerging Technology
Consultants, Post Office Box 12444, St. Paul, MN 55112.

Given that suitable media are not always available for training needs,
we are often faced with the task of producing custom-made software
locally. Certainly, teachers and trainers perform this task routinely
for materials such as overhead transparencies, slide-tape
presentations, and even modest television programs. Local
production is justified if instructional needs are sufficiently high to
justify production costs, if materials are not commercially available,
and if necessary expertise is available to produce the materials.

What are the costs involved in the production of videodisc software,
and how do these costs compare with other types of media? It
depends. Generally, production costs for videodisc can be compared
to those of high quality film or videotape production, although the
number of still frames employed and the complexity of the treatment
can increase the production costs of videodisc dramatically, whereas
linear media costs are more stable.

Costs for videodisc development diverge from other motion media
during post-production, and most of the reasons for this will become
painfully obvious as you consider the topics presented in the
videodisc production portion of this book. Videodisc is a radically
different medium, and during post-production, most of the costly
differences are realized. Some of the unique or significantly different
costs include:

- *Programming.* Multimedia applications require the development of computer code to drive the videodisc, and often computer-assisted instruction accompanies the video-portion of instruction. This component of development is becoming easier and less expensive, given the introduction of powerful and "friendly" authoring tools. But depending upon how elaborate the programming needs become, computer programming can be a time-consuming and costly enterprise.

- *Still Frames.* Sure, the combination of still and motion video is an attractive part of videodisc, but those still frames are expensive to produce. Some of the still frame costs are absorbed during preparation and production, but post-production costs will still rise. Some still frames will be created on a character generator during post-production. Extra attention will have to be paid to field dominance, and in some cases, frame accurate editing is required. These topics are addressed in detail later, but for now, realize that still frames increase post-production costs dramatically.

- *Mastering.* Although not unique to this medium, videodisc manufacturing includes a set-up charge for each disc side duplicated. This is a one-time-only charge from the manufacturer.

- *Check Cassette, Check Disc, Proof Disc.* Only the very brave or foolhardy approve a master for duplication without examining it first. Approval copies from each stage of mastering are available for your review.

- *Time.* Developing a videodisc is exacting and can be complex. Project management time will be longer than with other media, and inevitable delays will occur throughout the post-production process.

- *Duplication.* Once everything else has been completed, disc replication is relatively inexpensive.

- *Quick and Dirty.* Some companies can produce small quantities of videodiscs using real-time duplication. Videodisc recording units are also available. Both the cost of the hardware and blank discs for real-time recording are high at the moment.

In the final analysis, the production and duplication of videodisc software is cost-effective if a specific training need is met, large quantities of material must be stored in a small area, or a relatively large number of copies need to be made. For the casual producer, who may wish to reproduce a collection of slides in a video format, cost comparisons do not favor videodisc.

Interactive video is a different technology than film or linear video, and it is an important component of most multimedia systems. Directly comparing costs associated with developing each type of video (and other multimedia components, for that matter) is deceptive, because the end products differ substantially. If producers exploit the potential of videodisc, the result is a more powerful training medium than is possible with other motion formats.

A Brief History of Videodiscs

The standardization war over videodisc format was waged over a mercifully short period, and resulted in one clear loser and one apparent victor. For nearly a decade, starting about 1970, distributors of video equipment annually announced that the introduction of videodisc hardware was imminent, and that its introduction would revolutionize our concept of video. Skeptical potential users responded anxiously at first, then with patient acceptance, and finally stifled yawns as excuses and new promises were offered.

Finally, in the early '80s, a confusion of systems was introduced. The purchaser was faced with not only a radically different technology, but also had to choose from among optical-reflective, optical-transmissive, grooved capacitive, and grooveless capacitive systems. Each system touted unique features, down-played system-specific limitations, and was incompatible with all the others. Not surprisingly, potential customers were cautious. In addition, the delay in marketing viable consumer systems allowed videocassette systems to infiltrate home and educational markets. Because they permitted recording as well as the playing of programs, they gained such an advantage that videodisc may not influence the home market for a long time. It appears the industry was not "fast enough on its feet."

The first casualty in the standardization war was capacitive systems, most notably the RCA CED system. Capacitive systems used a stylus-in-groove technology, similar to that used by LP records in audio systems. Aimed primarily at the home entertainment market, RCA introduced their CED system about 1980, lost staggering sums, and, following an aggressive marketing campaign, withdrew their system from the market-place in 1984. The reasons for RCA's failure are probably varied. They include rigorous competition from the established home videocassette market, lower quality and durability of software compared to optical systems, and an inability to accommodate recording or interactivity.

Following capacitive systems, optical transmissive systems were withdrawn from the marketplace. Thomson CSF of France developed a system which could read either side of the disc without removing it from the player, merely by refocusing the light source on the disc from one side to the other. Its disappearance from the videodisc landscape has hardly been noticed, since it was marketed only to education, industry, and the military.

Optical-reflective systems are the apparent survivors of recent competition. This type of system supports interactive applications, provides impressive quality, durability, and capacity, and exploits training, industrial, and commercial opportunities. Optical-reflective systems allow rapid and accurate frame access unavailable in capacitive systems, and the laser-read hard disc is much more durable than either the stylus-read capacitive disc or the floppy-format optical transmissive disc. In addition, the optical-reflective systems allows either one hour of extended play per side (CLV) for linear viewing or 30 minutes per side (CAV) for random frame access and interactive applications.

An 8" format was introduced for shorter or more portable applications. An 8" disc is capable of 14 minutes of motion or 25,200 still frames in the CAV format and 20 minutes of continuous CLV playback. The format is compatible with existing players because players are designed to playback from the inside track, proceeding outward. Players are therefore capable of using any size disc which fits on the player. The 8" videodiscs are less expensive to manufacture per disc, but the cost per minute is substantially higher than their 12" counterparts. Therefore, taking only manufacturing costs (mastering and replication) into consideration, 8" discs are most attractive for applications confined to 14 minutes of playback.

Optical Reflective Discs

We will examine the optical reflective disc in greater detail, as it is the commonly accepted videodisc format. The optical reflective videodisc acts as a storage medium for encoded information (video and two tracks of audio control and program data) which can be processed by a videodisc player. The disc has two sides available for storing information, which are approximately 30 centimeters (12″) in diameter; 54,000 tracks per side are arranged in a continuous spiral which begins at the center and proceeds to the outer edge of the disc (Figure 3-1).

Figure 3-1. Videodisc track pattern: A spiral from the interior of the disc resulting in 54,000 circumnavigations from the center.

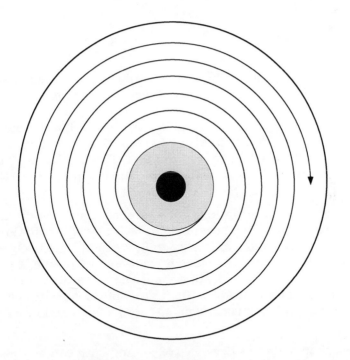

Within the tracks, data exist as microscopic pits or oval depressions in the inner surface of the disc. These pits are created by focusing a laser beam through a high-efficiency recording lens onto the surface of a photo-resist glass master as it rotates. The exposed glass master is developed to obtain a master disc (Figure 3-2).

Figure 3-2.   Stages in mastering.

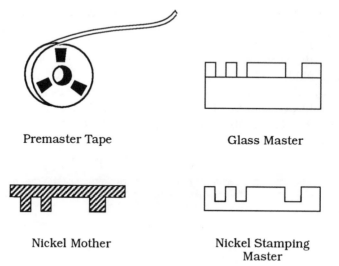

Premaster Tape   Glass Master

Nickel Mother   Nickel Stamping
                                 Master

The glass master is covered by nickel plating, and it is removed to obtain the mother disc. The mother is nickel plated again to obtain a nickel stamping master, which represents the fourth generation of the material (tape, glass master, nickel-mother, nickel stamper). Actual discs are molded by injecting or compressing a vinyl chloride polymer in contact with the nickel stamper. This produces a plastic version of the data which is then given a thin coating of reflective aluminum and covered by a protective layer of plastic.

The result of this is a recording which can be interpreted by reflecting a focused, laser-generated beam of light (actually split into three beams to detect the audio and video multiplex FM signal, focusing error, and tracking error). Because it is covered by plastic, and focusing actually occurs beneath the surface of the disc, the recording is extremely durable. The "frame" of video never comes in contact with a reading mechanism, so the image should never degrade.

Two types of optical-reflective discs exist, and both can be "read" by standard videodisc players. They are called CLV (Constant Linear Velocity) and CAV (Constant Angular Velocity) and they exhibit specific strengths and limitations. In order to make sense of the differences, it would be helpful to first review how video images are created and transferred to disc.

Video Frame-Field Representation

In video, each second of apparent motion is made up of 30 individual still frames or pictures. They are rapidly displayed and blacked-out sequentially, like an electronic zoetrope, to give the illusion of motion.

The North American standard video frame (NTSC) is divided into two fields and two vertical blanking intervals (VBI) containing a total of 525 lines of information (Figure 3-3).

Figure 3-3.   Field composition of video frame.

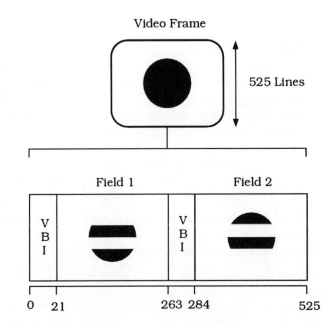

Each of the two fields which comprise a single frame contains half of the visual information necessary to create a complete picture. The fields are woven together such that lines 22 to 263 from Field 1 electronically scan the picture, leaving every other line of the picture missing; then, following a VBI, Field 2 fills in the gaps with lines 285 to 525, completing the picture. Interlacing Field 1 and Field 2 occurs in $^1/_{30}$ second, giving the viewer the visual impression of an integrated, continuous picture. Vertical blanking intervals occupy lines 0–21 and 263–284 in each frame. The VBI lines carry no visual information, but permit the inclusion of control information, recorded in an area which is not normally visible—unless your television has unstable vertical hold.

Types of Optical Reflective Discs

Understanding the discussion of frames, fields, and lines is essential to understanding how video is transferred to disc, and the strengths and limitations of available formats. Constant Angular Velocity (CAV) and Constant Linear Velocity (CLV) videodiscs differ only in the configuration of frames on the disc and therefore the playback characteristics of each.

Constant Angular Velocity (CAV)

The relationship between videotape and videodisc is visually apparent when you examine a CAV videodisc. Each video frame occupies a full track (360 degree segment of the track spiral). Two pie-shaped video blanking intervals are etched across the disc, clearly marking the location of the vertical blanking intervals. Fields 1 and 2 occupy opposite sides of the disc. Since there are 54,000 tracks on each side of a CAV disc, the same number of individual frames can be placed on a single side. Obviously, the frame length is much shorter near the center of the disc than near the outer edge (Figure 3-4).

The CAV disc is designed to rotate at a constant speed of 1800 rotations per minute. At 30 frames per second, this configuration will allow up to 30 minutes of continuous motion playback per side.

In the popular and commercial literature, a great deal has been made of the capacity of the videodisc to hold massive amounts of information, given its 54,000 available frames per side. Granted, that is a lot of frames, but the number is hardly astounding. Remember, a cassette videotape is capable of holding six hours of video at 30 frames per second, or 648,000 frames of information—and the package is even smaller than that of a videodisc. What is important about the CAV videodisc for multimedia instruction is how information can be accessed, manipulated, and used, coupled with the impressive quality of stored images.

Figure 3-4.   CAV disc format.

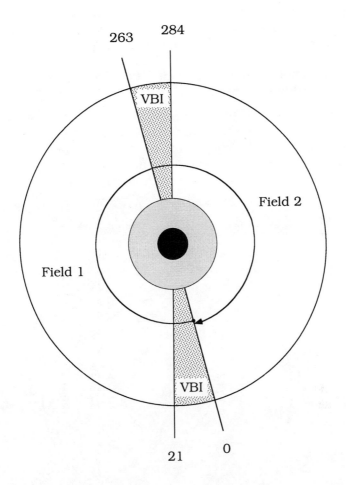

The concentric alignment of fields allows a number of functions which would otherwise be difficult. Each of the frames is identified by a unique frame number and other hidden code which resides in the VBI (including such things as picture stops and chapter numbers). Individual frames can be accessed by a program or user. Each time the laser completes a video field, it enters a VBI, and can be commanded to jump inward or outward to other tracks, permitted to continue to the next field, or continuously repeat the same track. This provides a level of flexibility unavailable with videotape.

Constant Linear Velocity (CLV)

Like a CAV disc, a CLV formatted disc has 54,000 tracks per side. Unlike the CAV disc, however, the CLV format uses a constant length for embedded frames, rather than always having one frame occupy an entire track on the disc. Thus, a single track on a CLV disc may contain more than one frame, and the result is an increase in playing time from 30 to 60 minutes per side (108,000 frames reside in the 54,000 tracks) (Figure 3-5).

A CLV disc is designed to be scanned at a constant linear rate which does not vary over the entire disc. To achieve this, the disc varies its speed of rotation from 1800 rpm at the center of the disc (scanning one frame per track) to 600 rotations per minute at the outside circumference of the disc (scanning three frames per track).

Figure 3-5.   Constant linear velocity (CLV) disc format.

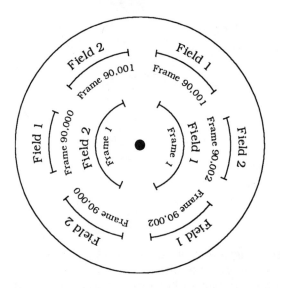

While the differences between CAV and CLV are not apparent to the casual viewer, several interactive functions are commonly available only in the CAV format. These are described in the next section.

Typical Videodisc Functions

Specifically, some of the functions which are possible with videodiscs include:

- *Still Frame.* Repeating the same track is possible with CAV playback, and with CLV using some players. Since each track contains only one frame of video, repeating it results in a still frame or freeze effect.

    When commanded to perform a still frame, the laser scans an entire track, then jumps back to the beginning of the track and repeats the scan. This can be accomplished for any of the 54,000 tracks, whether they are designed for still frame presentation, or appear as a single frame in a motion sequence. Since only a beam of light contacts the disc surface, unlimited repetition is possible without degrading the image. One caution must be mentioned. While continuously scanning a single image does not harm the videodisc, leaving a still image on a television monitor for a long period of time can damage the monitor. Ultimately, images can "burn" into the picture tube, and leave a ghostly image of the still picture as a permanent scar. We learned this the hard way; hope you don't.

- *Step Frame.* Step frame combines several still frames in sequence. A single still frame is repeated until the user commands the player to *Step*, at which point the player moves to the next track in sequence and repeats it as a still frame. This can occur in forward or reverse mode, but only in sequence.

- *Fast Motion.* Fast motion play is accomplished by reading only one field of each frame, and then moving to the next track. Not all players have this feature, or may only permit forward play.

- *Slow Motion.* Normal playback rate can be slowed by repeating individual frames within a sequence. A variable rate of slow motion is accomplished by increasing or decreasing the number of times each frame is scanned before moving to the next frame and repeating the process.

- *Scan.* Scanning a disc results in extremely rapid playback of visual information, allowing the viewer to "fly through" the contents of a disc quickly. It is accomplished by having the player skip over tracks, only displaying occasional frames as it traverses the disc.

- *Search.* Any resident frame can be accessed by entering the frame number and a search command from the keypad. With most players, the screen goes blank during the search, and once the requested frame number is located, the player scans that frame in a still frame mode. In some models of videodisc players, the last image is captured and displayed while the search is executed for the next location. When the new frame or sequence is initiated, it replaces the previous image. This results in "seamless" searching (the screen is never blank). With some players, CLV frames can also be searched by SMPTE time code location.

These features, available in CAV (and CLV in some players), are critical for interactive applications. They provide the instructional developer with a variety of tools to use for constructing exciting, varied instruction. Chapters (segments of video instruction) and frames can be combined in any order to capitalize on specific learner characteristics and responses. How a designer employs these features to do such things as provide different rates of presentation, practice, and feedback, and to relinquish control of instruction to the learner, will influence the effectiveness of instruction. Research is beginning to shed light on important design variables, and these will be discussed in detail later.

Videodisc Production

In order to produce a videodisc, visual material is commonly subjected to four production generations or steps (Figure 3-6):

- Original Source Media
- Edit Master Tape
- Disc Master
- Videodiscs

Your job as a developer will probably include the first two production generations. You will produce or assemble original source media and transfer them to an edit master tape. The tape is then typically sent to a production house, where a disc master is produced from the tape, and individual videodiscs are pressed from the disc master. When small quantities of discs are needed, you can purchase a videodisc recorder or send your tape to a production company which produces discs directly from tape. This process is similar to making a copy of a videotape from one VCR to another.

Figure 3-6.   Typical production generations.

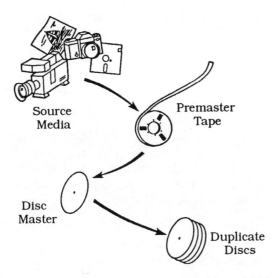

While the stages are simple to understand, the first can cause difficulties. Original source media exist in a variety of incompatible formats which must all be combined to exacting standards. An additional step in the process can be to convert the originally produced source media to a common format before assembling the pieces onto an edit master. This step includes transferring a variety of media to videotape, and does cost you an additional generation. However, transferring all source media to a common format can also save you many expensive hours of on-line editing.

Also, as you prepare source material for the edit master, you must consider some specific approaches to organizing material on the disc. These include both technical standards and conceptual decisions.

Original Source Media

Most production houses suggest that high-quality source material is required for conversion to the edit master and disc. The quality arguments are undeniable. The videodisc mastering process has an annoying habit of reproducing sounds and images precisely—even those of questionable quality. Disc manufacturing representatives live in daily fear of 8 mm film. Certain formats such as VHS and BETA videocassette, 8 mm film, and some computer graphics produce inferior resolution, and sometimes introduce image stability and audio synchronization problems.

Nevertheless, almost any original source material will work, as long as you are willing to live with the consequences, and can fight off the impulse to point an accusing finger at the mastering company for substandard images. The most desirable (and expensive, of course) format is 1″ type C composite NTSC 525 line, 60 Hz videotape. Actually, this is also the most common format used by professional production studios, so it poses fewer problems than one might suppose. Excellent results can also be obtained from:

- 1″ type B composite 525 line, 60 Hz videotape;
- 2″ helical and quad videotape;
- $^3/_4$″ professional NTSC 60 Hz videotape;
- professional Beta SP;
- 35 mm motion picture and slide film;
- 16 mm motion picture film;
- some computer graphics.

Be aware, however, that most motion picture film is shot at 24 frames per second (fps), and videotape displays 30 fps. This creates a simple technical problem for converting film to videotape, but it introduces a complex instructional design and financial problem for the author of the program. The technical solutions are dealt with in this chapter.

Finally, you must collect all of your original source materials in whatever formats you have chosen, and bring them to a post-production facility for conversion to tape. If you have a reasonable budget, this would be a good time to spend part of it. Video editing is not for the unskilled or fainthearted, and a good video editor can save you time, frustration, and maybe even money in the long run.

Converting Source Media to Tape

Usually, the first step is to take all of the source materials and convert them to a common videotape format. This is convenient and it simplifies some of the editing tasks when producing the edit master. Of course it costs you a generation for any material which is not already in the chosen format, but the convenience of working in a single format during the final stages of editing will probably outweigh any slight quality loss.

As mentioned earlier, quite a variety of original source materials can be transferred to tape. Some specific technical considerations for specific source materials follow.

Still Frame Media Transfer

Graphic and Text Frames. Camera-ready graphic art can be transferred to tape, and should follow guidelines for any video production. Black and white or full color art can be used, but major considerations for either include the aspect ratio of television display and the complexity of the graphic.

The aspect ratio for television is three by four horizontal—an inflexible fact of life. Artwork produced for television must conform to this standard to "fit" on the screen properly. Any size of artwork is acceptable, as long as the three by four ratio is not violated (Figure 3-7).

Figure 3-7.   3 × 4 aspect ratio—acceptable graphic format for television.

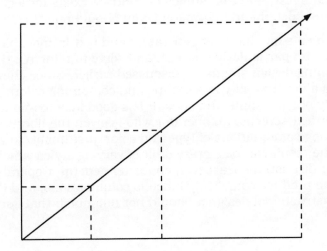

Even though the actual size of graphic art is not critical, it is a good idea to use a uniform size for all flats designed for a single production. This will reduce the amount of time devoted to resetting cameras for each graphic, an unnecessarily expensive annoyance. Whenever possible, provide a large border and work within a conservative "safe area," because television will crop about 10% of the edges. Allow graphic backgrounds to "bleed" into unused portions of the flat, rather than use boxes or border lines around graphics. Straight border lines seldom appear straight on video, and the extra background area will help ensure that shots stay within frame.

The complexity of the video graphic is another important consideration. Graphics should be simple and crisp, due to resolution and viewing limitations. Obviously, most textbook illustrations are inappropriate for conversion to video (aside from copyright concerns) because they often include too much detail. Pare down illustrations to the minimal amount of information necessary to ensure learning. Use bold lines and minimal text on a single graphic. Avoid the impulse to use an existing drawing from a print source "as-is," because it is likely that it will be too complex, or will violate the correct aspect ratio.

Text frames can be generated by preparing lettering on artwork, by a character generator, or by an external computer. Generally, a text frame should contain no more than 10–12 lines of text with 30–35 characters per line. A simple, legible type font is best, perhaps sacrificing some aesthetic appeal for instructional integrity. If text is to be used in combination with an illustration or superimposed over a video frame, ensure that there is ample "dead space" in the visual to accommodate text, and that sufficient contrast exists for legibility. For additional detail and information, you should refer to Chapter 11.

A few comments on character generators and text frames, based on experience, are particularly relevant, and serve to reinforce the notion of establishing design standards discussed earlier. Since character generators allow flexibility in selecting and combining colors, as well as a variety of types fonts and sizes, it is a good idea to standardize formats for text screens. An operator who is given the liberty to shift at will among combinations of type and color, just might, to your dismay. The result can be a crazy quilt of varying styles which can distract (or disgust) the learner. A character generator operator gone berserk can produce some truly hideous combinations, and the prudent instructional designer should not relinquish that control.

Character generators also produce highly saturated colors. As complete frames, this is hardly noticeable or distracting. But when character generated text is combined with another video frame, the difference is quite noticeable. This can be corrected by reducing color saturation of character generated material to about 60% when combining it with other material. This is a good idea to keep in mind when combining overlays from other media in multimedia systems too. It is possible to combine over-saturated computer graphics with video, so be careful to attend to the combinations.

One final and seemingly obvious concern deserves mention. Proofread all of your text frames carefully for spelling and grammatical errors. Any mistakes which slip through to the disc can only be repaired by remastering the videodisc. On our last production, it happened to us. The offending text frame read "Now its your turn," and it was a critical node in the production. Every member of the development and production teams (including two former English teachers with an embarrassing number of university degrees) overlooked the missing apostrophe. As you would conventionally do with other written material, it is a good idea to have someone unfamiliar with the content proofread your text frames. Another useful trick is to read the material backwards. This disrupts the continuity of the prose, and forces the reader to examine each word without imposing closure on mistakes.

In review, make sure that original graphics and text frames:

- conform to a 3 × 4 horizontal aspect ratio;
- use simple line drawings;
- provide large margins, and are confined to a "safe area";
- avoid using frames as borders around graphics;
- include simple, seriffed lettering;
- include no more than 12 lines of 35 characters each;
- insert text in visual "dead space" of video frame;
- have no spelling or grammatical errors.

Slides. Slides can be excellent source media for still video frames, as long as quality and format requirements are observed. Only properly focused and exposed slides should be used, although it should be noted that television is somewhat more forgiving toward slight overexposure than underexposure. Slides shown sequentially should not vary significantly in brightness level.

Slides exhibit a 2 × 3 aspect ratio, which can be either vertical or horizontal. Vertically formatted slides should be avoided for conversion to video, because they produce an image that is masked on either side. Horizontal slides also present an aspect ratio problem, but it is easily overcome by careful photography. When a 2 × 3 slide is converted to video, only the middle portion of the slide is visible. Photographing slides for conversion, the photographer must be disciplined to include important visual information within the "safe area" for video. Anything appearing outside the 3 × 4 area will not be visible on the television screen. The photographer should also remember the additional 10% cropping with television, so the "safe area" is even more restricted than appears in the illustration shown in Figure 3-8.

Figure 3-8.   Comparison of slide and video horizontal aspect ratios.

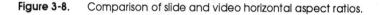
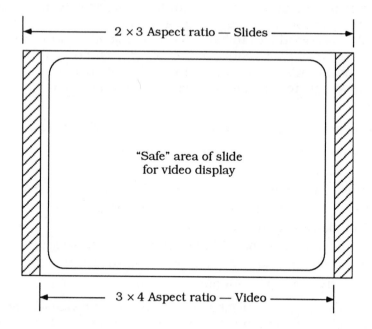

2 × 3 Aspect ratio — Slides

"Safe" area of slide for video display

3 × 4 Aspect ratio — Video

Filmstrips. Except for the 10% cropping loss inherent in video, filmstrips have the same aspect ratio as television. They can be easily converted to video, especially with the use of a 35 mm film projector. Filmstrips can be transferred at 30 fps if they are to appear in their original sequence, or individual filmstrip frames can be treated like slides.

If an external computer is to be used, and only some of the frames are useful, it may be economically wise to convert all of the frames to tape, and then program around them, rather than handle each frame individually. Still, if the *Step* feature is used, unwanted frames will interrupt the desired sequence.

Also, watch out for dated material in filmstrips. All too commonly, old automobiles, haircuts, and fashions disrupt an otherwise useful learning experience.

To summarize the major points concerning slides and filmstrips:

- materials should be focused and properly exposed;
- slight overexposure is preferable to underexposure;
- slides have a different aspect ratio than video;
- filmstrips can be transferred at 30 fps or by frame;
- filmstrips and video have similar aspect ratios;
- if *Step* function will not be used, transfer several duplicate still frames to tape to ensure an acceptable frame exists.

Still Frames with Audio. Recent technological advances in interactive video permit the display of video still-frames with accompanying audio. With older equipment, this feature required additional playback equipment, specifically an audio processor which is linked to the videodisc player. The audio processor retrieves and stores compressed audio from a portion of the videodisc, then plays the audio back as the videodisc player displays a still frame. This approach was seldom used, as it required additional hardware and a videodisc program produced with compressed audio. For a number of reasons few such applications were ever produced.

Conversely, newer videodisc players store and display a single video frame, and can simultaneously play an audio track from another part of the disc. This arrangement requires neither specialized hardware nor exceptional production techniques to take advantage of still frames with audio.

The production challenge this presents a developer is where to place the audio on the disc, as it will require much more linear space on the disc than the accompanying single video frame. If you are willing to sacrifice a stereo audio treatment, then one of the two resident audio tracks can be used to house audio for still pictures. The audio segments should be proximate to the referent still frame in order to minimize access time.

Motion Media Transfer

Videotape. Life would be easy if all original material were on videotape. The only special requirement for transferring tape in the CAV format is consistent field dominance if the user will execute the freeze frame option. As mentioned earlier, each video frame is made of two separate fields, each carrying half of the visual information which comprises a complete frame. Either Field 1 or Field 2 can be the first field of a new frame, and this characteristic is called field dominance. In order to use freeze frames, and see stable, coherent images, the premaster tape must identify the first field accurately, so that both fields viewed are from the same frame. Failure to do this could result in a flickering still image, as the player scans portions of two adjacent frames, jumping back and forth between two pictures at 60 cycles per second.

The effect of mismatched fields is not noticeable in motion sequences, as the progressive scanning of fields isn't affected by field dominance. Mismatched fields, however, are quite apparent when still frames are selected. As a source tape is assembled, it is possible that field dominance will shift between motion sequences unless field-consistent editing is maintained. If one segment is Field 1 dominant, and another is Field 2 dominant, then one of the two segments will suffer from image flicker on the disc. Correcting such problems after they occur is expensive (Figure 3-9).

Figure 3-9.   Shift in field dominance between two edited segments.

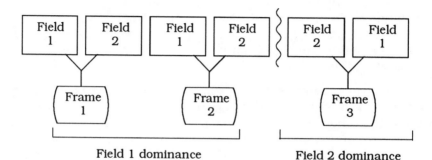

More information on field dominance appears later in this chapter. If you are considering a production with still frames or freeze frames, be sure to read it.

Motion Picture Film. Transferring film to videotape creates a technical problem. Film is typically shot at 24 fps and videotape is recorded at 30 fps. In order to accomplish the transfer, the incompatibility of film and tape speeds must be overcome. This requires a process known as 3–2 pulldown.

During a 3–2 pulldown transfer, every other film frame is duplicated as three video fields rather than the normal two fields. This is accomplished by duplicating the first field in that frame a second time, resulting in a series of film frames which contain three video fields, then two fields, three fields, two fields, three, two, and so on. Increasing the number of fields transferred in this fashion increases the equivalent number of video frames to 30 for every 24 film frames (Figure 3-10).

Figure 3-10.   3–2 pulldown from 24 fps film to 30 fps tape, resulting in some video frames with mismatched fields.

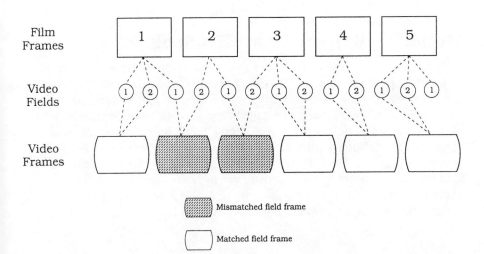

The limitation this imposes on resultant video is that mismatched fields produce frames which are unacceptable for freeze frame presentation. Mismatched frames produce images which flicker, rendering the second and third video frames in the above illustration useless as freeze frames. As described in the previous section, this is not noticeable in motion sequences, and skillful programming can choose the acceptable stills and jump over bad frames. Still, if *Step* mode is used, additional cues must be added during premaster tape assembly to identify the first field of each frame, regardless of field dominance. These field cues are sometimes called "white flags."

To summarize the major points in transferring motion source media to videotape:

- Professional quality tape-to-tape transfer is preferred.
- Consistent field dominance is important if still frames or freeze frames are used.
- Mismatched fields result in image flicker.
- For best freeze frame results, shoot original motion footage on film.
- If possible, shoot film at 30 fps.
- Film shot at 24 fps requires 3–2 pulldown for transfer to tape.
- 3–2 pulldown produces some video frames with mismatched fields, rendering those frames useless as freeze frames unless cues (white flags) are moved to identify the first field of each frame.

Motion/Still Real Estate Tradeoff

The maximum running time for a CAV disc is 30 minutes but most interactive videodisc treatments include a combination of motion sequences and still frames. Obviously, any disc space allotted to still frames erodes the amount of space remaining for motion sequences. The instructional developer must keep the 30 minute maximum in mind, and judiciously allot valuable disc space to both still and motion segments. One second of playing time liberates 30 frames for still frames. Extending the formula is easy, and will give you an accurate idea of how much space you can allot to each mode of presentation in a given treatment (Figure 3-11).

Figure 3-11. Still frame/motion sequence relationship.

Motion (minutes)	Stills (frames)
30	0
29	1,800
25	9,000
20	18,000
15	27,000
10	36,000
5	45,000
0	54,000

It should be apparent from Figure 3-11 that ample space for still frames can often be obtained by sacrificing only a modicum of motion time. Each minute of playing time releases 1800 frames of disc space—certainly adequate for most treatments. Because still-frame real estate is so plentiful, the cautious instructional developer may want to forget about frame-accurate editing and field dominance, and duplicate each still frame three times. This will ensure at least one "good" still frame, and only sacrifices the *Step* mode of presentation.

Producing an Edit Master

An edit master is also called a premaster. We've included both labels, and use the terms interchangeably, because you will encounter both when you begin a project.

Premastering involves assembling all of the original source material onto a single videotape, which can then be used as the source for creating a disc master. If you are planning to stay with a tape format rather than disc, this is the point at which many producers feel they can afford to get a bit sloppy.

This is not true, however. The post-production process is usually expensive and always critical to the quality of the final product. In the post-production/premastering process, you will:

- Assemble an edit master tape.
- Pilot test the tape format.
- Submit the edit master tape to a mastering facility.
- Test the encoded premaster tape.

Preparing material for premastering can be done at your own facility, or facilities and trained personnel can be obtained in most metropolitan areas.

Preparing video material for interactive applications is largely the same, whether you plan ultimately to master an optical videodisc from your final tape, or merely use a tape medium for presentation. Regardless of the final mode of presentation, you will probably test materials in a tape format initially, so it is useful to think in terms of high quality tape mastering from the beginning of the post-production process. Preparation of video material for reproduction on disc is extremely exacting, and especially if still frames are combined with motion sequences, there must be exhaustive attention to precise format specifications.

Once all of your source material is successfully transferred to tape, you will probably find yourself in a room surrounded by reels of the stuff, wondering how you got into this mess. Your next job is to assemble all the source tapes into a single premaster tape from which the disc will be mastered.

You have a number of options at this point:

	Option	Probable Outcome
1.	Hire a post-production house to assemble your edit master.	You will probably get an excellent edit master tape if you have been careful to outline the specifications for the post-production personnel. It would probably be worthwhile to contract with a facility with experience in interactive post-production. Commercial rates for post-production can be expensive, so it is important to establish the reputation of the facility for quality work and the credentials of the individual assigned to your project. If you have a complex treatment, costs can rise dramatically.
2.	Have your development team assemble the edit master tape, conforming to specifications.	If you have access to proper equipment and editing skills, you can save the project considerable cost and learn a great deal about the intricacies of interactive post-production.

3. Throw it together   Unless you are very lucky, one of two
    quickly, and hope.   things will probably happen. Either you
                               will assemble an edit master tape which
                               will not satisfy your instructional needs
                               adequately, or your edit master tape will
                               be rejected by the disc mastering facility.

Edit Master Tape Specifications

First of all, what are the format requirements for premaster videotapes to be used in mastering discs? Thankfully, the major producers
do not differ significantly in their specifications. You will probably be
safe if your premaster tape fits the specifications listed below, but
double-check with the mastering facility you choose just to be sure.

CAV and CLV disc premaster specifications:

- 1" C or $^3/_4$" Professional NTSC, 525 line, 60 Hz format tape;
- continuous, increasing SMPTE non-drop time code on audio
  channel 3, beginning at color bars and continuing through
  lead-out;
- continuous control track;
- color burst present;
- video signal $\leq$ 110 IRE luminance;
- chroma level $\leq$ 100% modulation;
- video signal to noise ratio $\leq$ 45 dB unweighted, 10 KHz to
  4.2 MHz at 50 IRE units flat field;
- consistent audio levels in segments with a reference of 0 VU,
  with short peaks $\leq$ 3 dB;
- color bars with 75% chroma and stated luminance reference;
- $\geq$ one minute of audio tone 1 Kh and 0 VU during color bar. 3M
  recommends staggering the start of channel 2 audio by about
  10 seconds so that the channels can be identified easily in
  post-production;
- one minute of black video, silent audio preceding and following
  the program;
- SMPTE time code reference noted for beginning and ending
  frames of the active program;
- edit points of source changes from 2–2 and 3–2 pulldown;
- chapter starting frames.

These specifications were drawn from the published requirements of leading manufacturers. Where stated requirements differed, the strictest specifications were selected. Most are more important to the video engineer than the instructional developer.

CAV premaster tapes must also specify field dominance, picture stops, and program dumps.

This adds up to a fairly impressive array of information which must be considered if you plan to master a videodisc. Most of the technical specifications are quite mundane actually, and should be imposed on any video production. There are companies which will accept most any kind of tape and dump it onto a disc for you, but of course, the quality of your product may suffer.

Edit Master Field Dominance

If you are producing a treatment with no still frames or freeze frames, this section is not important. If, on the other hand, you anticipate using still frames, or have transferred film to tape and want to be able to stop motion sequences and obtain solid frames, then field-consistent editing is necessary.

Field dominance is established on the edit master tape by identifying the first field of each frame as either Field 1 or Field 2. Most post-production facilities use Field 2 dominance as the default when actual dominance has not been specified, but either can be accommodated. If Field 2 dominance is specified, then a code is inserted in the VBI (Vertical Blanking Interval) called a *white flag*, which identifies Field 2 as the first field in a frame. Thereafter, every second field on the tape is flagged as the first field of a frame, unless otherwise specified (Figure 3-12).

In the still frame mode, Field 2 and Field 1 of the same frame (between white flags) are played back together. This will result in minimal image flicker in the still mode (Figure 3-13).

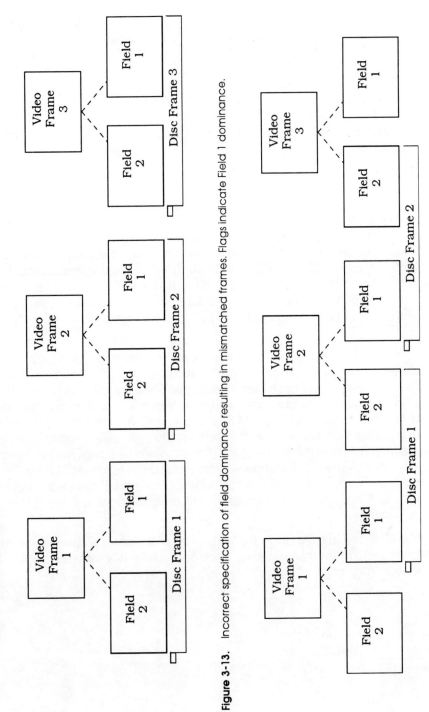

Figure 3-12. "White flag" placement identifying Field 2 dominance. Correct specification of field dominance resulting in matched premaster and disc frames.

Figure 3-13. Incorrect specification of field dominance resulting in mismatched frames. Flags indicate Field 1 dominance.

In the still frame mode, mismatched fields (Field 1 of Frame 1 and Field 2 of Frame 2) are played together as if they are from the same frame. If Frames 1 and 2 are quite different, this will result in a very pronounced flickering image. If Frames 1 and 2 are very similar, as with two adjacent frames in a motion sequence, the flickering image will be less prominent. The answer to this problem is to ensure that the fields are consistent throughout the edit master tape. Field-consistent editing is possible, given the proper attention, care, and equipment.

The problem is that the world is imperfect (you can quote us). Invariably, field dominance will change between two segments which are edited together, or film to tape transfer will be used, causing field dominance to shift repeatedly. If frame coherence is important, field shift can be achieved at this point by electronically changing the position of white flags each time field dominance changes. Cues can be inserted to identify which field should receive the frame address code when the disc is mastered. Thus frame correspondence is achieved between the edit master tape and the disc, regardless of shifts in field dominance on the edit master tape (Figures 3-14 and 3-15).

Cue insertion requires a specialized piece of equipment which can be obtained from mastering facilities, and requires that you identify the field dominance at each significant edit point. In complex treatments this can easily amount to several hundred edits, which can translate into a fair amount of time. Marking the shift points clearly on your Premaster Edit List will help speed up the process. The cue inserter is also useful for straightening out the problem of identifying coherent still frames from 3–2 pulldown film to tape transfers. It can be programmed to "ignore" the extra video field which appears in every other frame, and yield two significant disc fields for a given frame address.

If guidelines are carefully followed, you will master a disc in which every individual frame can be accessed, and will give reasonably stable images.

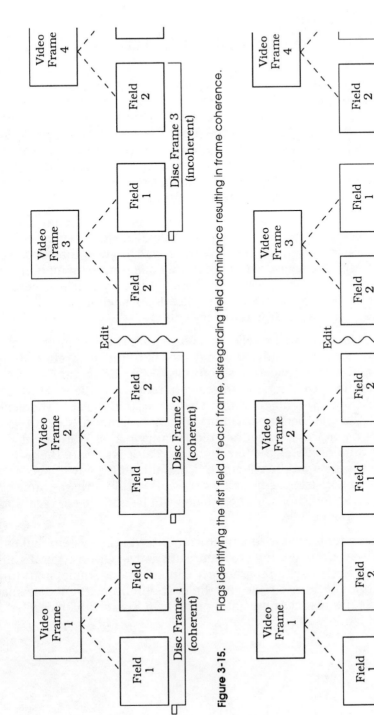

Figure 3-14. Field inaccurate edit causing a shift in field dominance and resulting in mismatched fields. Field dominance in this example is set at Field 1.

Figure 3-15. Flags identifying the first field of each frame, disregarding field dominance resulting in frame coherence.

Frame Accuracy

This section is important only if you are including still frames in your treatment.

Frame-accurate editing is necessary if you intend to use still frames and duplicate each frame only once on the disc. Frame accuracy requires sophisticated, computer controlled editing equipment and field-consistent video editing throughout the edit master tape. It does, however, enable the *Step Frame* command mode, permitting learners to move sequentially from one frame to the next without the aid of a host computer, and without encountering unstable images, a black interval between frames, or redundant frames.

This is an attractive alternative if disc space is at a premium, because redundant stills aren't consuming valuable disc space. There are few applications which require this level of frugality, given that 1800 still frames occupy the space required for only one minute of motion, and few applications require more than 1800 stills. Nevertheless, certain information storage and retrieval applications, such as visual databases, may use a large number of stills.

For typical treatments, however, which require the combination of motion and still segments, the annoyance of frame-accurate editing can be avoided by duplicating still frames a number of times. This confounds the *Step* function, unless you inform the user that several presses of the *Step Frame* button may be required to get to the next frame, or redefine the *Step* function in your program to step three frames for each press. Of course, redundancy makes editing quite a bit easier and increases the likelihood that at least one of the redundant frames will be coherent. It has the added advantage of making field-consistent editing less critical. Within a three-frame sequence, a solid frame with both fields will be addressed, regardless of field dominance (Figure 3-16).

Multimedia production with a microcomputer in the system makes non-frame-accurate editing even more attractive. Given several stills from which to choose, a programmer can select one frame, and "jump over" redundant frames to access the next still frame. So if disc space is available, frame-accurate editing may be a luxury which can be avoided (Figure 3-17).

Figure 3-16. Frame-accurate editing permits single still-frame duplication. Frame-redundant editing yields several duplicate still frames.

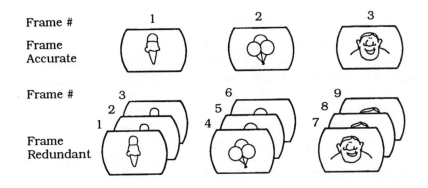

Figure 3-17. Frame redundancy permits selection of still-frame with either *Search* or redefined *Step* command.

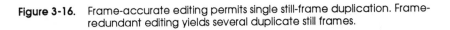

Chapters

Much like the chapters of a book, a videodisc can be divided into chapters. A videodisc chapter is any uninterrupted series of frames on one side of a videodisc. Thus, "chunks" of instruction can be identified by chapter number. For instance, an instructional treatment on "Preventive Dentistry" might be divided into the following chapters on a disc:

      Chapter 1: Introduction
      Chapter 2: Dental Deposits
      Chapter 3: Diet and Nutrition

Chapter 4: Plaque Control
Chapter 5: Fluorides
Chapter 6: Pit and Fissure Sealants
Chapter 7: Dental Health Indices
Chapter 8: Dental Health Education

For each frame on the disc, chapter number codes are placed in the VBI between the fields of a discrete frame. This enables chapter numbers to be displayed and the user can manually access any desired chapter of instruction. There is room for up to 80 chapters on a single side, but if they are used, every frame must carry a chapter number, chapters must be intact (in one area of the disc), and they must be numbered sequentially. You can start your numbering with any chapter number, but all subsequent chapters will be numbered sequentially thereafter.

Chapters can be quite useful, particularly if you are reviewing material, and want to access "chunks" of instruction quickly. Chapters can be accessed in one of two modes: Search or Scan.

Chapter Search

In this mode, the disc player moves to the first frame of the requested chapter, and displays it as a freeze frame. This is a very exact movement, and no allowance is necessary for error.

Chapter Scan

This is a very different mode, much more like taking a running jump into the chapter. When directed to conduct a Chapter Scan, the player moves rapidly through the treatment displaying some passing frames and skipping tracks. When the player detects a chapter stop code, which is positioned on the first 400 frames of a chapter, it halts. This provides very imprecise access to the beginning of a chapter, and mastering facilities recommend a 300 to 400 frame window of non-essential material which can act as a landing strip for the player as it scans. This represents almost 14 seconds of disc space, so if disc space is at a premium, it might be wise to ignore this feature and rely on chapter search.

Picture Stop

Occasionally, it is useful to have the player stop automatically on a single still-frame. This convention might be used at the end of a motion sequence, or at a menu or question. This can be programmed and externally imposed either from the player's built-in microprocessor or a host computer. Still, in some cases it might be convenient to have the convention activated without intervention. It is enabled by a picture stop code recorded in the VBI of the selected frame.

One thing to remember about encoding picture stops on the disc is that they are activated even if you override a resident videodisc program with your own microcomputer program (e.g., a HyperCard stack). If you intend to change your treatment from time to time, or create several different multimedia applications from a single videodisc, you would be well-advised to relegate all of your picture stop commands to the external microcomputer program for the treatment, rather than encode picture stops within the VBI throughout the disc.

Organizing Source Material

Before you set foot in a post-production facility, you must be organized. If you are the fastidious type, you have probably neatly labeled all of your source tapes and included detailed listings of the locations of all motion sequences and still frames. If you are like the other 90% of humanity, however, now is the time to begin the wearisome task of locating and recording all of the footage you intend to use.

Edit Decision List

For each reel of tape, review it and record each segment or still frame in sequence. Your form might look something like the portion reproduced in Figure 3-18.

Figure 3-18.   Edit decision list for source tapes.

Date_____   Source Tape # _____

Production Title_____   SMPTE __:__:__:__: to __:__:__:__

| SMPTE Location | | Still | Motion | Segment Description | Picture Stop | Cahpter # | Frames |
Start	Finish						
00:03:00:00		√		Title Frame		1	1
00:03:00:02		√		Main Menu-units of course	*	1	1
00:03:00:04		√		Unit 4 Objectives	*	4	1
00:04:30:00	00:08:00:00		√	Dental Therapy Unit		4	6300

Annotated Flowchart

A flowchart can be a useful tool during the post-production process. As a disciplined instructional developer, you probably used a flowchart to guide you during pre-production and production phases of development. In post-production you will continue to rearrange it until you are satisfied with its architecture. If you didn't construct a flowchart to guide you during pre-production and production, now is a good time to start one.

Whether you used a flowchart, algorithm, decision tree, or another strategy, your tool should identify each instructional element in your treatment, and should display relationships among elements. For post-production, this tool can be used in the following ways:

- as a master checklist to confirm that each element has been produced;
- to identify the SMPTE locations from source tapes for transfer to your edit master;
- to review the architecture of the entire treatment, and make placement decisions;
- to record disc frame locations for multimedia programming reference.

For multimedia development purposes, your flowchart should discriminate clearly among the sources (videodisc, CD-ROM, computer), perhaps by using different colors. This way, you may avoid the frustration of searching frantically for a video segment which doesn't exist, only to discover you intended to deliver it via the computer.

Another thing you will want to include in your flowchart is space for adding SMPTE or disc frame locations of the video segments. You will add location data to the flowchart from either the premaster tape, or from a "check" disc. This information is invaluable for completing multimedia programming. The SMPTE code can be used before you receive a check disc to test your program, and then exact frame locations substituted when a videodisc is available. This allows you to progress with your programming during inevitable manufacturing delays, so your project doesn't grind to a halt while you are waiting for a check disc. Much of your preliminary debugging can occur without the disc version, saving you time and frustration. When the check disc arrives, it will exhibit the exact frame numbers you can expect from later copies as long as you don't make changes at that point. Therefore, the check disc can be used to reference final programming decisions.

In the example in Figure 3-19, notice that different types of instructional elements are depicted with different shapes for easy identification. In addition, video frame numbers are added to each element for programming reference.

Figure 3-19.   Flowchart example (annotated).

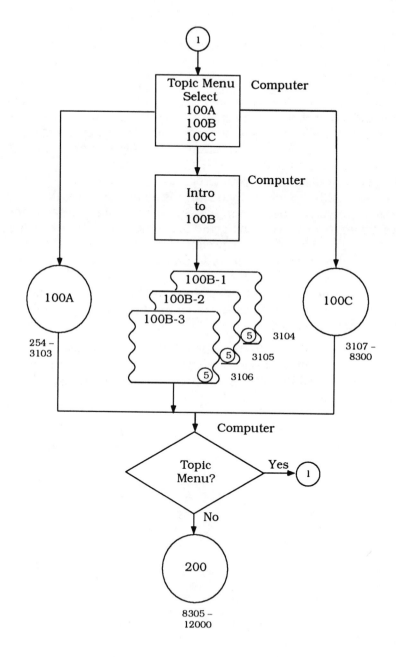

Conceptual Geography

The conceptual geography of a treatment refers to the rough layout of instructional events, such as motion segments, questions, clusters of remedial segments, and menus. It depicts the "neighborhoods" in which instructional pieces will be placed on a videodisc. The purpose of conceptual geography is to apportion the space on a disc to various events, and determine the time allotted to the total. Refinements to the order will be made later, but rough layout assignments should be made at this point.

To construct the conceptual geography, first refer to your flowchart and confirm that each video segment which should exist does exist. If segments have been overlooked, now is the time to find out.

After confirming that each element is accounted for, a useful step is to place each segment or still frame on an individual card. Placing each element of the treatment on a card will give you the opportunity to shuffle, add, or remove parts of the instruction until you are satisfied with the geographic structure of the treatment (Figures 3-20 and 3-21). Various types of color coding may be useful for your application, say,

- White = Computer-generated text or graphics
- Yellow = Motion sequence
- Blue = Still frame

Prominent letters, numbers, stripes, or symbols can be added to basic cards to discriminate chapters, questions, response feedback, timing, branching, and the like. For example:

- C1 = Chapter 1
- Q10 = Question 10
- M1 = Menu, Chapter 1
- FN2 = Feedback if wrong (no match) on second attempt
- #132 = Go to segment 132

On the back of each card, place the source reel number, the SMPTE location for the frame or sequence, and the total SMPTE code in minutes, seconds, and frames—or calculate the total number of frames.

The SMPTE time code can be used to estimate accurately the number of frames and total running time used by the treatment.

Figure 3-20.   Sample of post-production cards for motion, still, and computer segments.

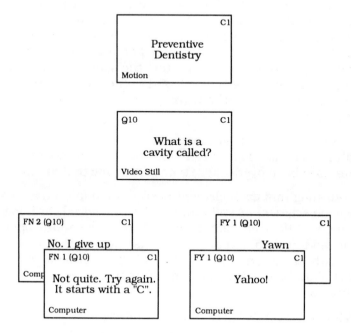

Figure 3-21.   Reverse side of post-production card.

Source Reel 2
SMPTE   From 00:03:30:05
            To   00:05:00:05

Total Frames: 2700
Total Time: 1:30

The eight digit SMPTE time code (e.g., 00:03:45:28) can be broken down as follows:

00:	03:	45:	28
hours	minutes	seconds	frames

This location is exactly 3 minutes 45 seconds and 28 frames from the first frame on the tape. Since there are 30 frames per second, moving the tape forward two frames would result in the SMPTE location:

00:03:46:00

SMPTE codes can also be used to calculate the number of disc frames by using the formula:

(Minutes × 1800) + (Seconds × 30) + Frames = Total # Frames

Thus, given the example of 00:03:45:28 from above, the videodisc frames used will equal:

(3 × 1800)	=	5400
+(45 × 30)	=	1350
+ 28	=	0028
		6778 frames

The sum of SMPTE totals or frame totals from the cards must not exceed 30 minutes or 54,000 frames. If there is a capacity problem, the designer must either decide what to eliminate from the treatment, or find a logical breaking point in the instruction and move part of the instruction to the other side of the disc.

One final important notion—*Katz's 54,000 Law.* Completely fill the disc with program material (L. Katz, personal communication, February, 1991). If any empty space remains on the disc once you have laid out the conceptual geography of your disc, find something else relevant to the topic to fill the remaining space. The cost of pressing and duplicating videodiscs is the same, regardless of the amount of program material contained on the disc. It only makes sense to pack as much material as possible onto the disc, even if you are not sure immediately how you will use it later.

Summary: Conceptual Geography

- Conceptual geography identifies the location of major sections of instruction.
- Conceptual geography decisions are used to conform production elements to your flowchart, and to make decisions about the location of video and computer segments.
- Placing elements on cards will allow you to move sections of instruction easily, and to experiment with combinations.
- SMPTE times can be totaled to ensure that the 30 minute time restriction is not exceeded.
- SMPTE times can be converted to disc frame numbers.
- Fill the disc with program material. If space remains following your treatment, find something potentially useful for another application to fill the space.

Tactical Geography

So far, you have determined that all necessary video elements exist, laid out the conceptual geography of the segments according to the flowchart, and calculated the space requirements for a disc. Now the layout of the instructional element must be refined. Following the layout of the flowchart provides a conceptual structure for major sections of instruction, but fine-tuning the order of the elements will result in an altered tactical structure of the elements.

One rule guides all decisions concerning the order of segments on the disc:

> The most heavily traveled paths through the treatment should also be the shortest paths.

In real life, it usually works the other way around—people choose the shortest paths, and therefore they become the most heavily trodden. In this instance, you must attempt to predict the most likely chosen directions through the instruction, and manipulate the order of the elements to make the instruction as efficient as possible. In other words, you predict which answer to questions, menu selections, and the like will be selected most often, and place them closer to the question or menu than elements which aren't encountered as often. The closer the physical proximity of elements on the disc, the faster the access, and the more professional the "look" of the materials.

Designing the location matrix for instructional elements is largely an art, with a liberal sprinkling of science thrown in for good measure. Three levels of decision can be made, based on intuition, logic, and elemental analysis. Although these will be discussed individually, most often a combination of the three is used to make final decisions.

Intuition

This is a very useful tool which can make the difference between excellent and uninspired designs. The intuitive instructional designer is skilled at assuming the role and personality of the learner, and viewing the instruction from that perspective. A point made earlier deserves repeating. From the perspective of the learner, you may be able to identify the most attractive options from a menu (which ones look interesting, easy, humorous). Strong distracters or obvious mistakes can be anticipated with some questions, and feedback can be constructed which seems almost clairvoyant. Instructionally this can be very powerful. For example, which of these is the stronger feedback segment?

> Segment 1: "Oops, you calculated the markup correctly by subtracting cost from retail, but you forgot to divide by the retail figure to get the markup percentage. Try again, and divide by retail this time."

or

> Segment 2: "No, try again."

Although you won't always be able to predict learner errors and patterns, a few intuitive bulls-eyes are easily programmed, instructionally sound, and give a treatment a personality. Constructing these types of segments requires a fairly intimate understanding of the content, or an open communication climate between the instructional developer and subject-matter expert. Another valuable source of information is typical learners during one-to-one formative evaluation of the materials. Having learners talk about their thinking processes will intuitively lead you to typical patterns of responses.

Certainly some things we call intuition are based upon experience, common sense, and an understanding of human behavior patterns. For example, it is quite common for individuals who don't know the answer on a test question to:

- Select "C" on a multiple choice question.
- Choose the longest multiple choice response.
- Pick an answer with a technical-sounding label.
- Answer false on true/false items.
- Locate syntactic cues which identify the correct response, or eliminate improbable answers.

These represent only a few possible notions you can consider when deciding the placement of elements on the disc. Whether they represent intuition, horse-sense, or experience, they can guide you to useful design decisions.

Logic

Closely related to intuition, logic is usually verifiable. Whereas intuition can point the designer in some likely directions, logic can sometimes be used to factually identify correct sequences. It can also be used to demonstrate the difference between conceptual and tactical instructional geography.

Let's use the example of a series of conditional responses to a question, based upon the number of attempts a learner has made. Asked a question, the learner could encounter a series of responses, based upon whether the answer is correct or incorrect, and the number of times an answer has been attempted. The conceptual geography, drawn from the flowchart, would resemble that in Figure 3-22, with correct and incorrect responses clumped together.

Figure 3-22.   Conceptual geography, with correct and incorrect responses clumped
                   together.

Question: Who is the Prime Minister of Canada?

Correct—first attempt:	Of course! Let's continue.
Correct—second attempt:	Yes. Take one Maple Leaf from petty cash.
Correct—third attempt:	Whew! That was close. The RCMP was asking for your citizenship papers.

Incorrect—first attempt:	Whoops! Take another look at the *Globe and Mail* article and try again.
Incorrect—second attempt:	No, but I'm sure that person would be flattered to hear it.
Incorrect—third attempt:	Sorry, let's have another look at the *Globe and Mail* article in this lesson, and see if you can pick out the Prime Minister's name this time.

This is a useful structure for examining the relationship among
elements in an instructional sequence, but it does not logically
provide the most efficient pattern for laying out the elements on disc.
A more efficient tactical geography would impose the structure in
Figure 3-23.

Figure 3-23. Tactical geography, with more efficient layout of correct and incorrect responses.

Question: Who is the Prime Minister of Canada?

Correct—first attempt:	Of course he is! Let's continue.
Incorrect—first attempt:	Whoops! Take another look at the *Globe and Mail* example, and try again.

Correct—second attempt:	Yes. Take one Maple Leaf from petty cash.
Incorrect—second attempt:	No, but I'm sure that person would be flattered to hear it.

Correct—third attempt:	Whew! That was close. The RCMP was asking for your citizenship papers.
Incorrect—third attempt:	Sorry, let's have another look at the *Globe and Mail* article in this lesson, and see if you can pick out the Prime Minister's name this time.

Logically, the student would have to encounter the incorrect first attempt response before possibly encountering either of the second or third attempt responses. The first attempt should therefore be located before the others to reduce the distance between question and response. Only those learners who missed the question twice would ever need to "jump over" the first four responses to receive a third attempt response. Obviously, most of the learners will get the answer correct on one of the first two attempts, thereby reducing the number of students exposed to the longer access periods. Alternative logical structures can be explored. Compare those shown in Figure 3-24, for example.

Figure 3-24. Alternative tactical structures for conditional response feedback.

Tactical Structure A		Tactical Structure B	
Incorrect	2	Incorrect	1
Incorrect	1	Correct	1
Question		Question	
Correct	1	Correct	2
Correct	2	Incorrect	2
Correct	3	Correct	3
Incorrect	3	Incorrect	3

Ask yourself, "Which of these structures would be more efficient if the learner is correct on the first try, second try, or third try?" The point is that the tactical structure used to organize elements on the premaster tape may be quite different from the conceptual structure of instructional elements. It may not look as pretty, but it works. (By the way, tactical structure A is more efficient than B, regardless of the number of incorrect attempts. Can you devise a more efficient tactical structure?)

Elemental Analysis

Where time, budget, and availability of subjects allow, pilot testing materials can provide extremely useful guidelines for making tactical geography decisions. This procedure requires a thoroughly written treatment with a script and storyboard, or preferably a completed version of the instruction with the computer program and edited trial videotape. Intuitive and logical tactical decisions will have been imposed on the materials, so that assumptions can be tested against actual pilot test results.

This type of formative evaluation also requires "typical" or representative subjects, and someone to monitor the subjects' paths through instruction.

The monitor should record each segment selected in order, menu selections chosen and ignored, and all question attempts and responses. The recording mechanism can be as simple as making a hash mark on each post-production card or the flowchart, or checking off instructional elements on a master post-production worksheet (Figure 3-25). Another approach is to use an audit trail tree, described more completely in Chapter 13.

Figure 3-25. Example of post-production worksheet used for formative evaluation.

Post Production Worksheet
Instructional Elements

	Element #	Description	Comment
√√√	1	Title	
√√√	2	Menu 1 — Drugs	
	3	Option 1 — Aspirin	
√√	4	Option 2 — Lanoxyn	Color too bright
	5	Option 3 — Tylenol	
√√	6	Option 4 — Ilosone	
√√√	7	Question — Drugs	
√	8	Correct 1	
√	9	Correct 2	
√	10	Correct 3	
√√	11	Incorrect 1	Misspelled
√	12	Incorrect 2	Insulting
	13	Incorrect 3	

A highly interactive treatment can easily contain several hundred elements and thousands of unique paths. This level of analysis will tell you which elements are receiving the most traffic and which are being ignored. Several specific approaches to analyzing paths, which we call audit trails, are discussed in Chapter 13.

The analysis does not produce absolute data, by any means, and you should be careful not to over-interpret tentative results. With only a few subjects participating, it would be unwise to eliminate instructional elements solely because they were not selected or encountered during the pilot test.

It is prudent to weigh pilot test data against intuition and logic to determine whether specific elements should be moved, edited, or eliminated. Other practical considerations will intervene, such as the amount of space available, the "look" of the material, and the complete marketing potential for the treatment, which may introduce a different mix of learners to the materials.

Still, carefully employed and interpreted, this type of elemental analysis can be successfully used to challenge previous design assumptions, and indicate areas for improvement. Discriminant analysis can be productively used to examine the relationships between various instructional elements in the treatment and overall learning. Asking the question "Did exposure to this sequence contribute to or interfere with learning?" can provide interesting (and sometimes frightening) food for thought.

Manufacturing Videodiscs

Once your final decisions are made about tactical geography, shuffle your post-production cards in order, or design a Premaster Edit List for studio work. On the Premaster Edit List (Figure 3-26), you will want to include the source reel number and SMPTE code for each segment in order. Also leave room to record the SMPTE time code on the premaster tape. This will be handy later, as you calculate disc frame numbers for the segments.

Submission, Review, and Approval

At this point, you have a completed edit master tape and are ready to submit it to the manufacturer for mastering and replication. The final activities are represented below. The activities are important, but represent each possible step in the process. You may be able to eliminate some of the steps, such as check cassettes, check discs and proof discs, depending on your project.

- Submission of edit master.
- Manufacture check cassette.
- Review check cassette.
- Manufacture check disc.
- Review check disc.
- Manufacture proof disc.
- Review proof disc.
- Replicate discs.

In any case, manufacturers request advance notice to schedule your project. Be sure your edit master arrives prior to the scheduled start date. Missing a deadline can result in losing your place in line, and this can be frustrating at the end of a long project. In most cases, manufacturing discs requires approximately 10 days, although 24 hour service is available.

Figure 3-26. Premaster edit list.

Premaster Edit List

Production Title _____ Premaster SMPTE Begin __:__:__:__

Field Dominance _____ Active Program End __:__:__:__

| Source Reel # | Segment SMPTE From Source | | Segment Description | Picture Stop | Chapter # * | Premaster SMPTE | |
	Begin	End				Begin	End

* 1st chapter frame

Check Cassette

Once the edit master is received by the manufacturer, the first step is encoding. You may receive a check cassette tape of the encoded tape in either $1/2''$ or $3/4''$ format. It will include a window dub identifying the SMPTE code, picture and chapter numbers, and the video field. Besides review, the check cassette is a useful medium for initial programming.

If you have an interactive videotape system, you can use it to test your computer code. This can save you a great deal of debugging time later, and is an efficient use of project time while you are waiting for the manufacturer to finish the final videodiscs.

Check Disc

After the check cassette is approved, a single check disc copy of the encoded master is available. The check disc is very useful for testing programs while waiting for the manufacturer to complete remaining tasks. Disc frame numbers are identical to those on later replications, although audio and video quality may not be as good as final copies.

Proof Disc

Yet another version of the treatment is available for review. The proof disc is the same as the check disc, except it also includes digital programs on Audio Channel 2 (program dumps). Unless you are using a Level II program, the proof disc may be unnecessary.

Other Video Formats

DRAW Videodiscs

Direct Read After Write (DRAW) technology uses an analog format to create videodiscs. Copies are made one at a time in real time, similar to duplicating a videotape onto a blank disc. As with their production-house counterparts, once the information is written, it cannot be erased or revised. This is an attractive option for small orders of discs or for in-house productions which require frequent updates. Motion segments and stills can be recorded quickly, without the set-up costs and inconvenience of working through production companies. On the other hand, if multiple copies are required, the cost per disc for DRAW technology quickly outpaces costs of manufacturing multiple copies. DRAW technology is also plagued by a lack of standardization in the industry.

Compressed Digital Video

As exciting and useful as videodisc continues to be, it very likely will not survive as the primary video source in interactive multimedia systems. Videodisc may coexist with compressed digital video for some time yet; indeed, component systems may dominate for the near future, requiring users to mix and match components when constructing systems. However, multimedia systems are rapidly becoming single packages, with the computer housing all sources. Our guess is that videodiscs will continue to serve stand-alone presentation and consumer markets for a long time, but will be less influential for multimedia instruction. Some form of compressed digital video will probably take its place in interactive multimedia systems. What is compressed digital video? A brief explanation is necessary.

Video is made up of analog signals. It is possible, as with audio technology, to convert analog signals to digital signals. Once in digital format, video can be handled very conveniently as computer files, thus folding the function of the videodisc player into the computer. The problem is that because video pictures include so much information, and they whiz by at 30 frames per second, in order to represent them digitally requires huge files. For example, 30 seconds of full motion color video requires approximately one gigabyte (1024 MB) of memory. Microcomputers are unable to store and retrieve video files efficiently, given the size of the data and speed of computers. The answer is to digitize video images and then compress them into a file size which can be managed by microcomputer systems. This requires compression technology, and also requires decompression technology for playing back the video in real time.

Compression is achieved by sampling video and specifically eliminating unnecessary portions of images. For example, one standard (DVI) uses a proprietary technique called *region coding*. Region coding identifies parts of video images which can be reduced to smaller numbers of data bits, say large monochromatic areas such as blue skies. In addition, a technique called interframe compression is used to eliminate duplication of the portions of frames which do not change from one frame to the next. This is the digital video equivalent of the cell animation technique of only changing the moving portions of characters on a static background.

There is a great deal of development activity in the area of digital video. One common technology is Digital Video Interactive (DVI) aimed at the PC market. It was developed by the David Sarnoff Research Institute at RCA, and later sold to Intel Corporation. DVI is a trade name for chips under development by Intel which compress video into files and decompress it for playback. The chips include a pixel processor which performs most of the decompression and special video effects and a display processor which produces video output (Arnett, 1990).

Compact Disc Interactive (CD-I) is another digital video technology being cooperatively developed by Philips, Sony, and Matsushita. It is based on the Motorola 68000 family processor and a real time operating system, so it is positioned to address the Apple Macintosh, Commodore Amiga, and NeXT markets. It is a compact disc format which includes audio, digital data, still graphics, and full motion video.

Common standards are being developed by the Moving Pictures Experts Group (MPEG) based on a video compression technique called Discrete Cosine Transformations. These are standards for motion video, and could be adopted as an international standard to which both DVI and CD-I could conform.

Generally speaking, compressed digital video is somewhat expensive to produce. Beyond the usual video production expenses, off-line compression of video costs approximately $250 per minute at the time of this writing (although costs will probably plummet as demand increases). Real time compression/decompression approaches avoid some of the off-line production costs, but the trade-off is lower image quality.

Magnetically-Recorded Video

We would be remiss if we did not mention the most common medium available for storing and retrieving television programming—

videotape. Videotape technology has been generally available to educators and trainers since the 1950s.

In interactive multimedia applications tape is usually used as an intermediate development medium, a place to record and store images until they can be converted to disc or to compressed digital video. In some cases, IMI systems may employ videocassette players, but in most cases videotape is used to perform formative evaluations prior to completing production in another format. A very brief discussion of the most common formats follows.

Open-Reel Videotape

Open reel units are still in wide use in professional television studios, particularly 1″ equipment. Generally speaking, the wider the videotape, the higher the quality of the image which can be recorded. Quality deteriorates with smaller tape, because there is less room on the tape to record information. Therefore, many professional studios still employ 1″ videotape recorders to ensure quality, facilitate editing, and allow quality duplicating. For accurate transfer of video from tape to disc technology, a 1″ tape is recommended by videodisc manufacturing companies, although other formats can be accommodated.

Videocassette

A minor revolution occurred in the early 1970s when videocassette recorders (VCRs) were introduced to the educational marketplace. The first popular format of videocassette recorders for educational purposes was $3/4$″, introduced by Sony in the early 1970s, and later produced by several competitors. High quality $3/4$″ videotapes still function as edit masters for videodisc manufacture, although 1″ is still the preferred format. In many cases, lower budget videodisc projects will rely on $3/4$″ systems for both source and edit master production. Some manufacturers require an additional set-up charge for $3/4$″ masters.

Just when educators were becoming comfortable with the $3/4$″ format, $1/2$″ videocassette recorders were introduced into the marketplace. Functionally similar to their larger counterparts, the $1/2$″ system was designed primarily for the home video market. There are two formats of $1/2$″ of videocassettes dominating the market—Beta and VHS. VHS dominates the home market today. A professional format of Beta is an industry standard for electronic news gathering, and offers excellent quality for transfer to other tape formats or disc.

References for Chapter 3

Arnett, N. (1990). Digital video arrives. *PC Magazine, July,* 152–153.

Arwady, J., and Gayeski, D. (1989). *Using video: Interactive and linear designs.* Englewood Cliffs, NJ: Educational Technology Publications.

Braden, R. (1986). Visuals for interactive video: Images for a new technology. *Educational Technology, 26*(5), 18–23.

Burger, M. L. (1985, January). *Authoring languages/systems comparisons.* Paper presented at the Annual Conference of the Association for Educational Communications and Technology, Anaheim, CA.

Galbreath, J. (1992b). The coming of digital desktop media. *Educational Technology, 32*(6), 27–37.

Gayeski, D. (1983). *Corporate and instructional video design and production.* Englewood Cliffs, NJ: Prentice-Hall.

Geber, B. (1989). Whither interactive videodisc? *Training, 26*(3), 47–49.

Iuppa, N. V. (1984). *A practical guide to interactive video design.* White Plains, NY: Knowledge Industry Publications, Inc.

Katz, L. (1992). Essentially multimedia: An explanation of interactive laserdisc and optical technology. *The Canadian Multi Media Magazine, 1*(1), 18-20.

Katz, L., and Keet, C. (1990). *Innovations in laser and optical disc technology.* Calgary, AB: Alberta Laserdisc Committee.

Pioneer Video. (1984). *Post-production and formatting information.* Montvale, NJ: Pioneer Video, Inc.

Sales, G. (1989a). An introduction to videodiscs III: Videodisc hardware. *Computing Teacher, 16*(7), 50–51.

Schwartz, E. (1987). *The educators' handbook to interactive videodisc* (2nd ed.). Washington, DC: Association for Educational Communications and Technology.

Schwier, R. A. (1987). *Interactive video.* Englewood Cliffs, NJ: Educational Technology Publications.

3M Corporation. (1981). *Premastering and post-production procedures for Scotch videodiscs.* St. Paul, MN: Optical Recording Project, 3M.

Weigand, I. (1985). Videodisc players: Pasts and futures. *Video Manager, 8*(3), 14–15.

Chapter 4

Audio

Although audio recordings have been around for a long time, some recent advances, notably in digital audio, have established new frontiers in the medium. Making recordings, especially recordings of music, is a complex and sophisticated business that is already well addressed by a vast literature, of which Huber and Runstein (1989) and Oringel (1989) are typical. This chapter deals only with some fundamental concepts of audio recording that transcend the medium holding the recording.

Audio includes the spoken word, music (instrumental and voice), natural sounds, and sound effects. Audio has been typically delivered in multimedia productions via videodisc, videotape, or audiotape (often audiocassette); more recently it has become possible to deliver it via computer technology, as well. Leaving aside such awkward delivery media—for the IMI environment, at least—as audiotape and videotape, current choices for audio delivery in interactive multimedia are:

- videodisc,
- compact discs (CDs), or
- digitized (computer-based) sound, either on magnetic media or on CD-ROM.

Both videodiscs and CDs are capable of binaural (stereo) sound; hence they each have two tracks. Where desired, a stereo track could be used to provide two monaural recordings instead; either track could be selected for playback. Sound recorded digitally on magnetic disks (floppies or hard disks) must be "played" through a microcomputer and is typically monaural, unless specialized hardware is added. On some brands of microcomputer, provisions are made to choose from among a small, relatively low-quality internal speaker, external headphones, or external output to high-fidelity amplifiers and speakers. In the Macintosh world, audio capability is built into all machines in a standard way. In the DOS world, audio is usually available as an add-on, with a variety of different formats and hardware/software combinations in existence. Planning audio for DOS platforms therefore requires more care in terms of specifying the hardware/software combinations that are supported.

There are two distinct methods of getting audio into a computer: MIDI and digitization. Before examining both methods, we elaborate on some basic audio concepts that transcend them.

Digital and Analog Audio

Sound travels in waves, through solids, liquids, and gases. For both simplicity and practicality, we will only consider sound traveling through the air. Objects producing sounds cause the air around them to be alternately compressed and rarefied, thereby creating the wave motion that travels to the ear; there, the eardrum vibrates in response to those compressions and rarefactions, and the result is interpreted by the brain as sound.

Because sound waves are invisible, it is useful to consider the analogy of waves in water: At a given location, the level of water will rise to a maximum height, then gradually fall, past the starting height, to a low point, then begin rising again until it reaches the starting point. If the height of the water (y axis) is plotted against time (x axis), the motion looks like the familiar sine wave (Figure 4-1).

Figure 4-1.   A sine wave.

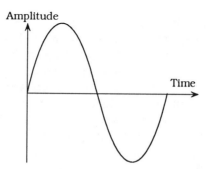

The wave plotted in Figure 4-1 has two important characteristics—its amplitude and its frequency. Its amplitude is the difference between its starting point and either its highest or lowest points, and corresponds, in audio terms, to the volume of the sound. Its frequency is the number of times a complete cycle (starting height to maximum height to starting height to minimum height to starting height) occurs per second. In audio terms, the frequency corresponds to the pitch of the sound.

A pure (single-frequency) sound produces a waveform that resembles that in Figure 4-1. However, few sounds are simple sounds. Most sounds have more complex waveforms, perhaps resembling the one in Figure 4-2.

Figure 4-2.   A complex waveform.

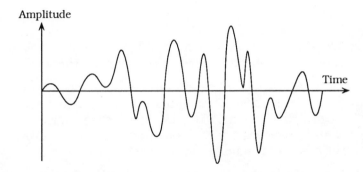

Sound is converted to electrical signals via microphones, in preparation for recording. Those signals can then be recorded using either analog or digital techniques. What makes an analog recording *analog* (as opposed to digital) is that the recorded signal continuously varies in strength, whereas a digital recording uses signals of constant strength.

Analog recordings are made when electrical signals of varying frequency and amplitude are converted into some other form, either:

- grooves (squiggles) on a vinyl record;
- magnetic signals on audiotape (either reel-to-reel or cassette), videotape, or magnetic-stripe motion-picture film; or
- variously-sized and shaped blobs on an optical sound track on motion-picture film.

Analog recordings are, as the name implies, analogous to the original sounds. Consider the case of a vinyl record, on which the squiggles constituting the grooves represent the sound: When the sound gets louder (i.e., the amplitude of the waveform increases), the amplitude of the squiggle on the vinyl gets larger; when the sound gets quieter, the amplitude of the squiggle gets smaller. Similarly, when the pitch of the sound increases (i.e., the frequency increases), the number of squiggles per unit of time (or length of groove on the record) increases, and vice versa.

A characteristic of analog recordings is that in addition to the signal (the sound being recorded), they typically include some noise (extraneous, undesirable sounds). Furthermore, additional noise is usually introduced every time the signal is processed (e.g., amplified, mixed, re-recorded, etc.). By using very high-quality equipment, the amount of noise relative to the amount of signal is minimized, but it is still there.

Digital recordings do not contain continuous signals; rather, they hold numerical representations of the sound waves. Since the numbers are binary-coded (i.e., ON or OFF, 1 or 0), the strength of the signal used is constant: it is either there or not there.

Digital recordings also do not deteriorate with age, so are infinite in life-span. Even if the physical medium on which the digitally-recorded materials begins to deteriorate, the data can be transferred to new media without loss or degradation. Furthermore, in digitally-recorded sound, error-correction schemes virtually eliminate dropout.

Digital recordings of natural (as opposed to synthesized) sounds are made on devices called sound samplers, through a process called quantization. Many microcomputers, fitted with a modicum of special equipment and using appropriate software, can act as rudimentary sound samplers. What samplers do is simply take many, many discrete samples of the sound waves every second (Figure 4-3). The samples are converted into numeric values, and stored.

Figure 4-3. Digital sampling (quantization) of a portion of a complex analog waveform. The amplitude (y axis) is broken into regions represented by a number. Samples taken periodically through time (x axis) are represented by those numbers (quantized values). For simplicity, the waveform here is represented by 4-bit digital numbers; actual CDs use 16-bit representations. Also for simplicity, only a short period of time is depicted in the figure; in CD production, 44,100 samples are taken per second.

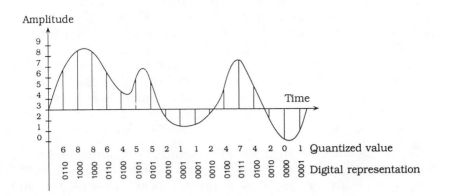

Because there are so many samples taken of the sound (44,100 per second, as explained below) and because they are made so close together in time, the net effect to the ear is one of continuity (much as many still pictures projected rapidly one after the other make motion-picture film appear to move). Digital recordings are thus able to be converted into either:

- on/off pulses on magnetic media (such as digital audio tape—DAT—or magnetic disks for computers, synthesizers, sound samplers, and sequencers); or
- pits on the surface of a CD, videodisc, or CD-ROM.

A large advantage of digital recording over analog is that the amount of noise introduced at each step of processing is virtually zero. Since the signals recorded are merely numbers, they can be copied and manipulated without any deterioration.

Playback can also be either digital or analog; generally speaking, the method of playback coincides with the method of recording (e.g., records and cassettes produce analog signals, and DATs and CDs produce digital signals). These signals almost always have to be amplified, and the amplification is usually analog in nature (although recently some digital amplifiers have come onto the home audio market). Ultimately (at the ear) everything must again revert to analog—because that's the way we hear—so if the signal is amplified digitally, there must eventually be a conversion to an analog signal which is sent to the speakers or headphones.

Of course, digitally-recorded sound may be re-recorded on analog equipment, and vice versa. In the normal course of production of CDs, for example, everything is kept in digital form, from the initial recording, through the mixing, to the pressing of the CD. However, as is evidenced from the many re-releases of pre-CD-era recordings, sounds that were originally recorded in analog can be converted to digital form, "cleaned up" electronically, and issued as a CD. Some of these re-released versions actually sound better than the originals: Since digital signals are merely ONs and OFFs, or 1s and 0s, they can be edited via computer programs. Clicks, pops, tape hiss, and other vestiges of the pre-high fidelity era of recording can be edited out.

Although digitally-recorded sound is commonly regarded as the "cleanest" possible today, there is a price to be paid: digital sound files are typically very large. Even a relatively short segment of sound can occupy many megabytes of computer disk space, particularly if it is recorded at the highest possible quality. For that reason, in the production of CDs, the recordings are usually made on digitally-encoded tape. (The actual production of CDs is based on the same methods as the production of videodiscs discussed in Chapter 3; virtually the only differences between CDs, videodiscs, and CD-ROMs—which we will examine in Chapter 5—are their sizes and the kinds of data encoded in certain tracks on their surfaces.)

Recording Quality

In analog recording, the speed with which the tape traverses the recording head has a major influence on the quality of the recording made. Generally speaking, if you keep the system quality—the hardware (recording and playback heads, tape transport mechanism, and electronic processing and amplification) and the type and size of tape used—constant, the higher the speed at which the recording is made, the better the quality of the recording. Thus a segment recorded on $1/4$" reel-to-reel tape at $7 \, 1/2$ inches per second (ips) will be acoustically superior to another segment recorded on the same system at $3 \, 3/4$ ips.

In digital recording, a parallel phenomenon occurs. However, instead of recording speed, sampling rate is the most crucial factor. Sampling rate is usually measured in kilohertz (kHz); one kHz is equal to 1,000 cycles per second. Hence a segment of sound recorded at a sampling rate of 11.0 kHz will be acoustically inferior to a segment recorded at 22.0 kHz.

The sampling rate determines the highest frequency that can be reproduced by the system. Indeed, slightly more than twice as many samples per second must be made as the highest frequency reproduced. In other words, to have a top frequency of 20 kHz, the upper limit of human hearing, requires a sampling rate of 44.1 kHz, the sampling rate used for CDs. Most microcomputer-based sampling programs work at sampling rates below that. For example, in the Macintosh world, one popular recording program offers users the opportunity to record at sampling rates of 22, 11, 7.5, and 5.5 kHz. The top of that range gives about the same quality as a good table-model FM radio, while 7-7.5 kHz yields approximately telephone quality. While most speech is quite intelligible at the lowest speed, music or subtle sounds require higher sampling rates. However, an increase in the sampling rate brings about a concomitant increase in the size of the file needed to record a given sound. Thus, higher-quality recordings take more file space than lower-quality recordings of the same sound.

Actually, there is a second critical factor that determines the quality of digitized sound—the resolution, or number of bits used per sample—but that is generally a constant for a given microcomputer, unless special hardware is added. The resolution determines the dynamic range of the recording, which is the difference between the loudest and quietest sounds that can be recorded by the system. Sixteen-bit machines are used for professional CD-quality recordings; Macintoshes without added hardware use eight bits, giving them the equivalent dynamic range of an inexpensive cassette recorder.

The amount of space taken to store a sound depends upon both the resolution and the sampling rate. For example, two minutes of 8-bit 22 kHz sound (as you might get on a Macintosh) requires about 2.5 MB; the same sound in 16-bit, 44 kHz (i.e., CD-quality) requires four times that amount, about 10 MB.

MIDI

One of the two basic methods for recording sound on a computer involves MIDI. MIDI stands for Musical Instrument Digital Interface, a set of standards agreed to nearly a decade ago by manufacturers of synthesizers and computers. MIDI specifies a common language, or protocol, for communication between synthesizers (and other electronic instruments) and computers manufactured by different companies.

A series—or sequence—of sounds created on a synthesizer or drum machine can be stored on a computer through the use of a particular kind of program called a sequencer. What is stored is not the actual sound itself, but rather a series of numerical notations that, taken together, completely describe the sound—pitch, volume, timbre, tempo, attack, and other such attributes—in the vocabulary of MIDI. The conversion takes place in a small, relatively inexpensive electronic device called a MIDI interface, placed between the synthesizer and the computer.

When the numbers are fed back out of the computer, through the MIDI interface, into the synthesizer, the sounds are reproduced in their original form. Since the stored information is essentially digital in nature, editing and manipulating MIDI sequences on a microcomputer is easy to do. Indeed, it is even possible to compose with the sequencer program. Sequencing programs typically offer the opportunity to record on a number of "tracks," much as studio recording equipment permits recording multiple tracks on tape. The tracks can be recorded one at a time, and played back singly or in multiples while recording a new accompanying track. Each track can be assigned the sound of a different instrument. The on-screen metaphor of a tape recorder makes the recording operation possible using familiar controls, and changing such characteristics as tempo is also relatively straightforward.

Digitizing Sound

The second major way of recording sound on a computer involves digitization. Digitizing sound on a microcomputer usually requires some specialized equipment—called a sound sampler or digitizer—to be used with the computer. This is typically a smallish electronic device whose price depends upon the quality of digitization it provides, ranging from quite inexpensive to very expensive. (However, some Macintosh models—beginning with the LC and the IIsi—have built-in sound digitizers, and come equipped with microphones.) In the Macintosh world, a popular, low-cost digitizer is the Farallon MacRecorder, which comes with its own software, SoundEdit. Although it cannot provide sound samples equivalent to CDs in quality, its output will suffice for most educational uses.

A digitizer connected to a computer can in turn be connected to either an external microphone or to a line input device such as a tape or cassette recorder, or a CD player. To make the recording, the sound source is activated, the software run, and the recording is digitized. It really is as simple as it sounds—it's no more difficult than using a cassette recorder!

The digitizer samples the sound waves produced (many times per second), and stores the samples as 1s and 0s; since they are in that form, they can be edited on a computer. Using a program such as SoundEdit on the Macintosh, you can take any sound segment and manipulate it—stretch it, condense it, re-shape it, mix up the order in which it occurs.

Note that the digitized representation of a sound is not the same as the representation employed by MIDI; hence you may not be able to use the same editing program for both types of sound files.

File Compression

One way of coping with the large files created by digitization of sound is to compress the files. Compression of files can be done with a variety of utility programs, which remove the "dead space"—space that includes redundant information—from files. Typically, such compression programs are used to create archive files of data—ones which you don't want to delete, but which occupy too much space to warrant their storage in normal (decompressed) form. Compression can result in substantial gains: It is not unusual for compressed word processing and graphics files to occupy anywhere from 35–50% of their original space, for example.

However, that kind of compression isn't too convenient for IMI: Imagine having to run a separate program to decompress an audio file each time it had to be used. What is more desirable is some kind of "on the fly" decompression.

Apple Computer has developed software routines called QuickTime, which are designed to do just that kind of on-the-fly compression and decompression of audio and video files. The microcomputer industry generally is currently paying a lot of attention to real-time audio and video compression. As a result, the whole nature of presenting audio and video in multimedia is changing dramatically. It is very likely that microcomputers will harbor all of the multimedia components internally in the future. Linking a batch of peripheral devices will no longer be necessary for many applications. But even given that welcome day, the design principles underlying multimedia development will survive. You will still need to consider the design and production of IMI components, although the finished products will probably be housed differently.

References for Chapter 4

Anderton, C. (1988). The MIDI recording studio. *Musician*, special edition, 22–27, 55.

Huber, D. M. (1991). *The MIDI manual.* Carmel, IN: Howard W. Sams and Company.

Huber, D. M., and Runstein, R. E. (1989). *Modern recording techniques* (3rd ed.). Carmel, IN: Howard W. Sams and Company.

Lehrman, P. D., and Tully, T. (1991). Catch a wave: Digital audio. *MacUser*, *October*, 94–103.

Oringel, R. S. (1989). *Audio control handbook for radio and television broadcasting.* Boston, MA: Focal Press.

Sinclair, I. R. (Ed.) (1989). *Audio electronics reference book.* Oxford: BSP Professional Books.

Watkinson, J. (1988). *The art of digital audio.* London: Focal Press.

Chapter 5

CDs, CD-ROMs, and Related Storage Media

As noted in Chapter 4, compact discs (CDs) represent a recent quantum leap in the technology of audio recording. Their compact size, relative robustness, long recording time, and, above all, their superior, digitally-encoded sound quality have made them the undisputed sound medium of choice for the home entertainment market, all within the space of a few years.

CD-ROM stands for Compact Disc–Read Only Memory. (A read-only memory device is one from which a user can access and read or copy information, but cannot add to, edit, or delete from. Books and phonograph records are read-only media; videotapes and audio cassettes are not, although both can be made virtually read-only by removing the little plastic tabs which permit recording.) A CD-ROM is a digital recording, essentially the same technology as an audio CD. However, rather than being intended to be converted to analog audio for interpretation by the human ear, it is designed to remain in digital form, and therefore understandable by computers. CD-ROMs are physically identical to CDs: The only difference between them is in terms of what is encoded on the headers to their tracks. The standards defining CDs and CD-ROMs are basically the same, except that those for the CD-ROMs are more extensive (i.e., the standards for CDs are a subset of those for CD-ROMs; there is more stringent error-correction involved in CD-ROMs).

Both CDs and CD-ROMs are 12-cm plastic discs, with a silvery finish and a spiral CLV track, just like videodiscs. Indeed, except for the difference in size and the fact that CDs and CD-ROMs are encoded on one side only, while videodiscs may be encoded on both sides, the two media are virtually identical.

At the most basic level, it is convenient and intuitive to use a metaphor to describe the way in which digital data are encoded on CDs and CD-ROMs: Think of two different levels of surface on the disc—called pits and land—as representing OFFs and ONs, or 0s and

1s, that are interpretable by a computer. (In reality, things are slightly more complicated than that. Transitions from pit to land or from land to pit are encoded as 1s and constant land or constant pits are encoded as 0s.)

Of course, at the working end, the difference between CDs and CD-ROMs is plain: The former sounds intelligible—usually even pleasant—when played on a stereo system, while the latter produces no sound; a CD-ROM contains information that a computer can understand, while a CD contains no information usable by a computer (unless a special program "tricks" the computer into behaving like a CD player, in which case the CD plays just as it would on a CD player). The recorded information on CDs is arranged in such a way that individual segments (equivalent to $1/75$ of a second each) can be addressed individually. This means that beginning or ending play on a single note of music is possible.

Both media share important attributes:

- They can store very large amounts of information (up to 74 minutes per CD; up to 660 MB of data for CD-ROMs).
- They can be produced at a relatively low unit cost.
- They are robust, inasmuch as they are constructed like videodiscs.
- They are a read-only medium, which means that, once pressed, they cannot be altered.
- They offer random access, albeit at a modest seek time (they are faster than floppy disks, but slower than hard disks).
- They are portable, both in terms of size and weight, and of compatibility across all brands of players.

CD-ROMs, like CDs, have specific sectors and fields that must contain certain kinds of data in order for them to work properly. However, by and large, a designer of CD-ROMs can ignore the technical details, leaving them to the manufacturer of the discs. Thus, designing a CD-ROM is really just a matter of creating the necessary files on a computer, then arranging them appropriately on a hard disk before having a manufacturer transfer them to the CD-ROM. (Some manufacturers will also accept other media, such as nine-track tape, as a mastering medium; check with them before proceeding, however.) This means that, first and foremost, you create all the necessary files, and you check and double-check to ensure that they work the way they are supposed to, and relate to one another appropriately. Index files, if needed, must be constructed and double- and triple-checked. Software and user interface decisions must be made, as must disc "geography" decisions similar to those necessary for videodiscs (see Chapter 3). With the possible exception of disc geography, however, the decisions are virtually the same as those that must be made if the final product were to exist on a hard disk.

If you are designing a CD-ROM that is intended to work on both Macintosh and MS-DOS platforms, the files must, of course, be tested on their respective machines.

Characteristics of CD-ROMs

CD-ROMs have a number of advantages, identified below. The advantages can be double-edged swords as far as instructional designers are concerned, however: While capitalizing on the strengths of CD-ROMs can lead to very effective interactive mediated instruction, failure to appreciate the implications of their characteristics can lead to sub-optimal designs. CD-ROMs:

- can hold huge amounts of data—up to 660 MB per disc when only digital data are encoded. That is equivalent to 825 double-sided Macintosh floppies! When such large quantities of data are placed on a single disc, careful planning is required with respect to its arrangement and to the relationships among the various files.

- are relatively inexpensive to produce, costing only a few dollars each when manufactured in quantity. Since—in quantity—a CD-ROM is not much more expensive than a floppy disk, but can hold so much more information, CD-ROM represents a very economical means of distributing courseware. Notice that the qualification *in quantity* forms part of the previous sentence. The one-time mastering charge makes CD-ROM cost-effective only when you have more than about 10MB of data and you need at least a couple of hundred copies.

- can be produced relatively quickly, with a turn-around time between finished original and multiple copies of about one and one-half weeks. Rush jobs can usually be accommodated to cut the turn-around time even more, albeit at a higher cost.

- can hold a variety of kinds of information. Because of the nature of encoding—digital—CD-ROMs can contain digital data (i.e., computer code and data), digitized music, and digitized video. Thus CD-ROMs are inherently multimedia. Designers can minimize the number of bits and pieces required for instruction—both in terms of hardware and software—by capitalizing on the "all-in-one" nature of the distribution medium.

- provide a robust, stable storage medium; they can't be overwritten, and they don't deteriorate significantly with age. The don't require as much care in handling as magnetic media. Their toughness makes them a viable alternative where more delicate media might suffer (e.g., field conditions). Although their read-only nature can be an advantage in some situations, not all applications require only reading of files.

- provide a standardized format. A file format designated High Sierra (or ISO 9660), which works with a variety of computer operating system, makes it possible for a CD-ROM to work properly no matter who manufactures the computer or the CD-ROM drive. Although technically speaking the High Sierra and ISO 9660 standards are actually slightly different, the latter being based on the former, they are similar enough that they are frequently both lumped together under the label "High Sierra". More importantly, the ISO 9660 standard is expected to be the standard of the future (Bechtel, 1989). Fortunately, both the Macintosh and MS-DOS platforms support both the High Sierra and ISO 9660 standards, and the standards themselves demand that redundant information be recorded to accommodate the different microprocessors in the two platforms, thus multi-platform compatibility is assured.

  On the other hand, if it is necessary or possible to limit access to the files to only one platform, using the platform's native format is also possible. For example, since HyperCard is available on Macintosh but not on MS-DOS, there is little point in taking the extra step of conversion to High Sierra/ISO 9660 format; rather, the files can be left in their original formats.

- provide random access to information stored on them. Although the seek times on CD-ROMs are not as fast as those on a hard disk, they are faster than those on a floppy, and are generally adequate for most purposes. Users will have a tendency to want to move files from the CD-ROM onto a hard disk, to increase speed of access. Many times, however, the files are too large to do that conveniently. It may be necessary to implement a system of installing and removing files from the hard disk. All things considered, CD-ROM is better as a distribution medium than as a real-time access medium. However, where speed of random access isn't crucial (e.g., large text databases), they can form a viable real-time access medium, as well. Audio and video will require better real-time compression techniques than are available at the time of writing before CD-ROM is viable for their real-time access.

- CD-ROMs can contain both CD-ROM (data) tracks and CD (audio) tracks at the same time, but their placement is critical. (Be sure to check with the manufacturer regarding their correct placement if you want both included on the same disc.) This means you could, for example, include 330 MB of data and 30 minutes of audio on a CD-ROM.

Related Storage Media

Other storage media exist which are related to CD-ROM technology. These are not typically included in IMI applications at present, although later generations of similar technologies may be in the future.

WORM Recording

WORM (Write-Once, Read-Many [times]) recordings are another form in which large quantities of data can be stored. In this recording method, once information is written, it can be read many times, but cannot be added to, changed, or deleted.

WORM technology suffers from a lack of universal standards like those for CDs and CD-ROMs. Different proprietary systems may have different disc sizes and/or data formats. Furthermore, the way in which data are written to WORM discs can vary from one manufacturer to another (Tisdall, 1990). While some use a pulse from a laser to vaporize a dye film on the disc, others use the laser to burn a pit into the surface of the disk, exposing a reflective material. Still others melt the surface of a semi-metallic film, and the surface tension created forms a pit in the film which then solidifies as the film cools.

Thus WORM recording is generally confined to fairly specialized uses, where large quantities of data need to be recorded and stored without any possibility of making changes to it and where portability is not likely to be a problem (e.g., medical, legal, financial, and government records). With a 100-year expected shelf-life, WORM media are excellent for archives. WORM tapes, as well as discs, are available (Rizzo, 1990), but both media will likely be of limited use in instruction because of the lack of standardization.

Magneto-Optical Recording

As the name implies, magneto-optical recordings combine two technologies. The resultant storage media look similar to audio CDs or CD-ROMs, except that they are somewhat darker in color and come in plastic cartridges from which they are never removed. The cartridges have metal access doors and write-protecting devices, much like floppy disks do.

Magneto-optical recordings, however, are produced in a completely different manner than CDs and CD-ROMs, however. A laser operating at a high-power setting produces a series of heated spots on the special coating on the disc. As the disc rotates under an electromagnet before the plastic substrate cools, the electromagnet magnetizes the spots into either 1 or 0 representations. In read mode, the laser is used on a low–power setting, and the direction of rotation of polarized light reflected from the magnetized spots is converted back to 1s and 0s.

Magneto-optical recordings have a number of advantages:

- They offer a compact means of storing a great deal of data. The current 5.25″ discs store approximately 300 MB per side. At this writing, single-sided 3.5″ discs holding 122–130 MB are appearing on the market. The potential exists for four-fold increases in data density as better lasers are developed (Seiter, 1991).

- They are not susceptible to corruption by stray magnetic fields, since their magnetization is dependent upon the temperature of the medium. This makes them less susceptible to damage than floppies or hard disks.

- They are not susceptible to head crashes as hard disks are, since the read/write "heads" are kept a safe distance from the surface of the disc.

- They can be used over and over again—up to 10,000,000 erase/write cycles (Rizzo, 1991).

- They can be mounted and ejected like floppies. From a user's point of view, they appear to be large floppy disks. They can also be partitioned.

- They are a very economical means for storing large amounts of data (in a $/MB sense), compared to floppies or hard disk cartridges (e.g., Winchester disks). At this writing, however, the price of the drives is relatively high, although they are expected to come down as their popularity increases.

- Their durability makes them ideal for distributing data or creating archives. Physical shelf-lives of about 15 years seem likely; this is far longer than floppies or tape can be expected to last.

- Built-in error-checking schemes make the medium very safe in terms of data integrity.

Their disadvantages are:

- The aforementioned relatively high current price for the drives, as well as rapidly-dropping—but still relatively high—costs for each cartridge. Costs will likely continue to drop, but are unlikely ever to become as low as those for CD-ROMs.

- The discs have to be turned over manually to access all the data. That is, the devices appear as two separate volumes, each capable of holding 300 MB.

- Writing to them is considerably slower than reading from them, because the write mode requires an erase cycle, a verify cycle, and a record cycle. Although this may not be a big disadvantage in many instructional situations, it makes duplication in quantity more time-consuming. However, speed is a relative thing: magneto-optical drives are, at this writing, four or five times faster than CD-ROMs, and expected to get faster still in the years ahead, while CD-ROMs are limited to their current speed by the standards under which they are built (Rizzo, 1991).

Differences in approach to hardware and data formats by the various drive manufacturers seems to be a disappearing problem, as more recent models can at least read each others' discs. Furthermore, there seems to be a promise of technological convergence, eventuating in drives that will both read and write WORM, and read CD-ROM discs, as well as read and write magneto-optical ones (Rizzo, 1990; Seiter, 1991). Hybrids of CD-ROM and WORM (dubbed CD-WO—Compact Disc Write-Once) are beginning to appear (Harvey and Corbett, 1991). Some currently-available drives offer proprietary data formats as well as the International Standards Organization (ISO) format; obviously, the latter is preferred for data that will be shared with users owning other brands of drives.

Phase-Change Recording

Magneto-optical drives are commonly called erasable optical drives, and they are. However, there are other kinds of erasable optical drives, as well. They are all-optical in nature, and depend upon phase changes on the surface of the disc engendered by a laser beam. Phase-change technology employs a dual-power laser to convert the coating on the disc to either a crystalline or an amorphous state. Light reflected from the two kinds of surfaces exhibits differences in phase, which is then interpreted as binary information. Because no magnets are involved, the potential exists for phase-change drives to operate at higher speeds than magneto-optical drives.

Since the more-entrenched magneto-optical technology and the newer phase-change technology are both proprietary systems, the likelihood that one ultimately emerges as the more widely used may be an outcome of corporate battles reminiscent of the VHS/Beta wars for videocassette supremacy.

Preparing Files for CD-ROM

There are a few general considerations that apply to virtually any kind of content you might put onto a CD-ROM. These have to do with the way files are named and located.

File-Naming Conventions

Naming files is important because file names are the means by which the computer locates specific collections of information. Naming is important no matter which computer platform is involved, but particularly so if the High Sierra/ISO 9660 format is to be used on a CD-ROM, since both major platforms must be accommodated simultaneously. File names must be unique, yet within the restrictions of the host operating system, and there are major differences in those restrictions between the MS-DOS and Macintosh worlds.

MS-DOS

In the MS-DOS world, the names of files cannot exceed eight characters in length, and cannot include blank spaces, commas, quotation marks, colons, semi-colons, periods, question marks, or the characters >, <, |, /, \, [,], +, =, and *. Names are typically—but not necessarily—followed by a period and an extension containing up to three characters. There are a number of conventions in file extensions (e.g., BAT = batch; DAT = data; TMP = temporary; TXT = ASCII text), but it is not essential that the conventions be adhered to. Frequently, the extensions are used to differentiate similarly-named files according to function or form. Files should be given names that are as meaningful as possible, given the severe restrictions on naming them.

MS-DOS files are arranged into hierarchical tree-like structures called directories and sub-directories. The absolute, or complete, name of a file includes a specification of the directory/sub-directory path as well as the filename; it may also include the volume name. For example,

A: \FOODS\MUSHROOM\MORELS.DAT

specifies the file MORELS.DAT in the sub-directory MUSHROOM, which is in turn located in the sub-directory FOODS of the primary disk drive.

Macintosh

In the Macintosh world, any printable character except a colon (:) can be used in a file name, even ones with diacritical marks, like å, Ü, and ñ. Names can be up to 31 characters long and include spaces.

The concept of an extension to a filename does not exist in the Macintosh operating system.

In the Macintosh world, historically, two different systems have been used. In the early Macs, the Macintosh Filing System (MFS) was used. It was a simple, flat filing system that quickly became dysfunctionally slow and awkward with storage media larger than the 400K single-sided floppy disks used originally. MFS was superseded by the Hierarchical Filing System (HFS) upon the introduction of the 800K floppy disk drives. All Macs still accommodate MFS, but MFS is only used on the 400K, single-sided floppies; 800K and 1.4 MB floppies, and hard disks all use HFS. The user generally needn't be bothered with which filing system is in use; the Mac keeps track itself.

HFS uses a tree-like structure similar to MS-DOS, but it looks different to users because of the graphical user interface of the Macintosh: Sub-directories appear as folders. Opening a sub-directory in MS-DOS is functionally equivalent to opening a folder on the Macintosh.

The full or absolute name for a file in the Macintosh world consists of the filename preceded by the name(s) of any folder(s) housing it, preceded in turn by the disk or volume name, with all names being separated by colons. Thus, on a Macintosh, the filename equivalent to the MS-DOS one in the example above might be

Biology Disk:Foods:Mushrooms:Identification of Morels.

In both MS-DOS and Macintosh systems, there is no distinction between uppercase and lowercase characters in file names—they are considered the same. Thus STUDYONE, studyone, and StUdYoNe are equivalent to the computer, if not to the human eye.

Tips on the Size and Location of Files

- If you are designing on the Mac, use file-naming conventions that will accommodate the lowest common denominator, MS-DOS.

- To increase speed, arrange files contiguously on the disk. Before submitting hard disks directly to the CD-ROM manufacturer, use a disk optimizing program to arrange and de-fragment files. Since some disk optimizing software imposes its own preferences for locating certain types of files, you may find it necessary to copy files one at a time to a newly-initialized hard disk in order to achieve your particular tactical geography.

- Pre-compute and store as much as possible. CD-ROMs are large enough that you usually have space to spare, and pre-computation will free up the CPU for more important things at runtime. Locating a file containing the stored data will frequently take less time than computing it.

- HyperCard stacks should use absolute files names, since users are unable to change them, and space is plentiful. Finding a specific file is expedited when the absolute file name is used.

- Don't put too many files into one Macintosh folder, since the Finder is relatively slow at opening large folders. Rather, use more folders, organized logically.

References for Chapter 5

Bechtel, B. (1989). *CD-ROM and the Macintosh computer.* Apple Computer, Inc. Advanced Technology Group.

Harvey, D. A., and Corbett, J. (1991). Unlimited desktop storage: Optical drives that blow away the competition. *Computer Shopper, 11*(11), 230ff.

Miller, D. C. (1987). *Special report: Publishers, libraries and CD-ROM: Implications of digital optical printing.* Report distributed to the registrants of the Optical Publishing and Libraries: Cheers or Tears? Preconference Institute, 1987 American Library Association Conference, San Francisco, CA.

Rizzo, J. (1990). Maximum movable megabyte: Erasable optical drives. *MacUser, 6*(11), 102–130.

Rizzo, J. (1991). Multifunction optical storage. *MacUser, 7*(11), 108–114.

Seiter, C. (1990). Erasable opticals. *Macworld, 7*(3), 152–159.

Seiter, C. (1991). Optical outlook. *Macworld, 8*(6), 139–145.

Tisdall, B. (1990). Buyer's guide: Optical disk [sic] drives. *PC User, 137* (July 18), 74ff.

Chapter 6

Interfaces

An interface, simply stated, is any device which allows a user to communicate with a computer or other hardware. In the early days of computing, the main computer interface was a keypunch and card reader. The user sat at a keypunch machine and typed instructions on a typewriter keyboard. Each character struck on the keyboard produced a series of corresponding holes punched through a card. The combination of holes and non-holes in each column of the card created a binary representation of the character typed. A typing error meant the card had to be thrown away, and a new card produced. Once a program was completely written, the stack of cards was submitted to a card reader, which sequentially read the cards and passed along their instructions to the computer. Only the most dedicated or persistent survived the challenge.

As computers grew in sophistication and were joined by other media in multimedia systems, corresponding developments occurred with interfaces. In general, the trend in interfaces used in education and training has been toward *user-friendliness*, that is, making systems easier to use by requiring little or no technical knowledge. Ironically, as interfaces require less knowledge to use, the interfaces must become much more sophisticated. In this section, we will tour a range of interfaces, from the most mundane to the extravagant. You may notice we have not included any discussion of graphics tablets, joysticks and light pens. In our judgment these have waning significance for interactive multimedia systems, and thus have little importance for this discussion.

Remote Control Unit

Many devices have remote control unit (RCU) interfaces—video cassette recorders, video disc players, compact disc players, television receivers, sound systems, and garage door openers, to name but a few. A remote control unit is a hand-held command center which is capable of communicating specific instructions from a user to the equipment. The available command set is typically specific to a single piece of equipment, although universal RCUs are available which can control an array of equipment from a single device. These interfaces communicate with equipment via infra-red transmission or over wires. In interactive instruction, RCUs are most frequently used to make selections in Level II videodisc programs or develop user-designed control programs which can be stored and executed by a microprocessor in some players. For example, the following sequence of commands and numbers pressed on a Pioneer RCU will produce a small program which will execute a simple routine.

Press on RCU	This Happens
Program	Identifies upcoming sequence as a program to the player
6151 Search	Locates frame #6151 and freezes
1 Input	Pauses until a zero is pressed
7477 Autostop	Plays from current position to frame #7477 and freezes
Halt	Stops the program
End	Identifies the end of the program and stores the routine in the memory of the videodisc player
Run	Retrieves and executes the routine

An important disadvantage of using an RCU to produce interactive programs is that the program is stored only as long as the videodisc player is turned on. If power is lost, so is the program. The present system is also intolerant of errors. If an entry error is made, it cannot be erased. The entire program must be re-entered, so it is not likely that large or complex programs will be introduced this way. Both of these limitations may be improved in future generations of equipment, but at the time of this writing, they impose serious limitations on the use of an RCU as an interface for interactive multimedia instruction. But as a user interface for browsing through videodiscs and CDs, it has lasting utility.

Keyboard

Still the most common interface to most microcomputer systems is the keyboard. This interface is basically a typewriter-like platform of keys which permits the user to type individual characters and commands. Of course, a typical microcomputer keyboard also includes a number of additional features, such as control keys, function keys, and numeric keypads. These permit the user to carry out specialized functions which vary slightly from manufacturer to manufacturer, but the principle is still the same. On a microcomputer keyboard, the user must be able to type instructions, and this may require specialized knowledge of the program being used. Nevertheless, as an interface for interactive multimedia systems, the keyboard is very flexible. It allows a wide range of responses from the user, as long as the user and the system share the same vocabulary.

Mouse

A mouse is a push button mounted in a housing atop an omni-directional roller (ball). The "button on a ball" interface is moved around freely on the surface of a desk (or anything with a surface for that matter). As the mouse is moved, a cursor, marker or pointer on a screen makes corresponding moves. So, for instance, if you move the mouse until the pointer on the screen enters a target area and then you push the button, the program can execute whatever command is associated with that target.

The mouse is a very easy device to use, and it is not as intimidating as a keyboard or RCU for many users. Although it requires a modicum of physical dexterity to use well, most people acquire the skills quickly. As an interface for interactive instruction, a mouse is somewhat limited. It is primarily capable of three functions: pointing, clicking, and dragging.

Pointing is the act of moving the cursor on screen to a desired position. Clicking is the act of pressing the button. For example, you might use the mouse to point at an illustration of a kitten on the screen. Pointing at the kitten and then clicking the button on the mouse registers your cursor position with the instructional program. If the program has a command associated with the kitten's position (e.g., play the videodisc from frame 5000 to frame 5100 showing a kitten eating a mouse) then the command will be executed.

Dragging is the act of depressing and holding the button while you move the mouse. Dragging can be used for moving items on the screen. For example, if the program permits, you could point at the kitten, click and hold the button, and then drag the kitten to another position on the screen by moving the mouse. In similar fashion, the dragging function can be used to draw on the screen. The first click identifies the starting point and then moving the mouse will drag the line, box or circle to its end point or identify a second coordinate position.

Trackball

Functionally, the trackball is exactly the same as a mouse. Furthermore, a trackball looks and behaves something like a mouse—an upside-down mouse. That is, the unit remains stationary on the table, and the user manipulates a ball on its top surface to control the position of the cursor on the screen. Buttons near the ball provide for clicking and dragging. Since subtly different hand and finger motions are involved in using the two devices, user preference can be a major factor in the choice between the two devices.

Barcode

We have all become used to having a can of beans scanned at the supermarket checkout counter. It is routine technology. The same technology has been adapted to laser video systems, transforming a routine supermarket technology into a very useful instructional interface. Simply stated, a barcode interface for video allows a developer to write command sets in barcode hieroglyphics, and a user to sweep over the sets with a special scanning pen to execute the commands. A command set might look something like that shown in Figure 6-1.

Figure 6-1.   Barcode strip.

So, what's the big deal? To reiterate an earlier point, anyone who has used a remote control unit (RCU) to execute strings of commands realizes how cumbersome and prone to errors that can be. In order to do something simple, say find frame 2000, play from there until frame 3200 and stop, ten separate RCU keypresses are needed:

2
0
0
0
Search
3
2
0
0
Autostop

If any entry errors are made, the user must clear the entries and start over from the beginning. Multiply this by several command sets for a typical lesson, and the problem is apparent. Instructors using the system for group work, or students attempting to illustrate instruction independently, can easily make mistakes and either embarrassment or frustration can result.

A laser barcode system reduces the amount of information a user must manually introduce to the system. A single sweep of a barcode strip (followed by an audible 'beep' to announce the successful reception of information) and the commands are executed. A barcode system is made up of these parts:

- a videodisc player and monitor;
- a videodisc (of course);
- a barcode scanning pen (barcode reader);
- authoring software to generate barcode command sets.

Not all videodisc players support barcode systems; barcodes are still relatively new. Most older hardware, however, can be adapted, and we anticipate a brief transition time until all players are supported.

The barcode scanning pen (barcode reader or barcode wand) is an infrared or wired device which, when swept over a barcode strip such as the ones illustrated in Figures 6-1 and 6-2, transport serial commands to the videodisc player. The shape of the pen is familiar to users, and has the distinct advantage of not requiring special knowledge to use.

Much of the instructional videodisc software now being produced contains barcode indexes and common command strips (such as *Step Forward, Play, Scan*) (Figure 6-2). Still, to take full advantage of barcodes, it is necessary to print your own command sets on barcode strips. Authoring software is available for both Macintosh and IBM platforms to encode, rehearse, and print barcode command sets. A standard command set was established by the LaserBarcode Association in Japan, which includes companies such as NEC, Sony, Pioneer, Toshiba, and Sanyo. The standard command set is somewhat limited, as we will discuss below, but does ensure that materials developed which conform to the standard set will work with all LaserBarcode compatible players (currently all new Pioneer, and older adapted models). The set currently includes two search commands, two segment play commands, and 14 independent control commands.

Figure 6-2.   Selected commands for LaserBarcode systems.

<I Step Reverse

Step Forward I>

Play

Audio Stereo

Audio 1

Audio 2

The complete command set includes the following:

Frame Search (CAV)	*Video Off*
Chapter Search	*Video On*
Frame Segment Play (CAV)	*Play*
Chapter Segment Play	*Pause*
Audio Off	*Step Forward* (CAV)
Audio 1/Left	*Step Reverse* (CAV)
Audio 2/Right	*Reject*
Audio Stereo	*Marker Clear*

As mentioned earlier, this command set is limited. In fact, barcode systems do not, at this writing, include many useful commands which are available from the RCU (Zollman, 1991). Zollman pointed out that the barcode system does not permit the user to display frame numbers. This is a very useful feature for some instructional analyses, such as timing a heartbeat by counting the number of frames between beats and dividing by 30 (remember, 30 video frames = 1 second). He noted that even if you activate the frame display with the RCU, a barcode command turns it off automatically. Also, the system does not yet allow the user to vary the speed of play, play backwards, or conduct any time-searches or plays. Granted, these are not commands one uses as often as the others, yet for special instructional applications, they are unfortunate omissions. Enhancements to the command set are needed, and will probably be introduced to make the most of this innovative application of the technology.

Barcodes offer some very useful options for instructors and students beyond IMI applications. For group instruction, barcode strips can be placed in the margins of lecture notes or pasted onto a reference index. During a class, an instructor can select from a planned set of video illustrations without having to look up frame numbers and enter them with an RCU. Our experience is that this is a marvelous convenience, and it frees one to attend to the class instead of the equipment. We do, however, suggest you keep an RCU and comprehensive disc indexes available, as students have the uncanny ability to ask for illustrations you have not planned. For these, and similar, instructional situations, the flexibility of the RCU is welcome. Barcodes, by their very nature, are more useful for planned (or at least anticipated) instruction, rather than for flights of serendipity.

The highly touted self-instructional version of the above suggestion is the illustrated textbook for readers (a modest print and video multimedia system). In the margins of the textbook, or in the body of text, barcodes can offer illustrated sojourns for students through related video pictures and segments. This is indeed a useful application, and it couples a newer instructional technology with one of the oldest ones, resulting in a familiar, yet potentially highly interactive multimedia resource for learners. This also challenges instructional designers to learn more about text design and how to merge external media with text to create integrated learning systems.

Yet another instructional application of barcode systems is for multimedia classroom displays. A display of realia, say a human skeleton, could have barcode strips placed on or adjacent to specific features. When scanned, the student might receive some video instruction about the part or see the system in its living state. Barcodes can be attached to most anything (well, all right, fish are difficult), and realia can extend the learning offered vicariously through video. Using realia as part of a multimedia system can introduce immediate, concrete experiences for learners which are not necessarily subjected to the treacheries of generalization.

So, a barcode system is really just a flexible interface for learners. Can't a computer also do most of these things? Yes, and given the command set limitations, better. But a computer is more expensive, more difficult to transport, and for many people, still somewhat intimidating to use in public. For independent study and use with children, the barcode reader offers easy access to a wide range of material without dedicating a computer to a particular learning station, without spending a great deal of time training students how to use it, and without exposing more vulnerable systems to the rigors of a third-grader's onslaught.

Touch Screen

Touch screens are the finger food equivalent of the mouse. They are characterized by a frame mounted to the face of a display screen. Although the technologies vary significantly, all touch screens perform similar functions: they identify coordinate positions on the screen and report to a program when one of the positions has been trespassed. Individuals interact (make selections) in a program by directly touching the screen. Touch screens require little or no knowledge of special commands to use them effectively, and they free the user from looking back and forth from the screen to the keyboard, or coordinating actions with a mouse. They do, however, usually require specialized knowledge of a programming language to develop instruction. Because most applications are system specific, touch screen based programs are not very portable and are usually limited to more expensive systems. Touch screens also retain the same disadvantages as a mouse. User responses are limited to selecting items from the screen or tracing positions from one position to another on the screen. Still, touch screens are used in a wide variety of settings, but are particularly beneficial in training or public display programs, where the users may not be typists, may be techno-phobic, or may span a wide range of ages and abilities.

Three common types of touch screens are available: infrared (IR), membrane, and capacitive. Each has distinct advantages and limitations for interactive multimedia instruction. This section will briefly describe the features of the three systems and compare their relative strengths.

Infrared touch screens use several light emitting diodes (LEDs) on one side of the frame which are aligned with phototransistor detectors on the opposite side of the frame. Pulses are constantly sent from the LEDs to the detectors in straight lines. The same configuration is used on vertical and horizontal sides of the frame. When placed on the face of a monitor, this creates a lattice pattern of infrared beams in front of the screen.

Because infrared light is invisible, the gridwork of light covers the screen without obstructing the user's view of the program. When the screen is touched, some beams of light are interrupted. The coordinates of the interrupted beams are communicated to a program on a host computer, which carries out the command associated with that location.

Infrared systems have the advantage of offering an unobstructed view of the screen. No overlay is used, so the visual field, and therefore the quality of the image, is not affected. Also, infrared systems are comparatively durable, because users do not actually touch any part of the interface. The monitor screen may suffer the indignity of a sharp fingernail, but the touch screen will be unscathed.

The main disadvantage associated with infrared systems is parallax. Because LEDs are mounted above the screen, the relative position of targets on the screen, and the coordinates of the touch screen will change in position depending on the position from which the program is viewed. In effect, visual discrepancies occur when the angle between the user's line of sight and the user's finger vary. The greater the angle, the greater the likelihood that the finger will touch a different area than intended, but will appear correct to the viewer. This problem is aggravated when applications use small targets or when the touch systems have optical components mounted farther away from the screen.

Membrane touch screen systems place a membrane of plastic or glass over the display screen. An additional layer of film is also laid over the membrane and charged with voltage. Using either a conductive or resistive mechanism, a change in voltage at the point of a touch is indicated when pressure is applied to the membrane. The location of the voltage change is reported as an X and Y coordinate to a monitoring program, in much the same way the location of infrared touches are identified.

Capacitive systems have a thin coating of capacitive plasma covering a glass shield. Capacitive plasma is capable of storing a charge. A conductive stylus (such as your finger) is used to touch the coating, resulting in a change in capacitance at the location of the touch. The location is then communicated to the controller in a similar fashion to the other systems.

The advantage of membrane and capacitive systems is reduced parallax. Both types of systems conform more closely to the shape of the screen, and the active touch area is virtually on the surface of the screen. A disadvantage is a slight reduction of image quality due to the membrane coverings, but this reduction is usually slight. A more serious problem with membrane and capacitive systems is wear. Constant physical contact and damage can degrade the system over time, and these systems are reputedly more susceptible to oxidation, moisture, and static than infrared systems.

Voice Recognition

Voice recognition interfaces permit the user to give verbal instructions, commands, and responses to programs. Obviously, this is a desirable (almost transparent) interface; the user does not need to learn how to operate any external device or even make the effort to point. This type of interface would find tremendous application in an interactive multimedia environment in order to request information from a variety of sources.

Developments in voice recognition are just starting to make their way into mainstream instruction, most noticeably for individuals with physical disabilities which hamper fine motor activity necessary to manipulate a keyboard or mouse efficiently. Others of us dream of the day we can speak in natural language with a computer, and have it interpret our instructions conversationally.

Voice recognition systems require a user to speak into a microphone. Vocal input is represented as voice print patterns, and those patterns are compared to resident patterns. For example, if you said, "Save the file I am using," a numerical representation of that speech would be constructed. A programmer, anticipating this request, would have entered the phrase or key elements of the phrase for comparison. The input phrase would be compared to all resident elements, and if a match occurred, the command would be carried out.

One difficulty with voice recognition is in generalizing commands to several individuals because of differences in vocalization and pronunciation. With most programs in current use, one first records a series of commands or key words which become the resident voice print patterns for later comparison. In this way, you are matching your own voice when you input a command, but you are limited to phrases you entered or constructions from the phrases you entered. Voice print patterns also require a substantial amount of memory, a problem which file compression, sampling, and larger computers will reduce in the future. For now, the vocabulary of voice recognition remains small, but development is brisk in this area, and it is not unreasonable to expect free-form natural language interfaces to be available at some time in the not-distant future.

For instructional developers and researchers, voice recognition will open new areas of inquiry. A significant challenge will be to go beyond pattern recognition of a fixed vocabulary (the verbal equivalent of touch screen input) to derive contextual meaning from complex verbal input. Will systems ever be sufficiently sophisticated to deal with metaphoric, idiomatic, or colloquial speech, such as, "Hot dog, let's run this up the flagpole and see if anyone salutes?" Even if possible, would it be desirable?

Virtual Reality Interfaces

A virtual reality interface is a complete environment, one in which the user physically enters and interacts with the program. For example, if you were learning about landscape design in a virtual reality environment, you might walk around an area to be designed. You could pick up shrubs and plant them in various locations, lay a paving stone walkway, install lights, construct a water treatment, and then walk through your creation to view it from a variety of perspectives. Absurd? Not a bit. Virtual reality programs and interfaces already exist, and their sophistication is growing rapidly.

The interface to accomplish this type of interaction is specialized and usually specific to a particular treatment, although most interfaces include some combination of goggles and gloves or data suits. A great deal is written in popular, electronic, and computer publications about prototypes and visions of virtual reality, but commercial applications are just beginning to emerge.

A virtual reality system requires a presentation system and an interface for interacting with the system—no difference between this and other multimedia systems in that regard. The trick is to make the presentation system so complete, so absorbing, that the user can treat the simulated world as if it were real. Typically, this is accomplished by wearing a pair of goggles which places a small television in front of each eye, thus giving the wearer binocular, three-dimensional vision. The goggles sense the position of the head and communicate with a computer, which changes the perspective on the screen as you change the position of your head. When you want to see what is behind you, you turn and look. As part of the presentation system, the user also wears earphones of some sort, in order to introduce stereo sound into the system.

The user must also be able to use senses to operate in a virtual world. To one degree or another, all interfaces attempt to extend our senses. A touch screen extends our fingers; a keyboard extends our vocalizations. Virtual reality interfaces go one step further, from extending our senses, to mimicking our senses. With virtual reality interfaces, when you want to grasp an object, you physically reach out and grasp. The interface you use is a glove. While wearing it, if you extend your hand and wave, you see a computer animation of a hand waving. The glove interface allows you to reach out, pick up virtual objects, and manipulate them.

Work is currently being done on the sense of touch in interfaces. Tiny webs of vibrating nodes in gloves can selectively mimic many touch sensations, such as sensing the surface of a virtual object. The range of sensations we can attribute to touch are complex and varied, from the jolt of walking into the end of a low table to the breeze we feel on our faces when riding a bicycle. This presents a difficult challenge to research and development in virtual reality, and offers a most exciting vision for instructional design in the future. To quote Jaron Lanier, founder of VPL Research, from an interview in *Omni* magazine:

> Sometimes I think we've uncovered a new planet, but one that we're inventing instead of discovering. We're just starting to sight the shore of one of its continents. Virtual reality is an adventure worth centuries. (Stewart, 1991, p. 117)

References for Chapter 6

Alessi, S. M., and Trollip, S. R. (1985). *Computer-based instruction: Methods and development.* Englewood Cliffs, NJ: Prentice-Hall.

Borsook, T. (1991). Harnessing the power of interactivity for instruction. In M. R. Simonson and C. Hargrave (Eds.), *Proceedings of the 1991 Convention of the Association for Educational Communications and Technology* (pp. 103–117). Orlando, FL: Association for Educational Communications and Technology.

Fleming, M., and Levie, W. H. (1978). *Instructional message design: Principles from the behavioral sciences.* Englewood Cliffs, NJ: Educational Technology Publications.

Hannafin, M. J., and Peck, K. L. (1988). *The design, development, and evaluation of instructional software.* New York: Macmillan.

Heinich, R., Molenda, M., and Russell, J. (1989). *Instructional media and the new technologies of instruction* (3rd ed.). New York: Macmillan.

Helsel, S. (1992). Virtual reality and education. *Educational Technology, 32*(5), 38–42.

Miller, R. (1990). Introduction. In R. Bergman and T. Moore, *Managing interactive video/multimedia projects.* Englewood Cliffs, NJ: Educational Technology Publications.

Phillipo, J. (1989). An educator's guide to interfaces and authoring systems. *Electronic Learning, 8*(4), 42, 44–45.

Romiszowski, A. (1986). *Developing auto-instructional materials.* London: Kogan Page.

Shuping, M. B. (1991). Assistive and adaptive instructional technologies. In G. J. Anglin (Ed.), *Instructional technology: Past, present, and future,* pp. 292–301. Denver, CO: Libraries Unlimited.

Stewart, D. (1991). Interview: Jaron Lanier. *Omni, January,* 45–46, 113–117.

Zollman, D. (1991). What's m-ss-ng? *EBUG, 1*(1), 1–2.

Chapter 7

Authoring Programs

An authoring program is any computer program which can be used to develop instruction. For IMI development, authoring programs also tie together the various components of media in the system. Several authoring programs are available for the instructional developer to create the computer portion of an interactive multimedia treatment. They range from highly prescriptive and easy-to-use programs with a limited number of options, to fairly sophisticated programs which are only limited by the programming skills and equipment configurations of the user. In every case, authoring programs offer protocols for creating computer-based instruction, and most can be used to create interactive multimedia instruction. Authoring programs vary considerably in price, and most are specific to one or two types of computers. A fairly extensive list of authoring programs is identified at the end of this chapter, along with compatible computers and acquisition sources.

It is important to recognize that only some authoring programs are suitable for interactive multimedia instruction. Others are used exclusively for the development of computer-based instruction, and will not permit you to access peripheral devices. The list in this chapter includes only those which can be used for IMI development. Another important consideration is that certain combinations of equipment and software also require a custom interface (a device which facilitates communication between the computer and an attached peripheral), while other combinations employ standard interfaces. Custom interfaces can be expensive, and may only support a single function, while standard interfaces may be less expensive and perform a number of useful functions. When you are putting a system together, be sure to obtain a thorough under-standing of all equipment you will need to carry out your treatment, ensure that all components are compatible, and that your authoring program will perform all of the functions you will require. Also consider the end user of your material. Will the equipment requirements restrict the portability of, and therefore the market for, your work?

Don't rely completely on what you read or hear about a particular authoring program to guide a purchase decision. We have our own favorites and villains, and so does everyone else. Before adopting a particular system or language, spend time grappling with it on the hardware configuration you will use. Only then can you be reasonably certain it will do what you want, and even then you may encounter surprises. Changing authoring programs after a treatment has been completed is a very time–consuming task.

Basically, there are two major categories of authoring programs from which to choose: programming languages or authoring tools. (Some writers talk about *authoring languages* by which they mean programming languages used for authoring instruction. We use our terminology in the hope of avoiding terminological confusion.) Your skills and needs will determine which is more appropriate.

Programming Languages

Programming languages include programs such as BASIC, Pascal, and C. They allow the programmer to do a multitude of tasks by writing step-by-step instructions which can be interpreted by the computer. These tasks can include, but are not limited to, creating interactive multimedia instruction. The advantage of a programming language is the flexibility it gives a developer for designing instruction. The developer is not confined to the often prescriptive boundaries of an authoring system. An author using a language can get at the source code, and make modifications at that level, whereas many template-based systems do not allow the author access to the actual code (Hunka, 1989). This can be very important in large-scale projects which may require unconstrained development and the ability to customize instruction to various systems. On the other hand, a programming language can require a higher degree of sophistication from the author than authoring tools; languages are not very "user friendly." Also, authoring with a programming language can require much more time than authoring with a specific authoring tool, because of the time required to construct the syntax for simple commands (Figure 7-1).

Figure 7-1.   Example of programming language-based programs written in GWBASIC
to communicate with a touch screen and videodisc player.

Application Program Sample

Establishes the dimensions and locations of screen targets
which in turn activate the autostop subroutine listed below.

```
707 TARGET( C(24,60,14,710) C(58,60,14,720) C(90,60,14,730) )
708 IF(35,F,100)
710 SEARCH(7569,8138)
715 GOTO 705
720 SEARCH(8420,8900)
725 GOTO 732
730 SEARCH(8163,8385)
731 GOTO 705
732 SEARCH(8920,11880)
735 SEARCH(12472,0)
```

Source Program Sample

Autostop subroutine: searches for a frame and starts to play
from that frame until a specified ending frame is reached.

```
5110 AU=-1:GOSUB 5010
5115 I$="":J$=MID$(STR$(FRAME.E),2)
5120 For I=1 to LEN(J$):I$=I$+FNVD$(MID$(J$,I,1)):NEXT I
5125 I$=I$+"F3":PRINT #2,I$:FOR I=1 TO 100:NEXT:PRINT #2, "@1B"
5130 FOR I=1 TO 100:NEXT I
5135 I$="":J$="":PRINT #2,"@D3"
5140 IF EOF(2) THEN 5130
5145 I$=INPUT$(1,#2):J$=J$+I$:IF NOT EOF(2) THEN 5145
5150 J$=LEFT$(J$,4):J=4096*FNHX(LEFT$(J$,1))+256*FNHX
(MID$(J$,2,1))+16*FNHX(MID$(J$,3,1))+FNHX(RIGHT$(J$,1))
5155 IF J<FRAME.E THEN 5130
5160 FRAME.L=FRAME.E
5165 AU=0;FOR I=1 TO 40:NEXT:RETURN
```

Authoring Tools

Authoring tools are usually easier to use than programming
languages, and usually require less skill in programming to use
productively. Although they vary considerably in sophistication,
authoring systems can be thought of as templates into which you
place your instructions and text. Many use menus to prompt the user
for information, and most use a frame (a complete screen display) as

the basic unit of development. In essence, you are "filling in the blanks" with the information and commands you desire. This requires an understanding of the command structure used by the authoring system, but in most cases, the commands are iconic or mnemonic and easy to execute, and help directories are available if you forget how to do something. You design text screens, graphics, question frames, and branches the way you want them to appear to the user. So, as you design a frame, you get a reasonably accurate idea almost immediately of what the learner will see. This is known as the principle of WYSIWYG (pronounced *wissy-wig*, and derived from What You See Is What You Get). While the principle is well-known and sought after by instructional developers, relatively few authoring programs adhere to it. We suggest it is one of the most important features of an authoring tool from an instructional developer's point of view.

Hypertext Authoring Tools

If you already have some experience with writing computer programs (almost any language), then you are a candidate for using a hypertext-based authoring tool. These programs were not created specifically as multimedia authoring platforms; rather, they have been adapted to that purpose. Such programs usually combine many of the features of database programs, hypertext programs, graphics programs, and authoring programs.

To describe hypertext-based authoring tools, we will use Apple's HyperCard as an example, because it was the first such program, and remains the most popular today. Similar programs exist in the MS-DOS and Commodore worlds. HyperCard uses the metaphor of a stack of cards to describe its shape. When you write a program, you create a stack of cards. Each card in the stack contains information. That information can include any combination of text, graphics, animation, sound, and buttons. The buttons (either apparent or hidden behind text or objects) can be programmed to transport the user back and forth among other cards in the same stack or other stacks, or activate additional animation, sound, or peripherals. Authoring with HyperCard or similar programs also requires familiarity with the underlying programming language, HyperTalk in the case of HyperCard. At this level, the programmer is scripting (writing) a program, giving a series of commands to be executed. HyperTalk is like almost any other programming language at the scripting level (although most would argue it is much more conversational), requiring a sequential command structure and logic (Figure 7-2). As mentioned previously, these tools were developed with multiple uses in mind; they are not restricted to interactive multimedia instruction applications.

Figure 7-2. Example of HyperTalk script. This script (or program) is associated with the button labeled "Click here" on the screen display below. When the user clicks on the button, the screen display is replaced with the contents of another card (in this case, Card 4844 in the stack named "Explain Task" The remainder of the script evokes visual and auditory effects to accompany the change of display.

```
on mouseUp
   Go to card id 4844 of stack "Explain Task"
   Visual effect wipe left very fast
   Play "Harpsichord" tempo 150 "e e e qc"
end mouseUp
```

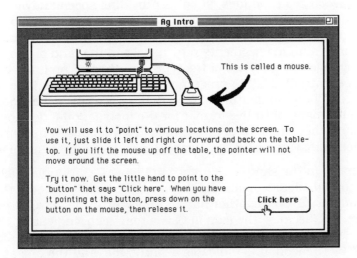

The power, ease, and significance of these programs led to widespread adoption by instructional developers. Thousands of shareware and commercial stacks are available. The relational database foundation of hypertext programs is consistent with the multimedia need to develop less restrictive navigational approaches in instructional materials.

Authoring Systems

The second group of authoring tools, authoring systems, consists of dedicated programs which were designed specifically to create computer-based instruction, and by extension, interactive multimedia instruction. The most popular of these are based on a series of icons which represent, for example, a screen of information, a question, a formula, an animation sequence, a sound sequence, or a video clip. The author typically selects icons from a palette and drags them onto a flowchart (Figure 7-3). The icons are opened, revealing the blank screen template to be filled, or presenting the controls associated with linking peripherals or performing specialized functions. For example, using Authorware Professional, when you click on a screen icon, you are presented with a blank screen and a tool box. The tool box permits you to create text in the screen, draw shapes, shade areas, and manipulate buttons, among other things. When you choose a television icon, you are given full control of a videodisc player. Most routine—and some not-so-routine—functions are linked to icons. For certain specialized functions, such as providing special navigation possibilities or linking to other programs, a conditional icon opens a window for writing programming segments to accomplish the task. Writing programming segments returns you to the land of program-ming languages. Regardless of the type of authoring program chosen, all roads eventually lead to programming if you intend to take full advantage of program features. Nevertheless, icon-based authoring tools offer a highly intuitive format for the instructional developer to exploit, and they are a far cry from the early versions of authoring languages and systems on the market just a few short years ago.

To illustrate, in the sample sequence in Figure 7-3, double-clicking on the icon labelled ① opens the display in Figure 7-4. Doing the same thing on ②, on the other hand, brings forth the flowchart shown in Figure 7-5 (because the icon at ② is a map icon, indicating that it contains a group of other icons). Opening ③ yields the display in Figure 7-6. The icon at ④ indicates a sound file, and the one at ⑤ represents a videodisc sequence. The display represented by the icon at ⑥ is similar to those in ① and ③, but doesn't permit learner input.

Figure 7-3.   Example of icon-based flowchart program. This flowchart represents the
highest level view of the sequence, showing the overall structure.

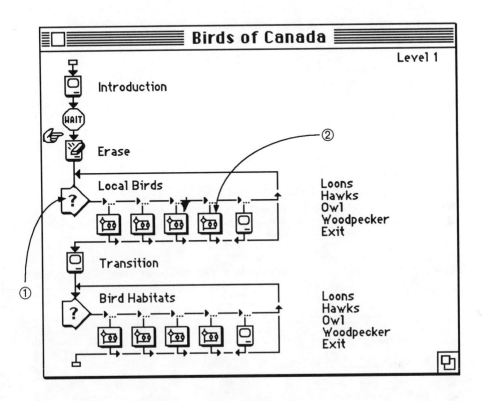

Figure 7-4.   This display is represented by the icon labelled ① in Figure 7-3.

Figure 7-5.   This flowchart represents the second level view of the sequence, exposing the contents of the icon marked ② in Figure 7-3.

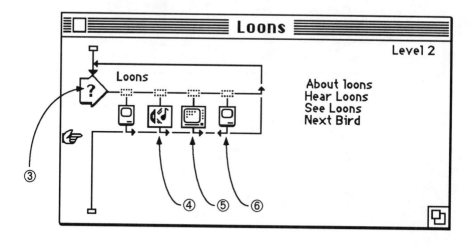

Figure 7-6.   This display is represented by the icon labelled ③ in Figure 7-5.

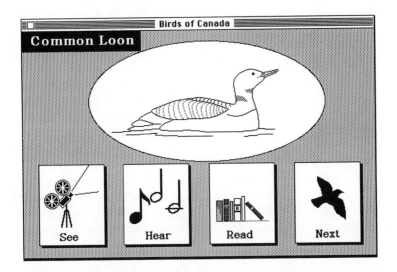

Selecting an Authoring Program

One important task is to select the appropriate authoring program for your situation. This is not an easy job. Many of the packages currently available are large, integrated programs, capable of performing an impressive array of functions. They often use product-specific terminology, and require a significant investment of time to evaluate. While we would not hazard a guess at which program will meet your needs, we will outline features to look for in an authoring tool. We will attempt to define some of the important characteristics, drawing on our experience and the substantial recommendations of others (e.g., see Hannafin and Mitzel, 1990; Hazen, 1987; Hunka, 1989; Maddux, 1992; Raskin, 1990; Richards and Fukuzawa, 1989). Your needs will determine the emphasis placed on any of these selection variables.

- *Portability* is an important issue for most developers, especially those working on commercial products. Portability is the relative ability to disseminate a product you've created. One portability issue is whether compatible systems exist in the marketplace. Especially in multimedia development at present, adding a wide range of components may limit the portability of the work. Potential users may not have the same configurations of equipment you do. Portability can be enhanced by choosing authoring programs which exist in competing environments, say, MS-DOS and Macintosh, for example. If the same, or very similar, programs can be used, development time in competing formats can be significantly reduced.

Another portability issue is whether or not the authoring program can create standalone run-time modules. Some programs (e.g., HyperCard) require that the ultimate user (i.e., the learner) have a copy of the copy of the same program as used to create it, just in order to run the instruction. Others (e.g., Authorware Professional) can "package" the instruction into a standalone unit (effectively making the instruction into an executable file) that has no such requirement. Both cost and convenience considerations may come into play here.

- *Licensing agreements* are another important feature of authoring programs. You will want to determine the costs associated with distributing products created with any particular authoring program. Some programs are more expensive to purchase initially, but they allow unrestricted distribution of products made using them. Other programs are less expensive to purchase, but distribution royalties must be paid for any programs you develop and sell. Still others require the developer to purchase special run-time discs on which developed programs must be distributed. In any case, your distribution needs may influence which program you should adopt.

- *WYSIWYG* (What You See Is What You Get). As mentioned earlier, this is, in our opinion, a critically important feature of authoring programs. If you are developing and editing material as it will be viewed by a learner, you are probably working in a much more efficient manner than if you must design the materials in one mode and convert it before you can view the result. We have used programs which require the developer to write instruction, then exit and run the product to see how it will appear to the learner. This can become tedious, time consuming, and frustrating if any significant amount of correction is necessary. We highly recommend you select a program which approximates a WYSIWYG environment. If this is not possible, select a program which allows you to move from an authoring to a run time mode easily and quickly.

- *Documentation* can be thought of as two distinct entities: protocols for documenting programs as they are written, and written and on-line information about the authoring program. If you intend to produce elaborate courseware, documenting it thoroughly is crucial. Documentation most often describes decisions made at various places in the instruction, and charts the choices made by the author. A different author, or for that matter the same author returning to the same program months after initial development, needs documentation to wade through new or long-forgotten territory. In addition, the authoring program you select should be well documented itself. Most of us have had negative experiences with reference manuals and tutorials received with programs. You will want to determine whether a program has features such as a reference section, concrete examples, an index, and on-line help.

- *Flexibility.* Sophisticated authoring systems should be able to accommodate a variety of approaches to developing instruction; that is, they should allow an author to work from strengths. Some authors like to work from flowcharts, others like templates, and still others prefer scripting approaches. An authoring system you choose should either emphasize your preferred style or be flexible enough to support the styles of everyone using the system.

- *Variable levels of expertise* may be possessed by different authors using the same program. Does the program support this? Privilege levels or variable support structures may be a very useful feature of programs used by various authors or by the same author over an extended period of time. For example, a novice author may find copious windows, advice, and help files very comforting. The same author, several weeks later, may find the same features unnecessary and annoying.

- *Integration of peripherals.* An important feature of authoring programs for multimedia development is the number of peripheral devices which can be tied together by the system, and the ease with which it is accomplished. Once you determine the external devices you will want to use for instructional input, you will need to see whether your program can accommodate them. Some such devices could include videodisc players, video cassette players, CD-ROM players, audio cassette players, video digitizers, synthesized audio boards, and full-motion video boards.

- *Text* composition and editing features can be significant, and you may want to find an authoring system which approaches a full range of word processing features. For example, some hypertext tools restrict the use of special text styles, such as boldface and italics, in a single body of text. You may want to consider features such as flexibility, cutting, pasting, importing text, fonts, and styles.

- *Graphics* are fundamental to screen design, so an authoring program should have the ability to create, edit, and/or import graphics easily. When selecting an authoring program, you might consider whether the program gives you access to drawing tools, vector-based drawing, clip art, palette editing, cut and paste functions, fat-bit editing, and importing from standard graphics packages.

- *Animation* features can be very important to some productions, and not as important to others. If you have need of animation in any of your products, you will want to determine the capabilities of your system and program for accomplishing two-dimensional animation, three-dimensional animation, cel animation, sprint animation, and path animation. In addition to creating animation you will also want to determine the program's compatibility with external animation programs, the range transition effects it offers, and the speed at which it is able to access and execute animation routines.

- *Audio* features may be partially associated with other features of the program, and the peripherals attached to the system. Still, it is worth determining whether the authoring program will accommodate analog source input, digital source input, and a MIDI interface. Another significant feature is sound editing. Some programs will permit you to visually edit a waveform display of a sound file, giving you a great deal of control over recorded audio.

- *Video* is commonly available from authoring programs as either a programming feature of the programs, or by linking the program to another program which handles video. In selecting an authoring program, you may want to consider the capability and ease with which it handles full screen motion video, motion video in a window, full videodisc control, and multiple video inputs. Also consider whether any of these features require additional hardware.

- *User control* is a critical feature of any program. What range of user control options are supported by the program? Some of these will be system-dependent. For example, touch screen applications are easily accommodated in a Windows system, but not as easily in others. Find out whether the authoring program will support a keyboard, mouse, graphics tablet, light pen, touch screen, speech recognition, barcode, or virtual reality interface. You will also want to determine the range of available buttons, menus, and similar program control functions which are easily supported by the program.

- *Performance tracking* is an important part of most instructional and training programs. If you are developing resource bases, this feature may not be as important to you. Still, for most applications, features such as answer judging, formula insertion, intelligent scoring, audit trails, and reporting can be very significant. Many programs contain a list of system variables which are automatically calculated while a program is used, such as the amount of time a learner uses a program and the number of questions answered correctly during instruction. Such variables can be a welcome addition to a program, and can save long hours spent developing them from scratch.

- *Programming features* include such things as high level programming language, editing/debugging tools, and bridges to external programs. Other programming features mentioned previously include the ability to test a prototype while authoring, and whether a program permits the creation of a standalone, run-time version of products.

- *Advanced author support* includes features such as on-line instructional design advisement. These program features would assist the author to maintain instructional integrity by imposing or suggesting approaches to designing instruction or teaching content.

- *Networkability* can be a key feature for some development projects. We have encountered significant problems networking some versions and types of software, ranging from slow access time to program crashes. If networking is anticipated, we recommend trying sample programs in the exact network environment for which the product is anticipated.

Authoring Tools

Figure 7-7 summarizes authoring tools available for the various microcomputer systems.

Figure 7-7.   Authoring tools available.

Program	Distributor	System
Authorware Professional	Authorware, Inc.	PC, Macintosh
Guide	Owl International Inc.	PC
IconAuthor	Aimtech Technology	PC
Instant Replay Professional	Nostradamus, Inc.	PC
Multimedia ToolBook Integrated	Asymetrix Corp.	PC
Quest	Allen Communication	PC
TIE	Global Information Systems Technology	PC
Course Builder	TeleRobotic	Macintosh
HyperCard	Apple	Macintosh
MacroMind Director	MacroMind, Inc.	Macintosh
Mentor	Edudisc	Macintosh
AmigaVision	Amiga	Amiga
Animation: Sound Track	Hash Enterprises	Amiga
Deluxe Paint III	Electronic Art	Amiga
MovieSetter	Gold Disk	Amiga
Photon Video: Cel Animator	Micro-Illusions	Amiga
The Director	Right Answers Group	Amiga

References for Chapter 7

Barker, P. (1990). Designing interactive learning systems. *Educational and Training Technology International*, 27(2), 125–145.

Black, T. R. (1987). CAL delivery selection criteria and authoring systems. *Journal of Computer-assisted Learning*, 3(4), 204–213.

Bork, A., and Promicter, N. (1990). Practical techniques useful in authoring technology-based learning material. *Journal of Computer-Based Instruction*, 17(2), 53–60.

Brandon, P. R. (1988). Recent developments in instructional hardware and software. *Educational Technology*, 28(10), 7–12.

Cook, E. K. (1990). The use of Macintosh authoring languages in effective computer-assisted instruction. *Journal of Educational Technology Systems*, 18(2), 109–122.

Crowell, P., and Bork, A. (1989). Authoring systems. *Instruction Delivery Systems*, 3(2), 10–15.

Dean, C. T. (1988). Storyboarding for computer-based training: A technique in transition. *Performance and Instruction*, 27(5), 8–14.

Eckols, S. L., and Rossett, A. (1989). HyperCard for the design, development, and delivery of instruction. *Performance Improvement Quarterly*, 2(4), 2–20.

Hannafin, K. M., and Mitzel, H. E. (1990). CBI authoring tools in postsecondary institutions: A review and critical examination. *Computers and Education*, 14(3), 197–204.

Hazen, M. (1987). Criteria for choosing among instructional software authoring tools. *Journal of Research in Computing in Education*, 20(2), 117–128.

Hunka, S. (1989). Design guidelines for CAI authoring systems. *Educational Technology*, 29(11), 12–17.

Kearsley, G. (1988). Authoring considerations for hypertext. *Educational Technology*, 28(11), 21–24.

Li, Z. (1990). Transaction shells: A new approach to courseware authoring. *Journal of Research on Computing in Education*, 23(1), 72–86.

Maddux, C. D. (1992). User-developed computer-assisted instruction: Alternatives in authoring software. *Educational Technology*, 32(4), 7–14.

Merrill, M. D., and Li, Z. (1989). An instructional design expert system. *Journal of Computer-Based Instruction*, 16(3), 95–101.

Phillipo, J. (1989). An educator's guide to interfaces and authoring systems. *Electronic Learning, 8*(4), 42, 44–45.

Quinn, K. (1990). Expert system shells: What to look for. *Reference Services Review, 18*(1), 83–86.

Raskin, R. (1990). Multimedia: The next frontier for business? *PC Magazine, July,* 151–192.

Richards, T. C., and Fukuzawa, J. (1989). A checklist for evaluation of courseware authoring systems. *Educational Technology, 29*(10), 24–29.

Rode, M., and Poirot, J. (1989). Authoring systems—are they used? *Journal of Research on Computing in Education, 22*(2), 191–198.

Sales, G. C. (1989b). Repurposing: Authoring tools for videodisc. *Computing Teacher, 16*(9), 12–14.

Taylor, T. D., and others. (1987). Interactive video authoring systems. *Optical Information Systems, 7*(4), 282–300.

Underwood, J. (1989). HyperCard and interactive video. *CALICO Journal, 6*(3), 7–20.

Whiting, J. (1989). An evaluation of some common CAL and CBT authoring styles. *Educational and Training Technology International, 26*(3), 186–200.

Section III

Designing Interactive Multimedia Instruction

Chapter 8

When to Use Interactive Multimedia Instruction

Analyzing an Interactive Multimedia Instruction Problem

Your first challenge in any development effort is to determine whether or not you have an instructional problem; only then do you examine whether IMI is a potential solution. Instruction is not a panacea, and often problems can be addressed effectively with a variety of solutions, from job aids to organizational sanctions. The following discussion will assume you have conducted a needs assessment, and have already identified a legitimate instructional problem. If you want some background in conducting a needs assessment, try these two books:

Rossett, A. (1987). *Training needs assessment*. Englewood Cliffs, NJ: Educational Technology Publications.

Mager, R. F., and Pipe, P. (1970). *Analyzing performance problems or 'You really oughta wanna'*. Belmont, CA: Fearon Publishers.

As with the selection of any single medium during instructional development, some interactive multimedia components and combinations are more appropriate for specific problems than others. Chosen appropriately, interactive multimedia can provide powerful instructional treatments. Chosen inappropriately, training via interactive multimedia can range from glossy and needlessly expensive white elephants to truly hideous interventions. This chapter will identify some of the characteristics of instructional problems which lend themselves to interactive multimedia solutions. The list of characteristics discussed is representative, but not exhaustive. As an instructional developer, you will need to weigh the unique characteristics of your projects against the items mentioned, and incorporate other variables which intervene.

Characteristics of IMI Problems

Once you have determined that you have an instructional problem, the instructional developer is faced with the problem of determining the solution set of media which can effectively address the instructional requirements. What clues may indicate that interactive multimedia can or should be used? Specifically, let's consider characteristics of the media, content, learners, and learning climate.

Media

Interactive multimedia instruction, at its best, capitalizes on the advantages of several media and compensates for the weaknesses of individual media. If you are reading this book linearly, you have already encountered the characteristics of each medium, so you have a sense of their various advantages and limitations. A useful, if simplistic, principle to use to approach the problem of media selection is reduction. What is the simplest, least expensive combination of media available to address the problem? If print alone is adequate, why bother with more elaborate solutions?

Content

Several characteristics of the content determine its suitability for IMI:

- Is it capable of being segmented?
- How complex is it?
- How important is realism?
- How stable is the content?

One of the first considerations is whether the content will lend itself to segmentation. Is there a series of discrete components within the content which will permit breaking it into "chunks.?" This can be determined on a casual level in most cases, as the segments will be evident at a glance. But, like peanut butter, content seems to come in both chunky and smooth varieties. For example, *Macbeth* may appear to be chunky because it is neatly divided into acts and scenes. But its content is decidedly linear, and tampering with the flow of the play may disrupt some subtleties of learning and appreciation, particularly for individuals who are unfamiliar with it.

On a more formal basis, the developer could use task analysis procedures to examine the content. Techniques such as matrix analysis (Davies, 1976) provide a visual representation of the content, allowing the developer to identify strings, concepts, multiple discriminations, and principles, as well as how these components of content are related to one another. Be forewarned, however, that formal task analysis procedures can be tedious and time-consuming. If your only purpose is to determine whether you are working with smooth or chunky peanut butter, you may be advised to start casually, and become more formal by necessity. Nevertheless, other purposes can be served by formal task analysis. For a recent project, we spent two full weeks conducting a task analysis on very elaborate content. Several benefits were realized in terms of our understanding of the content, and our efficiency in designing treatments later. Certainly, formal task analysis is often a good investment which can be amortized over the life of a project. Many approaches to task analysis are available to you, and they are described in the recommended chapter below.

Jonassen, D. H., and Hannum, W. H. (1991). Analysis of task analysis procedures. In G. J. Anglin (Ed.), *Instructional technology: Past, present, and future* (pp. 170-187). Englewood, CO: Libraries Unlimited.

Another consideration is the complexity of the learning task. If the content is quite difficult, you may anticipate the need for remedial instruction or review of some components. Interactive multimedia environments are ideal for providing these types of options for the learner. As with segments, complexity can be determined casually by examining the content and discussing impressions with subject matter experts, or it can be formally determined through learner analysis and content analysis procedures.

The need for realism should be considered as well. Video provides a high degree of realism, and if the learner will benefit from this type of treatment, then interactive video may be appropriate. It may be worthwhile to temper some of the enthusiasm for this medium at first, however, and consider less elaborate (and expensive) media. Will written materials do the job? Can videotape be used to provide the bulk of instruction without interaction with the learner? Can computer-generated graphics and animation provide sufficient detail, and perhaps be superior to highly realistic video presentations? Given the seductive and "glitzy" nature of multimedia, we can be easily lured into developing elaborate and expensive (albeit beautiful) solutions to simple problems. These are judgment calls which can seriously impact the cost of a project and the credibility of an instructional developer. Tread carefully.

 Reiser, R., and Gagné, R. (1983). *Selecting media for instruction.* Englewood Cliffs, NJ: Educational Technology Publications.

What about the stability of the content? Is the material likely to change frequently? If so, media such as interactive video and CD-ROM are at a disadvantage to other media, because once material is recorded, it cannot be revised quickly and inexpensively. Generally speaking, it is a good idea to place stable information on read-only media, and relegate volatile information to other, more easily alterable formats such as computer-assisted instruction and print.

Learners

Learner characteristics that influence the suitability of IMI include:

- heterogeneity,
- number of learners involved, and
- location of the learners.

Studying the audience will also provide some indications as to whether interactive multimedia is necessary or desirable. Again, this may include a mixture of formal and informal learner analysis.

Because interactive multimedia instruction can be designed to provide a variety of paths through instruction, it is one of the better media available for dealing with heterogeneous groups of learners. By pretesting scripted material with typical learners who represent the range of abilities you are likely to encounter, you may isolate difficult or confusing portions of instruction which require remedial sequences. The main point, however, is that the wider the range of abilities and aptitudes exhibited by the target audience, the greater the advantages of interactive multimedia over more conventional media. With well-designed interactive multimedia, it is possible to accommodate the needs of various learners within a single treatment through the use of remedial segments, flexible ordering of presentation, options for bypassing unnecessary instruction, and variable feedback. This does not necessarily preclude media such as print; some excellent examples of interactive and branching treatments are available in print-based programmed instruction. Nevertheless, computers, videodisc, and CD-ROM lend themselves naturally to the problem of designing multiple trails through instruction.

The number of potential learners is also a significant selection variable. Although there are no absolute numbers necessary to justify production of various configurations of IMI, generally speaking, the greater the number of potential learners, the more closely the cost-per-learner of IMI approaches traditional approaches such as print or classroom instruction. Large-scale interventions are usually more cost-effective than smaller projects, so in our "bottom-line" society the size of the audience becomes a factor.

The location of the audience can also be important. If learners are centrally located, then many types of training approaches are possible, including such things as classroom instruction and site visits. But if the audience is dispersed, located over a wide geographic area, then an individualized approach which has the potential for power, immediacy, durability, and flexibility of interactive multimedia becomes more attractive. Multimedia can provide a cost-effective means of distributing instruction, especially considering the savings realized from travel and lodging expenditures often associated with events centrally offered.

Learning Climate

Learning climate factors also intervene to support or restrict the introduction of IMI as an alternative delivery mode. One environmental factor is the organizational climate. Development of interactive multimedia can require a substantial dedication of resources, so a positive commitment is needed organizationally. If interactive multimedia, and indeed instruction, is considered to be a frill, then lengthy and costly development efforts may be hampered. Before undertaking a development project of this magnitude, make sure that the necessary budget and organizational support are in place.

It is also useful to analyze the current approach to instruction and training in an organization. Many ideas for interactive development may be drawn from the successes and problems of current approaches.

Bergman, R. E., and Moore, T. V. (1990). *Managing interactive video/multimedia projects.* Englewood Cliffs, NJ: Educational Technology Publications.

References for Chapter 8

Bergman, R. E., and Moore, T. V. (1990). *Managing interactive video/multimedia projects.* Englewood Cliffs, NJ: Educational Technology Publications.

Davies, I. K. (1976). *Objectives in curriculum design.* New York: McGraw-Hill.

Dick, W., and Carey, L. (1990). *The systematic design of instruction* (3rd ed.). New York: Harper Collins Publishers.

Hazari, S. (1992). Multimedia: Is it the right tool for your instructional application? *Journal of Educational Multimedia and Hypermedia, 1*(2), 143–146.

Iuppa, N. V. (1984). *A practical guide to interactive video design.* White Plains, NY: Knowledge Industry Publications, Inc.

Jonassen, D. H., and Hannum, W. H. (1991). Analysis of task analysis procedures. In G. J. Anglin (Ed.), *Instructional technology: Past, present, and future* (pp. 170–187). Englewood, CO: Libraries Unlimited.

Mager, R. F., and Pipe, P. (1970). *Analyzing performance problems or 'You really oughta wanna'.* Belmont, CA: Fearon Publishers.

Reiser, R., and Gagné, R. (1983). *Selecting media for instruction.* Englewood Cliffs, NJ: Educational Technology Publications.

Romiszowski, A. J. (1986). *Developing auto-instructional materials.* New York: Nichols Publishing.

Rossett, A. (1987). *Training needs assessment.* Englewood Cliffs, NJ: Educational Technology Publications.

Chapter 9

Designing an Interactive Multimedia Treatment

After the decision has been made to select interactive multimedia to address an instructional or training problem, designing the treatment begins. The first step you will take in the design process is to decide what psychological orientation to adopt. Then you will perform a task/content analysis, attempting to ferret out all of the elements to be offered in the instructional treatment. In addition, you will attempt to place instructional components in a logical sequence and identify entry, subordinate, and superordinate skills and knowledge. Perhaps you already performed much of the content analysis during your selection process, but now is the time to become detailed. You will gather all of the reference materials available and digest them (some are more palatable than others). You will also work closely with a subject matter expert, who may be the individual responsible for delivering the material in its present form. If possible, it is often useful for instructional designers to actually participate in an existing instructional or training program. This not only enhances under-standing of the content, it also helps identify deficiencies in the instruction, and exposes the designer to participants who may provide invaluable applications, stories, and ideas for the project. You may want to think of yourself as a detective at this stage, tracking down elusive suspects (content) by gathering and examining as much evidence as possible.

Psychological and Philosophical Orientations to Instructional Design

Increasing attention is paid in the literature to the need for theoretically and philosophically grounded approaches to development. Without a stance, the developer is in danger of indiscriminately sampling convenient approaches and techniques, perhaps leading to a confounding mess of incompatible strategies.

> The process of planning the instructional enterprise can begin only after the planner meets the dual requirements of understanding both the systematic nature of the design process as well as particular theoretical orientations that explain how learners do learn, might learn, can be motivated to learn, etc. Without these prerequisite understandings, it is difficult to "plan" or "design" effective instruction to meet the individual need of the client. (Wildman and Burton, 1981, p. 11)

> To the extent that instructional systems are designed without regard to a cohesive learning theory (or theories), the decisions within components risk being inconsistent (and arbitrary), resulting in varying degrees of incompatibility among the components. (Wildman and Burton, 1981, p. 6)

Wildman and Burton (1981) further implore instructional developers to select a single learning theory as a starting point for development. Guidance is available. Some exceptional articles articulate different psychological and philosophical perspectives, and reveal several implications for instructional practice (Hannafin, 1989; Hannafin and Rieber, 1989a; Hannafin and Rieber, 1989b; Jonassen, 1991). Should you choose to adopt a behavioral, cognitive, or constructivist posture in a particular project, maintaining the fidelity of strategies with any of the orientations is possible.

While we acknowledge the utility of a clear orientation, we are not quick to adopt a single-theory posture in our recommendations. Different theoretical orientations can result in similar or compatible recommendations for practice. For example, providing the learner with frequent opportunities to respond to instruction can be justified from reinforcement (behavioral) or depth of processing (cognitive) theoretical stances. Another reason for rejecting a single-theory driven design is that the nature of the learning task and characteristics of learners will also guide strategy decisions

(Jonassen, 1985a; Lucas, 1992). For example, an unmotivated learner may benefit from a high degree of reactive interaction during initial instruction, while a highly motivated learner may benefit from open-ended strategies; learning precise basic skills may require highly prescriptive sets of drills, whereas creative writing might benefit from generative approaches. Given the capability of multimedia systems to house massive quantities of information and to construct complex delivery systems, it seems reasonable to encourage the development of instructional systems which contain more than a single cognitive orientation. In this way, the designer can impose consistency between the cognitive orientation and different learning tasks, and also capitalize on the possibility of designing instruction which is compatible with learning styles and preferences.

Interaction is the major difference between traditional instruction and instruction delivered via newer technologies. The quality and influence of interaction is explained from at least two theoretical perspectives, each of which illuminates the practice of instructional design. While bifurcation of theory into behavioral/cognitive or quantitative/qualitative categories oversimplifies the argument, it provides a convenient framework for discussing instructional design implications for multimedia.

Traditionally, the nature of interaction (i.e., our understanding of how it should be used within instruction) has been theoretically driven by reinforcement principles derived from behavioral psychology. Inter-action is viewed as stimulus-response-reinforcement encounters between the learner and instruction. The purpose of interaction is to shape behavior (which serves as evidence of learning). Reinforcement given in an encounter can be either fixed (regular) or variable (inter-mittent), and may be given on a ratio schedule (after a number of responses) or interval schedule (after an amount of time). Acquisition of knowledge (and other complex behaviors), is considered possible through the acquisition of chains of simple behaviors. Some examples of behavioral orientations to instructional interaction include:

- designer imposed pacing,
- overt responses,
- immediate feedback,
- knowledge of results,
- controlled sequencing,
- small step size,
- prompting, and
- confirmation.

Instructional designers embraced the practices implied by reinforcement theory. Researchers had a field day. A multitude of studies investigated such things as the effects of adjunct questions, grouped questions, and levels of questions on question-specific and incidental learning. Efficiency studies were conducted to determine the proper saturation levels of interactive events in instruction. A great deal was learned about the nature of interaction through test-like events in instruction, but this orientation did little to acknowledge the learner as an active contributor in the learning enterprise.

Enter cognitive theory. A cognitive orientation emphasizes understanding the internal workings of the mind, and how information is selected, perceived, processed, and retrieved. From a cognitive perspective, the individual is considered an important mediator of learning, and the role of instruction is to encourage meaningful engagement of content and stimulate the learner to invest effort in processing information at deeper and deeper levels. From a cognitive perspective, knowledge can be represented as propositions (single ideas), productions and production systems (procedures), images, or schemata (organized networks of prior knowledge). Processes which seem to be crucial to encoding and retrieving knowledge include:

- elaboration,
- organization, and
- spread of activation.

Elaboration includes using existing knowledge to enhance, extend, or modify new information. For example, you might use a metaphor of communication at a construction site when describing the component activities of protein synthesis to a group of construction workers. Organization includes the internal shaping of information into meaningful units. This might include something like developing an acronym to embrace a series of components. Spread of activation is the process of making linkages among existing related propositions. Cognitive mapping activities, for example, offer an example of this type of process.

In order to promote cognitive engagement in interactive multimedia, Hannafin (1989) offers a sample of activities. He suggested these serve as examples of both mathemagenic and generative strategies which will enhance the degree to which lesson content is meaningfully engaged and content processing deepened. Some activities include:

- fault-free questions (complex questions requiring a high degree of integration and synthesis, but which are not evaluated);

- queries (learners pose questions based on their own schemata, using approaches such as keyword searches);

- real-time responding (students respond to events as they unfold during instruction, either dealing with instructional situations or controlling the amount and sequence of instruction);

- note taking (by taking electronic notes, such as selecting portions of a script for later review or annotating instruction, the student generates a personal notebook of elaborations of instruction);

- predicting/hypothesizing (learners generate propositions, thereby organizing a schema, which can be compared to new information);

- hypertext (depending on the structure of the learning task or content, learners strike imposed, derived, or unencumbered pathways through instruction);

- cooperative dialogue (dyads or small groups of individuals collaborating on instruction can enhance the range of elaboration possible, but note the debate about functional group sizes later in this chapter).

Yet another view of instructional design proposes that behavioral orientations and most cognitive orientations represent an objective philosophical stance (Jonassen, 1991). From this point of view, one believes there is an externally defined, objective reality, and the primary role of education is to reveal that reality to learners. Students learn the instruction prescribed to them, and therefore become educated about the "real world" By comparison, others adhere to a constructive philosophy. Constructivism emphasizes that reality is internally defined, and is unique to individuals who "construct" their individual realities from perceptual experiences. Given this view, learners would be encouraged to construct their own meaning and interpretation of instruction, rather than be encouraged to learn what is presented to them. Jonassen (1991, pp. 11–12) suggests four fundamental changes to instructional practice which would accompany constructivist assumptions:

- Instructional goals and objectives would be negotiated, not imposed.

- Task and content analysis would focus less on identifying and prescribing a single, best sequence for learning.

- The goal of IST [Instructional Systems Technology] would be less concerned with prescribing mathemagenic instructional strategies necessary to lead learners to specific learning behaviors.

- Evaluation of learning would become less criterion-referenced.

None of these orientations is exclusive. The potential for hybrid strategies is high. Certainly behaviorally oriented strategies such as prompting and confirmation can coexist quite peacefully with cognitive strategies such as queries and note taking. Constructivism offers new ways to think about many of our more generative approaches to instructional multimedia. As our understanding of the philosophical and psychological foundations of interaction expands, so will our range of available strategies, and our confidence in strategies already employed. This area of study is vitally important if the practice of instructional design for interactive multimedia is to keep pace with technological capabilities.

Specifying Content

Most projects will result in a glut of information you need to organize. In fact, one can argue that instructional design is largely the process of organizing, rather than creating, opportunities for learning. One method useful for organizing material is a content outline. Many formats will work well, but the notion is to outline, in as much detail as possible, the components which will comprise the training treatment. A suggested format might include the objectives, related content, and treatment ideas in columns, as shown in Figure 9-1.

Figure 9-1. Sample content outline.

Objective	Content	Treatment
Assess methods of facilitating social adjustment of exceptional children in the regular classroom	Increase knowledge of exceptionalities • visitors, visits, films, books • prepare class for introduction of special needs student • student simulations Encourage support and acceptance • establish "buddy" system • sociometric techniques • recognize abilities of exceptional • sharing strengths and weaknesses • structured affective programs (DUSO, classroom meetings) • teacher modeling	Narrators introduce, followed by menu of two main areas. Narrators introduce each area with submenu allowing learner to select examples of each. Location shots.

The format in Figure 9-1 permits the instructional designer and subject matter expert to deal with all of the potential segments of instruction in a concise fashion prior to scripting. The document can be used to review what is included and missing, test assumptions, clarify thinking, and make initial suggestions about possible treatments. Each of the components is critical, and displaying them in this manner allows the designer to examine objectives along with their associated content and possible treatments. Looking for congruence among objectives, content, and treatment will help to avoid problems later in the project.

Two cautions must be raised regarding the use of a content outline. First, the content outline will impose an illusion of linearity on the content. The order in which objectives and content appear on paper may appear logical, yet be completely inappropriate for an interactive treatment. The instructional designer must struggle to maintain "segment-think" to deal with the components of the content rather than the structure appearing on paper. The final treatment will be segmented, and in many cases the learner will determine which subset of segments is encountered and how all the segments fit together. The flow of content implied by the juxtaposition of objectives and content on the content outline will likely be disrupted by interaction with the learner. Even worse, the implied linearity may seduce the designer into imposing a linear structure on the final treatment, thus undermining the power of the medium to deal flexibly with a variety of learners.

Another caution concerns the content—does it warrant an interactive multimedia treatment? Once an objective and content appear on a document, they seem to adopt a level of legitimacy. One of the purposes of the content outline is to help decide what should be included, excluded, or relegated to another medium for delivery. The instructional developer must often be ruthless about eliminating content which is either unimportant or could be dealt with better in another format of instruction. It is possible to waste precious resources on content which would be more effectively handled by a printed job aid. Continually remind yourself to examine content skeptically for unwanted stowaways in your outline.

The first component of the outline is the objective, one of the most value-laden and vehemently-argued components of instruction among otherwise sane instructional designers. The objective should be a clear statement of intended outcomes for the learners. Some designers argue that it must be behavioral, and include a statement identifying the audience (the learner), behavior (will be able to compute operating income), conditions (given a sample store operating statement listing income and expenditures), and degree (to the nearest dollar 100 percent of the time). Certainly this is a valuable approach to writing objectives, as behavioral objectives lend precision to understanding intended outcomes, and they can guide the developer in the design of instruction and evaluation. Nevertheless, others argue that generally stated objectives such as "understand the three main uses of the charge gross report" are sufficient to provide direction to developers and learners. Rather than fuel the debate here, it is enough to mention that the competing philosophies exist, and you will want to adopt the approach that meets the learner's needs, your style, and the client's requirement.

Yes, objectives are tedious to write, but they provide clear direction for further development. Often, you will want to share the objectives with learners. That means the hard work you put into the content outline will be translated directly into instruction later. How many do you write? There is no easy answer. If you intend to evaluate performance following instruction, each component you intend to assess should be represented by an objective. If not, you will want to have enough objectives to address every main topic you intend to cover. In an elaborate treatment, that can add up to a lot of objectives.

The objectives will lead you to the content necessary to achieve them. When outlining the content, ask yourself, "In order to perform the objective, what will the learner need to know or do?" Then list each element in order. It would be a good idea at this point to work in point form, listing only the points which will be embellished later during scripting. Try to include every idea which will be included in training.

Finally, it is also useful to leave room for treatment ideas. You will probably think of a number of useful ideas for presenting content as you complete the outline, and placing them next to the content in the outline provides an excellent reference later as you consider treatment decisions. If you fail to jot down your treatment ideas as they come to you, you will find that many excellent ideas are lost later. Remember, treatment ideas are tentative at this point, so you may want to list several alternatives.

Design Specifications

While building a program framework, a protocol for development is useful to ensure consistency throughout the treatment. The problem is that several people are involved in making creative decisions in most interactive multimedia projects, and each person probably has a unique way of presenting information. To help avoid obvious difficulties, design specifications can offer prescriptions for using elements in the treatment. These include technical standards, instructional formats, and aesthetic considerations. Agreement on how to approach key components should be reached prior to development. The purpose is not to stifle creativity, but rather to preserve the coherence and credibility of the product. For instance, without clear design specifications one part of a script might be written in a casual tone and another part in a formal tone; or in a single treatment you might find key words emphasized by variously using color, underlining, or boldfacing at different places in text frames. The result can be unsettling for the learner. It is also quite difficult to edit inconsistencies if they occur throughout a treatment. Once problems slip through to the edit master tape, they are costly and irritating to fix.

Your list of specifications will be different for each project and client you encounter. Still, some examples of technical, instructional, and aesthetic design specifications are included in Figures 9-2, 9-3, and 9-4 for your consideration.

Figure 9-2.   Sample of technical standards for design specifications.

Component	Example of Design Specifications
Writing Style	The writing style will be as simple as possible, and will include only the content necessary to meet objectives. The tone will be formal. Narration will be written in the first person.
Screen Format	Text screens will be limited to a single idea and no more than eight lines of text. Each text screen will carry a banner heading.
Grammar	No contractions will be used in text screens, although they will be permitted in printed material.
Numbering	Wherever possible, bullets (•) will mark points presented in lists. Questions will be numbered.
Layout Restrictions	Textual overlays on video will appear in blank areas of the visual. They will be computer-generated.
Abbreviations	After introduction to each abbreviation, SOS will be used interchangeably with Store Operating Statement, and CGR with Charge Gross Report.

Figure 9-3.   Sample of instructional formats for design specifications.

Component	Examples of Design Specifications
Strategy	The treatment will consist of six simulations, each introduced by narrators. Background information and suggested readings will be provided in a manual.
Menu Organization	Each chapter of the treatment will be preceded by a menu of entry points and access to other chapters.
Length of Segments	Each topic will be restricted to five minutes of videodisc space, although slight variations will be accommodated by shifting space among topics. In general, additional instruction will be provided via CD-ROM and the manual.
Reading Level	Textual material should be appropriate for an eighth grade reading level. All material will be presented as audio (in English, French, or Spanish) stored on CD-ROM for individuals who choose an audio treatment.
Test-like Events	All questions must permit touch-screen responses, either identifying the location of an answer or a timed response. At least three questions will appear for each topic and be embedded within the instruction.
Feedback	Unique remedial responses will be given. Following first incorrect attempt, the correct answer and explanation will be given. The tone of feedback will be compassionate.

Figure 9-4.   Sample of aesthetic considerations for design specifications.

Component	Example of Design Specifications
Screen Text	Font, Geneva. Normal text, 12 pt. plain. Titles 18 pt. bold.
Color	All menus will use white text on a red field. Question frames will be white on blue. Computer-generated text frames will use yellow lettering on black field. At no time in the program will more than three colors occupy text or graphics screens simultaneously.
Computer vs. Video	Wherever possible, video will take precedence over computer. Computer segments will be limited to those remedial segments which are seldom chosen.
Music	Beyond title music, only a three-note passage will be played following a correct response to a question.
Illustrations	All illustrations will be black-and-white line drawings on graphic cards.
Visual Cues	For illustrations, color will be used to highlight key elements. In text, key words will be highlighted in a contrasting color.

Many other categories and examples of design specifications could be added to the list. The important point is that you consider the technical, instructional, and aesthetic aspects of the project which would suffer from inconsistent treatment. Consider only the important components, and leave as much creative license as possible to the discretion of the instructional developers. Then, before production begins, reach agreement among development team members and the subject matter expert on how the selected components will be presented. Give everybody a copy of the design specifications, and occasionally check to see that procedures are being followed.

Program Elements

Once you have approved your content outline, after adding forgotten components and pruning unnecessary items, you have the substance for development. It is now necessary to construct a framework for the content. In this stage of development you will make decisions about how the interactive treatment will be constructed, and you will provide detailed design specifications. Typically, in large projects, several individuals are contributing to the final product, and an accepted format or template for development will make development easier, reduce inconsistencies among developers, and save a great deal of time in editing later.

What types of presentation elements comprise a typical interactive application? When you begin actual construction of a program, it may be useful to conceptually lump your development efforts into five piles: core instruction, complementary instruction, management elements, navigation elements, and interactive elements.

Core Instruction

Core instruction includes the elements or "nodes" which contain all of the expository material the learner would encounter in a single "path" through the instruction, without diversion. As you think in terms of modules or chunks of instruction, each module may include introductory segments, core instruction, and summary segments.

Introductory segments are included to orient the learner to the instruction which follows. Typically, they may include an overview of the content, procedures to follow during the program, objectives for the module, or an advance organizer for the material. When considering the design specifications for the entire interactive multimedia treatment, you may want to decide on a standard approach to be followed in each module. This will give the program a characteristic "look" and will allow several developers to work simultaneously on different modules without violating the format.

Core instruction frames include what is typically thought of as instruction. The "meat" of the content is presented in these segments (enough mixed metaphors?). This is also one area which permits a great deal of creativity and personal expression. You may go beyond straight exposition or linear presentation into the full range of presentation strategies. A successful interactive multimedia treatment may also include elements of drama, mystery, simulation, demonstration, discovery, and human interaction. In many modules, you may find yourself developing characters, and charting the components of an intricate plot. This is not to downplay the value of straightforward instruction, but you will want to avoid using the medium solely as an electronic page-turning device. You have the capability with this medium of devising problems for the learner, offering vicarious experiences which can approach reality in the hands of a skilled writer. After posing problems, the learner can propose solution strategies and see the consequences of various choices. This type of "segment-think" exploits the unique power of interactive multimedia, and besides, the writing becomes much more fun and challenging. There are many approaches to instruction, and one good source of ideas is the Arwady and Gayeski book listed below.

 Arwady, J. W., and Gayeski, D. M. (1989). *Using video: Interactive and linear designs.* Englewood Cliffs, NJ: Educational Technology Publications.

Summary segments allow you to crisply reiterate the main points of instruction. These may not follow each module, but rather summarize the critical information from several modules. They may appear as either motion or still sequences, and you may wish to leave their presentation under the control of the learner. Nevertheless, if you consider summaries as part of the core instruction, they may be mandated by the designer.

Complementary Instruction

Because interactive multimedia permits flexible presentation of segments and modules in the core instruction, there is a high degree of probability that learners will require additional help in order to learn effectively. Additional segments can be readily incorporated to augment core instruction, sometimes available at the discretion of the learner, and sometimes imposed on the learner based upon responses to problems.

Complementary instruction can be broken into three categories: help segments, remedial segments, and additional information segments.

Help segments offer additional information which embellish ideas originally presented in core instruction. Perhaps they include some background or detail that most learners will not need. In your design specifications you will decide where help segments will be made available to the learner, and also where instructions for accessing help will be presented in the treatment. Help segments are often designed so that a single keystroke will activate the subroutine to present the segment, and then return the learner to the point of departure. The segment may be motion video, still video frames, computer-generated text, graphics, print, or a combination of these. Relegating help screens to the computer or CD-ROM conserves videodisc real estate for core instruction, but may also undermine the impact of these valuable components. If the frames offered by the computer are not compelling, accessing help segments may seem more like punishment than support. Think about it.

Remedial segments are just that—remedial. They should not be confused with review segments, which merely repeat content which probably was not understood the first time it was viewed. Remedial segments are usually designed to respond to apparent deficiencies in learner understanding, judged from a response to a problem or question. As such they offer the designer unique opportunities to exercise intuition (and field testing data when it is available), and predict problems learners are likely to encounter. Once the problems are identified, remedial segments are designed to specifically address the weaknesses. The designer should constantly be asking, "What could go wrong here, and why would it happen?" If you pilot test your material with a group of typical learners prior to final release, you may be able to perform an item analysis to identify those incorrect responses which indicate a pattern for remediation. Frequently selected incorrect responses may warrant remedial segments presented on videodisc, while rare problems may be more efficiently remediated with computer-generated text and graphics. Still, the same caution mentioned above concerning video versus computer segments applies.

Additional information segments are particularly popular in hypermedia settings. By clicking or touching a target, the learner is given access to elaborative or tangential material. These can occupy a significant amount of development time, and result in instruction which often remains hidden from the typical learner. At the same time, additional information segments permit learners to follow interests and construct their own learning experiences—often powerful motivational strategies. This type of segment also introduces an additional layer of interest to the program, resulting in an intellectually three-dimensional treatment. A concomitant problem is that some learners may become bogged down or lost in the instructional tributaries and forget about the main instructional river.

One final point should be made about complementary instruction components, whether they contain helpful, remedial, or additional information. All exist outside the primary flow of instruction. Needless to say, complementary segments should be context-sensitive, otherwise they wouldn't be complementary. The closer you can tie complementary instruction meaningfully to the point of departure in the program, the more sophisticated the treatment will appear to the learner.

Management Elements

Management segments include brief test-like events, problems, and evaluation items which are used to assess learner progress, determine the direction (or path) the learner should follow through the program, and reinforce learning. They are generally made of two components: items and feedback segments. The items may be traditional test items such as multiple-choice items and true/false, or selecting the best solution from among choices for a simulated problem. For some applications, the learner is restricted to a keypad or a touch screen, restricting the types of questions possible. Other applications permit a wider range of open responses, due to the expanded capability of the computer keyboard, voice synthesizer, or virtual reality interface to facilitate expression and interpret input.

The trick with writing test-like events for interactive multimedia is to capitalize on the medium's ability to present complex problems. You are not restricted to composing clever multiple-choice items to test knowledge (e.g., audio-based testing can be used in language lessons; animation can simulate simple motion for the learner to diagnose). Through motion video segments which simulate human problems or demonstrate difficult procedures, you can ask the learner to exercise judgment based upon experience and information gained during instruction. Segments can be produced which accurately depict the interaction of variables you want to emphasize, require the learner to evaluate the situation, and take appropriate action. In fact, using a subjective point of view with the camera, the viewer can be placed into the situation to be evaluated. For example, you might be placed in a board meeting—with the camera serving as your eyes while individuals at the table argue points—and ultimately ask you for information or a decision. You might be able to type a response with the keyboard, speak a response as voice input, or pound your fist on the table with a virtual reality interface. This not meant to suggest that there is no place for traditionally presented test items, but rather to emphasize that the medium allows greater latitude, and system capabilities to interact more naturally with learners will continue to grow.

Based upon the decision made or the solution chosen to a test-like event, the learner encounters a feedback segment. The purpose of a feedback segment is to provide information to the learner about the quality of the response to the test-like event. The feedback should go beyond the "hooray" and "not quite, try again" variety, and attempt to identify what caused the error as specifically as possible, and point out remedial action to the learner. A response such as, "You probably didn't notice that the operating expenses were negative, resulting in a net gain to operating income" allows the learner to consider the likely source of an error, and makes the designer look a lot more intelligent. The challenge is to try to anticipate typical mistakes the learner might make, and then create a feedback segment which mimics how a good instructor would respond in each case.

But some learners will either purposely or unintentionally give outrageous answers to questions. For instance, if you ask the learner to press 1 to 5 on the keypad, someone will probably press 9, either accidentally, or just to see what will happen. Be prepared for "out-of-range" responses, and create feedback for them. It might be as simple as describing an appropriate range of responses, or giving a clue. But what if the learner continues responding inappropriately, because it is more fun than learning? You might place a counter (described in the next section) on the segment, and if out-of-range responses happen more than twice, ignore them. Also, be prepared for the individual who misses the same question several times. With a counter, you can limit the number of attempts possible, and avoid a frustrating experience for the learner. In general, when designing feedback segments, you put yourself in the position of the learners, and try to anticipate every problem, error, and mischief possible.

Navigation Elements

Several other elements outside the realm of instruction comprise interactive video treatments. They give a program structure, perform housekeeping chores in the program, and provide the learner some control over events. Well contrived and properly executed, navigation and management features serve to enhance learning and make the interactive multimedia treatment easy to use. Sloppily executed or improperly contrived, they can serve to make an interactive treatment a nightmare for the learner. Let's examine a few of these elements.

The learner needs to be able to review information easily. Let's face it, attention spans are not very long most of the time. Your mind has probably wandered several times to your upcoming vacation or a problem with the kids as you read this chapter. That means you must either re-read the missed information, or ignore it. Wouldn't it be disconcerting if you didn't at least have the option to review? This can happen in interactive multimedia treatments as well. No matter how engaging your material, the viewer's mind may wander. The opportunity to learn that material is lost unless you build in an opportunity to retrieve the segment and review it. Review segments do not require additional writing or disc space. It is merely a matter of making the option to review a segment available to the learner, by including a subroutine in the program driving the presentation, and letting the learner know how to activate it. Review options can be offered for specified segments of instruction or made available anywhere in the instruction via a global function.

Menus afford the learner a limited amount of control. Generally speaking, a menu offers several choices of instructional segments, and the viewer is permitted to select topics for presentation, or skip over topics. After selecting an item from the menu, the learner is branched to the segment, or yet another menu, and returned to that point following presentation. Menus are usually presented as still-frames, and are either video or computer-generated. The amount of learner control is limited to the number of options presented on the menu. The instructional designer must be careful to preserve the integrity of the program, regardless of the order in which the topics are viewed. For instance, when writing Item 5 on a menu the designer cannot assume that the viewer has already selected Item 4.

One very useful control device for interactive programs is a global escape routine. The escape routine is designed to allow the learner to exit the program at almost any point. In interactive programs, the escape routine can be used to mark the viewer's location in the sequence and record the progress achieved, so that upon return to the program, the viewer can resume at the point of departure.

Another control device mentioned earlier is a counter. A counter is a "transparent" portion of the program which keeps track of the learner's progress in the program. For example, a counter might be used to maintain a record of the number of correct responses to questions, attempts at a question, or the amount of time spent on a particular activity. For interactive applications, the value of the counter can be recorded, and stored for future reference. In some authoring systems, several system variables are automatically monitored by the system. For example, Authorware Professional contains more than 100 such variables, including items as routine as the cumulative number of correct answers given by the student to all questions encountered (TotalCorrect), and variables as esoteric as the number of seconds from the last mouse click (ClickSeconds).

Yet another useful device is a navigational control panel. This could appear as a small control panel on screen displays, and it would give more complete control of the program to the learner. For example, a control panel could include a variety of buttons, such as an arrow to move forward or back, a magnifying glass to look at detail, a TV set to view a related video segment, or fully functional video controls for videodisc (Figure 9-5).

Figure 9-5.   An on-screen control panel.

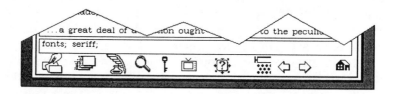

Made popular in hypermedia applications, these control panels are useful for most multimedia treatments. One caution: Learners who are unfamiliar with an instructional treatment can become disoriented or lost when they strike their own paths. The global escape mentioned earlier is just one method of permitting the learner a way out of the woods when lost. Another approach is to include a button which reveals a visual representation of the treatment and highlights the learner's location in the diagram (Figure 9-6). Of course, you should not assume that learners already know how to use even these features; instructions on their use should be given at the very beginning of the sequence.

Figure 9-6.   A "You are here" diagram.

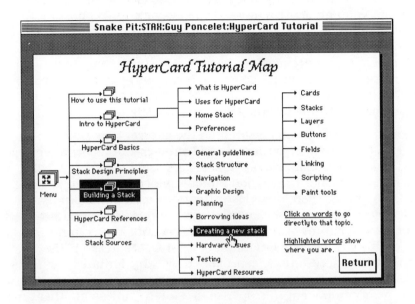

Interactive Elements

Borsook (1991) argues that in order for interactive instruction to be truly interactive, it should emulate interpersonal communication.

> We should aim to emulate in computer instruction systems [and by extension, multimedia systems], to the greatest extent possible, the richness and flexibility found in human/human interaction while concomitantly exploiting the unique capabilities computers have to offer. (p. 113)

He identifies seven key ingredients which are characteristic of interpersonal interaction. These include:

- immediacy of response,
- non-sequential access of information,
- adaptability,
- feedback,

- options,
- bi-directional communication, and
- interruptability.

Any program worthy of the label *interactive* will aspire to these ingredients, so it is worth considering the implications of each for IMI.

In any conversation, immediacy of response is assumed. If you ask a question, you anticipate a quick response, or else you assume something has gone awry with the communication system. Indeed, a parallel situation occurs in some IMI treatments. A learner selects a path and makes a decision or answers a question, only to wait while the program and hardware go through various gymnastics before responding. If the wait is too long, the learner may become impatient or assume something is wrong with the system.

Although we know of no research on the subject, our experience suggests that learners are increasingly intolerant of slow interaction times in instructional programs. Learners seem to expect quick response times, and frustration builds rapidly if a system is sluggish. In IMI programs, therefore, close attention to the conceptual and tactical geography of discs and the execution time of program elements will improve the quality of interaction. For example, at the time of this writing, one limitation of CD-ROM material is the relatively long access time, especially noticeable for large elements like digitized photographs. It would be unwise to branch learners to this type of component in response to a query, unless another type of communication could happen while the more time-consuming component is constructed. If long waits are unavoidable, at least warn learners that they will have to wait. That way, they may be more tolerant. Giving them something—anything—to watch during the wait may help, as well. For example, having a sliding scale, or a greyed-out bar that gradually changes to indicate progress can be helpful in dealing with impatience (Figure 9-7).

Figure 9-7.   Various progress-indicating devices.

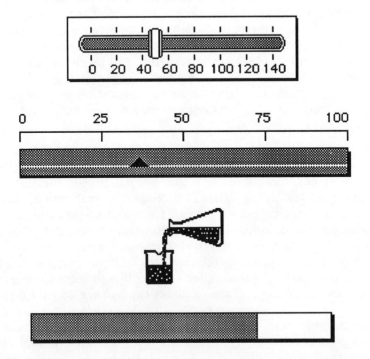

Non-sequential access of information, interruptability, and adaptability are interrelated concepts which can also be promoted in IMI design. In a truly interactive conversation, an individual should be able to interrupt a speaker and to change topics, and by virtue of these actions, influence the content and shape of communication. For IMI design, this is promoted through the sophistication of the navigation system and the quality of the feedback offered learners. By promoting full access and interruption, the designer empowers the learner to control a great deal of the learning environment, even though this is not always the intention of the designer or the best set of conditions for learning (see discussion of learner control later in this chapter). Still, where it is well-advised, these characteristics can be included in the design of a treatment. With an open architecture design, learners can be given access to any of the pieces of instruction. *Pause* and *Escape* buttons and context-sensitive help segments which are always active can help make interruptions available and fruitful for the learner.

The ability of the program to adapt to the situation or learner, just as we adapt to a speaker during a conversation, is dependent on the ability of the instructional designer to anticipate the types of learner responses and characteristics possible in the program. At a rudimentary level, a program can provide unique responses to a set of choices. By making a choice from a menu, and receiving the instruction tied to that choice, a learner is experiencing a program adapted to that individual. But depending on the choices which were available at that position, the program may or may not adapt successfully or meaningfully to an individual's needs.

More sophisticated designs are possible which increase the number of options for learners and which identify trends, and alter the path of instruction to accommodate the trend. For example, hypertext environments allow the designer to include *hot spots* for virtually any position on a given screen, which can transport the learner to additional, remedial, tangential, or explanatory resources. This type of arrangement allows learners to elaborate the instruction specifically as needed or desired, resulting in instruction which is molded by the learner. Yet another approach is to record tendencies in responses, and either advise or direct the learner based on these tendencies (see the discussion of audit trails in Chapter 13). For example, an individual might consistently choose video examples of concepts presented in instruction, and avoid textual explanations. Once the trend is identified, it can be pointed out to the learner and a video-enhanced path offered, or perhaps the program will require the learner to deal with some print instruction (if appropriate). Either result is an example of an adaptation made to learner characteristics.

As another example of adaptation, it is possible to identify (within reasonable limits of confidence) those students who have clearly mastered the content—or those who have clearly not done so—with far less effort than is usually devoted to conventional computer-based testing. In other words, it isn't necessary for a learner to endure, say, 25 test items in order to determine that he or she knows the content to a mastery level (or, conversely, that he or she hasn't got a clue about it). By using decision-making algorithms such as those developed by various researchers (e.g., Frick, 1989, 1990a, 1991; Kingsbury and Weiss, 1983; Luk, 1991; Novick and Lewis, 1974; Tennyson and Park, 1984; Tennyson, Christensen, and Park, 1984; Weiss and Kingsbury, 1984), it is possible to shorten considerably the testing time that most learners must endure. Put simply, the length of the test adapts to the knowledge the learner has about the subject matter. The clear-cut cases of masters and non-masters are decided within the presentation of only a few test items; the intermediate students require more items for the decision to be made.

Of course, adapting interactive instruction is based on bi-directional communication and feedback. Bi-directional communication implies dialogue, a worthy goal for a truly interactive treatment. In order to simulate dialogue, a program must be able to interpret input from the learner (or at least categorize a response) and provide feedback in the form of a logical response. Of course, lacking natural language recognition, we are unable to do these things completely, so the goal is somewhat futuristic.

Finally, as options characterize interpersonal communication, IMI should include many avenues for expression. Options in IMI should be many and varied. In highly communicative instruction, students should be able to freely move about the instruction without severe limitations. In other words, learner control is an inherent feature of well-designed IMI, and it is discussed more specifically later. There are at least two principal features of IMI where options can be expanded or restricted. One feature is content: it can be narrow and focused, resulting in precise but restricted instruction; or it can be broad and layered, with tangential appendages, resulting in instruction which is potentially rich but perhaps less focused. For interaction to be dynamic, it is necessary to build content for the varied directions the instruction may follow. This means developing a great deal of content which any particular learner may never see. Furthermore, learners can be presented with options as to which content they want to deal with. For example, in a math drill, it really matters not to the multimedia designer whether the numbers being added or multiplied are baseball batting averages, wingspans of model airplanes, profits from a lemonade stand, or weights of dinosaurs. However, it may make a great deal of difference, motivationally, to the learner.

Another feature to which options may refer is modes of interaction (interfaces) in IMI. Learners may be able to choose from keyboard, mouse, touch-screen, barcode, voice, or virtual reality modes of interaction with programs. While in most cases, hardware restrictions will determine which options are made available to learners, an instructional designer needs to consider which modes are instructionally appropriate.

Summary: Design Principles for Interactivity

- Control tactical geography of discs to promote fast access to elements (see "Tactical Geography" in Chapter 3).

- If access must be slow, include "wait" messages or other progress-indicating communication while the slow portion is accessed.

- Where appropriate, empower the learner to control the sequence of instructional components.

- Provide the learner opportunities to interrupt instruction and gain context-sensitive help.

- Provide ample opportunities (paths) in the instruction to adapt to anticipated learner differences and needs.

- Give feedback to learner input which is personalized and logically related to the context of the interaction.

- Build in as many options for interaction as possible, including breadth of information available and modes of communicating with the program.

Practice and IMI Design

Practice and interaction are not the same, although they certainly occupy similar territory. Practice is a larger construct which subsumes a much wider range of activity than just interaction. However, one of the principal functions of interaction is to require learners to practice using a skill or new knowledge. Instructional theories provide ample recommendations for dealing with practice and feedback. In fact, recommendations from various camps often overlap significantly, despite being labeled or rationalized differently. Salisbury, Richards, and Klein (1985) published a seminal article on the subject of extracting recommendations for practice from major instructional design theories.[1] While the focus of their article is practice (a somewhat larger issue than interaction), several of their observations apply specifically to the design of interactivity. They

---

[1] We recommend you take a good look at this excellent article, particularly Table 1 on page 11. It outlines specific recommendations for different types of learning at initial, intermediate, and final stages of practice.

concluded that instructional design theories concerning practice are complementary rather than antagonistic for the most part. For example, from a behavioral perspective, Gropper (1976) identified six tools which can be used in designing instruction:

- the amount of cuing,
- the size of units to be practiced,
- stimulus and response modes,
- variety,
- type of content, and
- frequency of practice.

From a cognitive perspective arose the notions of:

- automaticity,
- interference,
- spaced practice,
- spaced review, and
- making meaning.

While differences and unique contributions exist, particularly when applied to different learning tasks, a consensus of common practice can be derived.

> Different instructional theories often use different terms to refer to the same phenomenon which tends to make the knowledge base for designing practice to appear more complex than it really is (Salisbury, Richards, and Klein, 1985, p. 18)

We will draw upon this document and other sources, and attempt to distill some generalized principles for the design of practice in IMI.

Principle 1. **Practice during instruction should be varied, not constant.**

An instructional developer should consciously monitor the cadence, quantity, and type of interactive events available to learners at different stages of instruction. We recommend variety.

Principle 2. **As familiarity with the learning task increases, so should the difficulty of practice increase.**

Difficulty of interactive events, such as questions or practice of skills, should gradually increase as learners gain facility with the knowledge or skills. One way to increase the challenge level of practice is to increase the size of the practice task. As learning sub-skills progresses, the sub-skills can often be linked to form chains of complex activity.

Principle 3. Learners should be weaned from prompts as their facility with knowledge or skills increases.

In early stages of learning, give several cues, prompts, hints, and helps. As learning progresses, crutches should be gradually reduced, until they are completely removed. In many multimedia environments, optional help is continually available, and chosen by the learner. This approach has many strengths (need-orientation, adaptability, flexibility) but in some cases, learners rely too heavily on the help segments and therefore don't expend the cognitive effort needed to achieve deeper levels of processing. In such cases, multimedia instruction may want to use advisory messages linked to help routines. For example, a message like, "This is the fifteenth time you have asked for help with this exercise. Why don't you try it on your own this time, and see how you do" may promote self-weaning.

Principle 4. Use practice often during the early stages of learning, and gradually lengthen the space between practice sessions on a particular topic as instruction progresses.

Initial acquisition of knowledge or skills can benefit from frequent practice during early stages of learning. While a modest amount of overlearning facilitates retention, the instructional payoff of continual practice is lessened once a learner has acquired a particular skill or knowledge, and too much redundancy can become boring. It is a good idea, however, to return occasionally to the original material, and use practice as a "booster shot" to maintain learning. As new chunks of information are added to the instruction, it is a good idea to review old information to reduce the possibility of retroactive inhibition.

Principle 5. For some types of learning, practice should progress from accuracy to speed to automaticity.

Remember math drills in your early years of schooling? It wasn't enough to just know multiplication tables; you were expected to do speed drills with them. For some types of learning, this is sound, and can certainly be built into interactive multimedia contexts. In some cases, taking the next step to automaticity is desirable (performing the skill while performing a secondary task). For example, you may learn how to juggle three balls in a cascade pattern (accuracy); then juggle faster in a tighter pattern (speed); finally, juggle the balls while looking away and reciting the alphabet (automaticity). Automaticity has greatest relevance for psychomotor skills; for some types of learning, such as literary criticism or social analysis, we believe this progression has less utility.

Principle 6. Review segments can be used successfully in place of questions.

Review segments are not necessarily interactive, although they promote cognitive engagement. Some research suggests that review frames may be as effective as questions for recall learning (Schwier and Misanchuk, 1988; Tovar, 1989). We speculate that individuals, particularly motivated learners, may generate their own covert strategies for assimilating redundant information which are successful for lower levels of learning. Review frames may provide a novel change and be used interchangeably with more interactive strategies to create more variety. This suggestion may not hold for some learners and tasks. Questioning may be more effective for highly motivated learners (Schwier and Misanchuk, 1988). Passive review strategies (review segments and freeze frames) may be more effective than recall questions for teaching procedures using interactive video (Tovar, 1989).

Principle 7. Feedback should identify the successful and unsuccessful features of the interaction and describe why incorrect responses or omissions are insufficient.

This is probably self-evident, and echoes some of our earlier suggestions. In interactive multimedia contexts, it is important to tailor feedback to the response, and provide meaningful strategies for the learner to make improvements.

Principle 8. Learners can benefit from memory or organizational strategies to make information more meaningful.

Mnemonic devices, concept maps, epitomes, analogies, and outlines all serve to emphasize or construct meaning. Use them liberally, especially in cases where learning is complex.

Principle 9. Practice events should require learners to use information and discover and derive new relationships in information.

This principle is derived from component display theory (Merrill, 1983). Merrill describes three levels of performance: remember, use, and find. Generally speaking, learners should encounter practice events at the *use* and *find* levels as much as possible to increase meaningful engagement.

Principle 10. **Practice should be designed to motivate learners.**

Keller's model of motivation (Keller, 1983) includes four categories of motivation with design implications: attention, relevance, confidence, and satisfaction. With this in mind, practice events in IMI should:

- gain and maintain interest (attention);
- be directly related to the content and larger instructional context (relevance);
- provide a challenging but comfortable level of difficulty with ample instructional support (confidence);
- reward successful performance (satisfaction).

Learner Control

The topic of learner control is central to the design of interactive instruction. As the previous discussion revealed, the options for turning control of instruction over to the learner are many and growing in number. Does that mean a prudent instructional designer should relinquish control of instruction? Does unreigned and undirected control over the instructional landscape offer a healthy experience for learners? Of course, these are simplistic questions, but in most instructional development projects which allow any type of meaningful navigation and interaction, an instructional developer will struggle with the fundamental issue of how prescriptive to be with the instructional treatment.

The term *learner control* appears to have been defined and operationalized in a number of ways in the literature, and may refer to the learner selecting one or more of the following:

- Content to learn—a hypertext environment may provide many options from which the learner chooses one or more options, in an idiosyncratic order. Alternatively, learners may choose items from a menu of objectives.

- Context within which to learn—some skills can be taught using a variety of subject-matter. For example, Ross, McCormick, and Krisak (1986) designed a CBI sequence to teach statistics using examples from either education, business, or sports, and in one variation, provided the learner with the opportunity to choose the preferred context.

- Method of presentation—the same material may be presented either inductively or deductively; the presentation strategy might use either a generalization followed by an example (ruleg) or one or more examples followed by a generalization (egrule).

- Provision of optional content—introductions, overviews, supplementary information, and content maps are some of the possibilities.

- Sequence in which to learn—although some subject-matter is sufficiently hierarchical in nature that there is an optimal presentation sequence, many times the learner can be permitted to choose the order in which subordinate skills and knowledge can be learned.

- Amount of practice to undertake and/or the amount of time devoted to practice items.

- Level of difficulty of the instruction and/or exercises.

Furthermore, any of those kinds of learner control enumerated above can be granted with or without advice. That is, the control can simply be turned over to the learner, or the control can be turned over along with some advice. For example, a sequence can keep track of an individual learner's responses heretofore, perhaps factor in some background knowledge about the learner's conceptual style or aptitudes, and provide the learner with the probabilities that the various choices will lead to success. Those probabilities, of course, will be based on the degree of success experienced by previous learners with similar preference and performance characteristics.

While research in the area of learner control in IMI is relatively new, some initial directions have emerged. For the time being, particularly given the wide variety of definitions of the term *learner control*, these should be considered broad generalizations which may inform the design of interactive instruction.

- Learners who are generally high achievers or who are knowledgeable about an area of study can benefit from a high degree of learner control (Borsook, 1991; Gay, 1986; Hannafin and Colamaio, 1987).

- Naive or uninformed learners require structure, interaction, and feedback to perform optimally (Borsook, 1991; Carrier and Jonassen, 1988; Higginbotham-Wheat, 1988, 1990; Kinzie, Sullivan, and Berdel, 1988; Schloss, Wisniewski, and Cartwright, 1988).

- Learner control with advisement seems to be superior to unstructured learner control for enhancing achievement and curiosity, promoting time-on-task, and stimulating self-challenge (Arnone and Grabowski, 1991; Hannafin, 1984; Mattoon, Klein, and Thurman, 1991; Milheim and Azbell, 1988; Ross, 1984; Santiago and Okey, 1990).

- Courseware should be adaptive. It should be able to alter instruction dynamically, based on learner idiosyncracies (Borsook, 1991; Carrier and Jonassen, 1988).

- The effectiveness of learner control is mitigated by such learner characteristics as ability, previous knowledge of the subject matter, and locus of control (Santiago and Okey, 1990).

- Learner control of presentations has been shown to be beneficial with respect to text density (Ross, Morrison, and O'Dell, 1988) and context conditions (Ross, McCormick, and Krisak, 1986).

- Learner control may permit students to make poor decisions about how much practice they require, which are reflected in decremented performance (Ross, 1984).

- Learner control may provide motivation (Santiago and Okey, 1990; Steinberg, 1977).

- Learner control does not necessarily increase achievement and may increase time spent learning (Santiago and Okey, 1990).

The conditions, amounts, and types of learner control which may be relinquished to the learner under various instructional conditions will be studied and debated for some time to come. For example, Higginbotham-Wheat (1988; 1990) argues that learners should be given control over contextual variables such as text density, fonts, and backgrounds, but not over content support variables such as pacing, sequence, and examples.

Learning in Groups

It is easy to conceive of individualized multimediated instruction as a solitary activity; even the very name suggests isolation through use of the adjective *individualized*. And indeed, many times it is. However, individualization has also frequently been the goal of computer-based instruction, and several studies have shown that pairs of learners could learn effectively with that medium (Carrier and Sales, 1987; Dalton and Hannafin, 1987; Johnson, Johnson, and Stanne, 1985; Justen, Thomas, and Waldorp, 1988; Sanders, 1988). It seems reasonable to speculate that multimediated instruction can be effective with multiple learners, as well.

Early evidence on having two or more learners working together on multimediated instruction is mixed. Clark and Romaniuk (1989) had individuals, pairs, and triads work with an interactive videodisc tutorial. They found that while there was no difference in either post-test or retention achievement for the individuals and pairs, triads showed significantly lower retention scores. Furthermore, learners in triads took significantly longer to complete the module, hence had lower productivity ratios than either the individuals or pairs, who did not differ from each other. On the other hand, Cockayne (1991) found no such decrement when she compared learners undergoing instruction from interactive videodisc either individually, in groups of two or three, or in groups of four or five.

There is also some evidence that the gender of dyads using interactive video might be a significant factor. Dalton (1990) found differences in both behavior and attitude among female/female, female/male, and male/male dyads, extending the observations of gender differences found earlier by Webb (1985), Johnson, Johnson, and Stanne (1985), and Dalton and Hannafin (1987). This may represent just one gender issue among many, as Canada and Brusca (1991) have identified several social, situational, and environmental variables which result in a "technological gender gap" in educational settings.

References for Chapter 9

Arnone, M. P., and Grabowski, B. L. (1991). Effect of variations in learner control on childrens' curiosity and learning from interactive video. In M. R. Simonson and C. Hargrave (Eds.), *Proceedings of the 1991 Convention of the Association for Educational Communications and Technology* (pp. 45–67). Orlando, FL: Association for Educational Communications and Technology.

Arwady, J. W., and Gayeski, D. M. (1989). *Using video: Interactive and linear designs*. Englewood Cliffs, NJ: Educational Technology Publications.

Bergman, R. E., and Moore, T. V. (1990). *Managing interactive video/multimedia projects*. Englewood Cliffs, NJ: Educatonal Technology Publications.

Borsook, T. (1991). Harnessing the power of interactivity for instruction. In M. R. Simonson and C. Hargrave (Eds.), *Proceedings of the 1991 Convention of the Association for Educational Communications and Technology* (pp. 103–117). Orlando, FL: Association for Educational Communications and Technology.

Canada, K., and Bruska, F. (1991). The technological gender gap: Evidence and recommendations for educators and computer-based instruction designers. *Educational Technology Research and Development, 39*(2), 43–51.

Carrier, C. A., and Jonassen, D. H. (1988). Adapting courseware to accommodate individual differences. In D. H. Jonassen (Ed.), *Instructional designs for microcomputer courseware*. Hillsdale, NJ: Lawrence Erlbaum Associates.

Carrier, C. A., and Sales, G. C. (1987). Pair versus individual work on the acquisition of concepts in a computer-based instructional lesson. *Journal of Computer-Based Instruction, 14*(1), 11–17.

Clark, M. L., and Romaniuk, E. W. (1989). The effects of groups sizes on achievement and attitude using interactive videodisc courseware. In *Transitions: Proceedings of the AMTEC '89 Conference*. Edmonton, AB: Association for Media and Technology in Education in Canada.

Cockayne, S. (1991). Effects of small group sizes on learning with interactive videodisc. *Educational Technology, 31*(2), 43–45.

Dalton, D. W. (1990). The effects of cooperative learning strategies on achievement and attitudes during interactive video. *Journal of Computer-Based Instruction, 17*(1), 8–16.

Dalton, D. W., and Hannafin, M. J. (1987). Examining the effects of varied computer-based reinforcement on self-esteem and achievement: An exploratory study. *Association for Educational Data Systems Journal, 18*(3), 172–182.

DeBloois, M. L. (1982). *Videodisc/microcomputer courseware design*. Englewood Cliffs, NJ: Educational Technology Publications.

Frick, T. W. (1989). Bayesian adaptation during computer-based tests and computer-guided practice exercises. *Journal of Educational Computing Research, 5*(1), 89–114.

Frick, T. W. (1990a). A comparison of three decision models for adapting the length of computer-based mastery tests. *Journal of Educational Computing Research, 6*(4), 479–513.

Frick, T. W. (1991, February). *A comparison of an expert systems approach to computerized adaptive testing and an item response theory model.* Paper presented at the Annual Conference of the Association for Educational Communications and Technology, Orlando, FL.

Gay, G. (1986). Interaction of learner control and prior understanding in computer-assisted video instruction. *Journal of Educational Psychology, 78*, 225–227.

Gronlund, N. E. (1985). *Stating objectives for classroom instruction* (3rd ed.). New York: Macmillan.

Gropper, G. L. (1976). A behavioral perspective on media selection. *AV Communication Review, 24*, 157-186.

Hannafin, M. J. (1984). Guidelines for determining locus of instructional control in the design of computer-assisted instruction. *Journal of Instructional Development, 7*(3), 6–10.

Hannafin, M. J. (1989). Interaction strategies and emerging instructional technologies: Psychological perspectives. *Canadian Journal of Educational Communication, 18*(3), 167–179.

Hannafin, M. J., and Colamaio, M. E. (1987). The effects of variations in lesson control and practice on learning from interactive video. *Educational Communications and Technology Journal, 35*(4), 203–212.

Hannafin, M. J., and Rieber, L. P. (1989a). Psychological foundations of instructional design for emerging computer-based instructional technologies: Part I. *Educational Technology Research and Development, 37*(2), 91–101.

Hannafin, M. J., and Rieber, L. P. (1989b). Psychological foundations of instructional design for emerging computer-based instructional technologies: Part II. *Educational Technology Research and Development, 37*(2), 102–114.

Higginbotham-Wheat, N. (1988, November). *Perspectives on implementation of learner control in CBI.* Paper presented at the Annual Meeting of the Mid-South Educational Research Association, Lexington, KY. (ERIC Document Reproduction Service No. ED 305 898)

Higginbotham-Wheat, N. (1990). Learner control: When does it work? In M. R. Simonson and C. Hargrave (Eds.), *Proceedings of the 1990*

Convention of the Association for Educational Communications and Technology. Anaheim, CA: Association for Educational Communications and Technology. (ERIC Document Reproduction Service No. ED 323 930)

Johnson, R. T., Johnson, D. W., and Stanne, M. B. (1985). Effects of cooperative, competetive, and individualistic goal structures on computer-assisted instruction. *Journal of Educational Psychology, 77*(6), 668–677.

Jonassen, D. H. (1985a). Interactive lesson designs: A taxonomy. *Educational Technology, 25*(6), 7–17.

Jonassen, D. H. (1991). Objectivism versus constructivism: Do we need a new philosophical paradigm? *Educational Technology Research and Development, 39*(3), 5–14.

Justen, J. E., Thomas, M. A., and Waldorp, P. B. (1988). Effects of small group versus individual computer-assisted instruction on student achievement. *Educational Technology, 28*(2), 50–52.

Keller, J. M. (1983). Motivational design of instruction. In C. M. Reigeluth (Ed.), *Instructional design theories and models: An overview of their current status* (pp. 386–434). Hillsdale, NJ: Lawrence Erlbaum Associates.

Kingsbury, G. G., and Weiss, D. J. (1983). A comparison of IRT-based adaptive mastery testing and a sequential mastery testing procedure. In D. Weiss (Ed.), *New horizons in testing* (pp. 257–283). New York: Academic Press.

Kinzie, M. B., Sullivan, H. J., and Berdel, R. L. (1988). Learner control and achievement in science computer-assisted instruction. *Journal of Educational Psychology, 80*(3), 299–303.

Lucas, L. (1992). Interactivity: What is it and how do you use it? *Journal of Educational Multimedia and Hypermedia, 1*(1), 7–10.

Luk, HK. (1991, April). *An empirical comparison of an expert systems approach and an IRT approach to computer-based adaptive mastery testing.* Paper presented at the Annual Meeting of the American Educational Research Association, Chicago, IL.

Mattoon, J. S., Klein, J. D., and Thurman, R. A. (1991). Learner control versus computer control in instructional simulation. In M. R. Simonson and C. Hargrave (Eds.), *Proceedings of the 1991 Convention of the Association for Educational Communications and Technology* (pp. 481–498). Orlando, FL: Association for Educational Communications and Technology.

Merrill, M. D. (1983). Component display theory. In C. M. Reigeluth (Ed.), *Instructional design theories and models: An overview of their current status* (pp. 279–333). Hillsdale, NJ: Lawrence Erlbaum Associates.

Milheim, W. D., and Azbell, J. W. (1988). How past research on learner control can aid in the design of interactive video materials. In M. R. Simonson and J. K. Frederick (Eds.), *Proceedings of the 1988 Convention of the Association for Educational Communications and Technology* (pp. 459–472). New Orleans, LA: Association for Educational Communications and Technology. (ERIC Document Reproduction Service No. ED 295 652)

Morrison, G. R., Ross, S. M., and O'Dell, J. K. (1988). Text density as a design variable in instructional displays. *Educational Communications and Technology Journal, 36*(1), 103–115.

Novick, M. R., and Lewis, C. (1974). *Prescribing test length for criterion-referenced measurement* (Tech. Bull. No. 18). Iowa City, IA: American College Testing Program.

Ross, S. M. (1984). Matching the lesson to the student: Alternative adaptive designs for individualized learning systems. *Journal of Computer-Based Instruction, 11*(2), 42–48.

Ross, S. M., McCormick, D., and Krisak, N. (1986). Adapting the thematic context of mathematical problems to student interests: Individual versus group-based strategies. *Journal of Educational Research, 79*, 245–252.

Ross, S. M., Morrison, G. R., and O'Dell, J. K. (1988). Obtaining more out of less text in CBI: Effects of varied text density levels as a function of learner characteristics and control strategy. *Educational Communications and Technology Journal, 36*(3), 131–142.

Salisbury, D. F., Richards, B. F., and Klein, J. D. (1985). Designing practice: A review of prescriptions and recommendations from instructional design theories. *Journal of Instructional Development, 8*(4), 9–19.

Sanders, J. (1988). *The effects of pairing students for work on a graphically-oriented CAI simulation.* Unpublished M. Ed. thesis. Edmonton, AB: University of Alberta.

Santiago, R. S., and Okey, J. R. (1990, February). *Sorting out learner control research: Implications for instructional design and development.* Paper presented as the Annual Conference of the Association for Educational Communications and Technology, Anaheim, CA.

Schloss, P. J., Wisniewski, L. A., and Cartwright, G. P. (1988). The differential effect of learner control and feedback in college students' performance on CAI modules. *Journal of Educational Computing Research, 4*(2), 141–149.

Schwier, R. A., and Misanchuk, E. R. (1988). The effect of interaction and perceived need for training on learning from computer-based instruction. *Canadian Journal of Educational Communication, 17*(3), 147–158.

Steinberg, E. R. (1977). Review of student control in computer-assisted instruction. *Journal of Computer-Based Instruction, 3*(3), 84–90.

Tennyson, R. D., Christensen, D. L., and Park, S. (1984). The Minnesota adaptive instructional system: An intelligent CBI system. *Journal of Computer-Based Instruction, 11*(1), 2–13.

Tennyson, R. D., and Park, O. (1984). Computer-based adaptive instructional systems: A review of empirically based models. *Machine-Mediated Learning, 1*(2), 129–153.

Tovar, M. (1989). Effects of active vs. passive review strategies on recalling information from an interactive video instructional programme. *Canadian Journal of Educational Communication, 18*(3), 181–192.

Webb, N. M. (1985). The role of gender in computer programming learning process. *Journal of Educational Computing Research, 1*(4), 441–457. Cited by Dalton, D. W. (1990). The effects of cooperative learning strategies on achievement and attitudes during interactive video. *Journal of Computer-Based Instruction, 17*(1), 8–16.

Weiss, D. J., and Kingsbury, G. G. (1984). Application of computerized adaptive testing to educational problems. *Journal of Educational Measurement, 21*(4), 361–375.

Wildman, T. M., and Burton, J. K. (1981). Integrating learning theory with instructional design. *Journal of Instructional Development, 4*(3), 5–14.

Chapter 10

Flowcharting and Branching

Branching is used in multimedia programs to permit variation in the presentation. As learners respond differentially to the instruction, they choose (if permitted to do so by the program designer) or are caused (by the design imposed on the sequence by the program designer) to travel different paths, or branches, through the instruction. To keep track of where each of the different paths may lead, flowcharts—visual representations of the branches—are often used.

Flowcharts

Once segments have been identified in the content outline, and rough treatment ideas are isolated, a visual representation of the program elements is needed. Remember, the content outline displays program components linearly. Reading a linear document, it is easy to get lost in the complexity of interactive branching and overlook key elements in the design. Your ideas are probably still tentative at this stage, so you primarily want to display the main elements and avoid too much detail. A flowchart is a useful device to accomplish this (Figure 10-1). Its purpose is to represent visually the architecture of the treatment, and show how elements fit together. Certainly other approaches can be used to accomplish the same thing, but in interactive multimedia, a flowchart is an accepted convention.

At this stage of development, the flowchart is simple, displaying only key elements to help you initially examine the treatment structure. You can use it as a guide to decisions concerning the aesthetic and technical construction of the program.

The content of the flowchart is not static. As your ideas mature, so will the flowchart. During production/post-production, a detailed and

Figure 10-1. A sample flowchart.

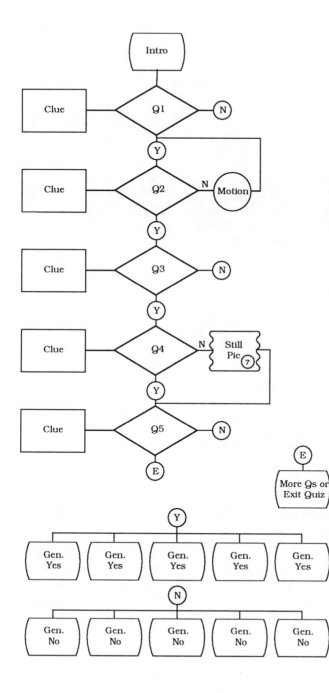

annotated flowchart can be used to identify and locate each element
in the treatment. For now, you may include only segment titles,
question points, and branches, and add detail as the project
continues. To facilitate and encourage continual changes, it may be
helpful to place elements on index cards which can be moved, edited,
added to, and deleted. You may also want to clear some wall space to
display the cards. This results in an unsightly mess for a long period
of time, but it is very functional. Computer-based flowcharting and
planning programs may also be useful, since they dynamically
accommodate the changes that are virtually certain to occur.
However, they are sometimes limited in their ability to portray the
whole picture at once, due to relatively small screen size.

Beware those who worship the flowchart as an aesthetic masterpiece,
rather than the visual working document of structure it should be. As
with the content outline and other development documents, inclusion
in the flowchart can imply that an element is inviolable, thus
hindering the chart's usefulness as a design tool, and perhaps
introducing premature rigor mortis to the treatment. If you start
flowcharting early in the design stage and let the flowchart evolve
along with your decisions, it can provide useful service to you
throughout a project.

You may want to design your own icons to represent single frames,
motion sequences, questions and timed stills, computer text,
graphics, or animation. For example, the symbols shown in Figure
10-2 might be used. These symbols will be useful when you begin
writing a multimedia program, because they will indicate the type of
code needed to perform the associated function. For many
treatments, the flowchart will become quite elaborate. When
examined as a whole, it can give you a feel for the variety or "flow" of
the overall treatment. You can tell at a glance whether there is a
mixture of visual experiences for the user, whether elements are
roughly where you want them, and whether you are using questions
at appropriate intervals. It's not important what your symbols look
like, as long as they are easy to discriminate visually, and you find
them useful.

Figure 10-2. Example icons for flowcharting.

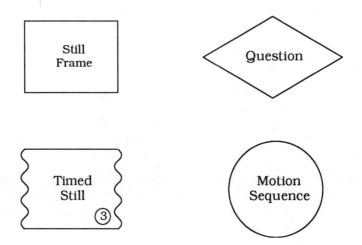

Types of Branching

Branching is the art of moving from one place to another in a treatment. Interactive multimedia systems permit elaborate branching configurations, based on a wide variety of conditions and levels of learner control. There are a number of basic branching configurations: linear, user-directed, review, remedial audio, single remediation, multiple remediation, and hypertext. These basic configurations, of course, are often combined with one another into a single multimedia presentation.

Linear Branching

Linear branching is sequential, unidirectional, and predetermined by the producer. Every user travels the same path through the treatment. This is the least complex form of branching, and the easiest to program, but hardly qualifies as interactive. There is no opportunity for remediation based on learner input, nor is the learner permitted any choice of direction (Figure 10-3). Indeed, because it is linear and unidirectional, calling this design "branching" is a bit of a misnomer.

Figure 10-3. Linear branching.

Before you blithely discard linear branching as an option because it is too simplistic and elementary, recall that it may be appropriate for portions of an otherwise highly interactive treatment. There may be portions of any treatment you want learners to march through in lockstep regardless of their previous skills or knowledge, such as an introduction to using unique course materials. Placebo questions may interrupt long segments, merely to break up the instruction and keep learners stimulated, rather than to assess and redirect learning.

User-Directed Branching

User-directed branching provides the learner with choices of direction, and the learner's selections determine which of several paths are traveled (Figure 10-4). Usually choices are provided by menus, and users must select from a predetermined number of segments.

Figure 10-4. User-directed branching.

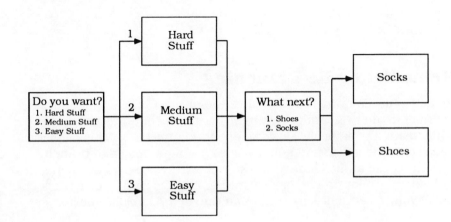

The purpose is not remedial. Rather, the purpose is to give the learner as much control as possible over content. With multimedia systems, menus can be delivered by the computer, directing the learner to instructional segments on videodisc. This avoids the relatively expensive construction of a single frame on videodisc, and also gives you the flexibility to update or revise menus and paths. Most interactive treatments employ user-directed branching liberally.

Review Branching

Review branching gives the user another look at the same material, as a result of an incorrect answer to a question, or upon retrieval (Figure 10-5). Formally, this would not be considered remediation, because the learner encounters nothing new. This strategy is not usually preferred for instruction, because if the user is unable to learn from the material the first time, a second strategy should be attempted. However, the learner's attention can wander, and it is often comforting to have the option of re-reading a portion of the instruction.

Figure 10-5. Review branching.

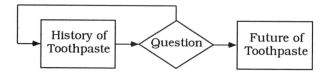

Remedial Audio Branching

Remedial audio branching switches the player to the second audio channel to alter the audio treatment for the second presentation while using the same visual component (Figure 10-6). This conserves space on a videodisc and still provides a unique remedial branch. Switching the audio channel works well with voice-over segments, but watch out for on-camera narrators. An alternative voice track can make your treatment look like a bad dub of a "Godzilla" movie.

Figure 10-6. Remedial audio branching.

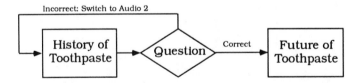

Single Remediation Branching

Single remediation branching assumes that an incorrect response to a question should result in a unique remedial segment (Figure 10-7). It is used when a single remedial branch can be used for any incorrect response. Either the question is structured as a limited response item such as true/false or yes/no, or the content limits the number of remedial opportunities available. Often space constraints on a disc will limit the number of remedial segments you will want to introduce. You must ask yourself, "Is the extra instruction worth the real estate devoted to it.?"

Figure 10-7. Single remediation branching.

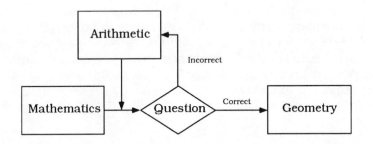

Multiple Remediation Branching

Multiple remediation branching is a powerful architectural approach to responding to student input. It is used when, based upon the response of the learner, the remedial instruction is tailored to repair the specific deficiency noted (Figure 10-8).

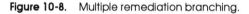

Figure 10-8. Multiple remediation branching.

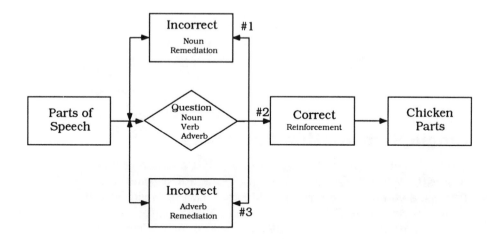

This is a powerful device because it gives the instruction a personality and pinpoints needs more accurately than possible with single remediation branching. Multiple remediation branches are often determined by anticipating common errors which learners might make, such as forgetting a minus sign in a mathematics problem, or transposing two similar-sounding concepts. The instructional developer assumes these will happen, and constructs a remedial branch for each anticipated difficulty. A skillful developer can correctly anticipate many difficulties a learner will encounter. Usually, there are few degrees of freedom. Through pilot testing, it may be possible to isolate the most attractive distractions, and allocate disc space only to the most likely remedial needs. Less popular remedial segments can be delivered by the computer, conserving valuable disc real estate, and extending the variety of remedial choices.

Hypertext Branching

Hypertext branching involves moving from any given screen display to (potentially) any other one. In practice, however, the number of potential targets is usually more limited. In building a hypertext branching network, the designer provides a means of moving from one display to another one, typically a button on the screen to click with a mouse. While future hypertext programs and systems will undoubtedly approach the hypothetical, at present the designer of a hypertext collection of information must specify in advance what links between various screen displays are allowed. That is, each card (the metaphor used by HyperCard, one of the most widely-used hypertext programs, to describe a screen display) is linked to a number of other cards in the collection. In addition to being able to accommodate all the different branching types described above within a collection of information, hypertext permits "jumping out" to other collections of information (also known as stacks), or to video or audio sequences. Then, at the click of a mouse or the press of a key, the learner is able to return to the point of departure in the first collection.

Because hypertext branching is thus "three-dimensional," it is difficult to represent adequately in a diagram. Nevertheless, Figure 10-9 provides some notion of how hypertext displays are linked. Each connection between screen displays represents alternative path choices open to the learner. In addition, some hypertext programs permit the learner to re-trace his or her steps sequentially.

Figure 10-9.   Hypertext branching.

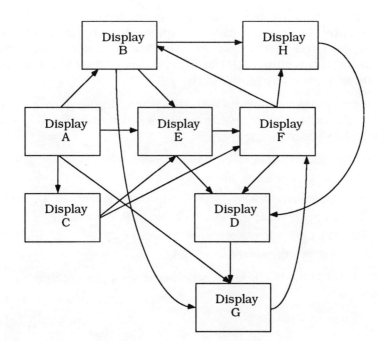

Branching Problems

A looped branch is one in which the user is directed to review a previous segment, usually because of an incorrect response to a question. Particularly with fill-in-the-blank questions, the learner may struggle finding the exact word for matching, and as a result, continually be re-routed through the same instructional segment.

Frustration will build quickly to unmanageable levels, and the learner will either quit or take the frustration out on the equipment. A safety valve measure can be built into the program in the form of an answer counter or an exiting routine. An answer counter can be used to branch the user out of the offensive loop after a predetermined number of incorrect responses.

Another safety valve is an exiting routine, which can be used at any point in the instruction to return the user to a topic menu or leave the instruction, as mentioned earlier in this chapter. For example, on a control panel which always remains on the screen, the user can be given buttons to return to a topic menu or exit the program. With some tinkering, most authoring languages and systems enable these functions, and they enhance your chances for success.

Conditional branching locations can also create problems for the learners, either by forcing them through needless remedial segments or by skipping over instruction entirely. This is an easy error to make with complex branching patterns. Look at the portion of a flowchart, for example, shown in Figure 10-10.

There are two major problems with this branching sequence. Follow the path of a learner who never answers a question correctly. What happens? In sequence, the learner:

1. Receives instruction on CAMELS (A).
2. Answers a question incorrectly (B).
3. Receives one of three possible remedial segments (C, D, or E).
4. Answers another question incorrectly (F, G, or H).
5. Jumps to yet another remedial segment (J).
6. Answers a question (K).

All of this looks fine to the user, who never sees the problem. Can you?

Figure 10-10. Sample flowchart of instruction on camels.

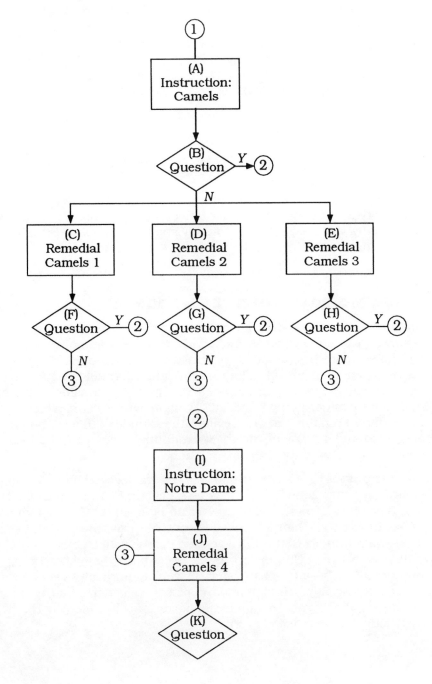

The first problem is that the learner never receives instruction about Notre Dame (I). For the second problem, assume the learner answers the first question incorrectly, but answers the second question correctly. In this case, the learner is given remedial instruction about camels (J) after successfully completing that topic earlier in the instruction (at either C, D, or E). The solution for both problems involves moving the remedial sequence (J) to a different position.

Branching Ideas

Answer judging and remedial branching are mundane topics. After all, this type of development is more tedious than creative. Still, given multimedia systems, some reasonably sophisticated and certainly interesting approaches can be used. Here are a few.

Same Melody, Different Lyrics

Already mentioned above, but worthy of second consideration, is replaying the same video segment with a different audio track or textual support. Program code can instruct the videodisc player to choose from among Audio Channel 1, Audio Channel 2, both simultaneously, or neither channel. This gives the designer quite a bit of flexibility in designing remedial segments with existing videodisc real estate. Probably the most elaborate example of this would be staggered audio segments on the two channels which can be used singly or in combination for remediation.

For this purpose, two synchronized audio tracks are laid down on Channels 1 and 2, and might look as shown in Figure 10-11. Given this type of construction, Channel 1 can be used for the original presentation and Channel 2 used for one remedial branch. But the interesting thing is that a third version can be constructed by switching between Channels 1 and 2 to combine the instructional portions of each—a very saturated, powerful approach. Also, a fourth version of visual instruction and music can be constructed, permitting the learner to supply the narration while viewing the instruction—a karaoke version.

Figure 10-11.   Alternate audio remediation.

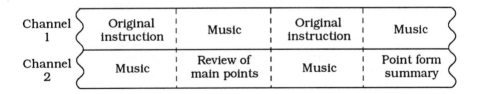

| Channel 1 | Original instruction | Music | Original instruction | Music |
| Channel 2 | Music | Review of main points | Music | Point form summary |

Beat the Clock

Most authoring tools give you the opportunity to time a user's response. In some situations this can be valuable information for potential remedial strategies. Let's consider the simple case of a drill and practice exercise for multiplication tables. Perhaps the user's score would be the number of seconds required to answer ten problems correctly. Based upon time categories, the learner would be routed into one of several remedial branches. Of course, a default category would be established for a maximum allowable time, so a user wouldn't be trapped forever trying to answer ten questions correctly.

Another version of this is to present a fixed number of questions, say ten, and divide the total number correct by the time used to get an efficiency index. The efficiency index is then used to route individuals into appropriate remedial experiences.

Yet another version of timed responses is asking the user to respond within an acceptable range of time. For example, in training baseball umpires, a learner could be instructed, "Press the space bar when you see an infraction of the rules." For each infraction, a range of acceptable response times is programmed. The user is judged correct if the space bar is pressed within an acceptable range, and routed to a remedial branch if an infraction is overlooked, or if the space bar is pressed at an inappropriate time.

Executive Summary

Often, a learner's response indicates only a minor deficiency, and it seems inappropriate to require a lengthy review of a motion sequence. A point-form summary may be adequate. This can be accomplished by selecting a few illustrative freeze frames from the original motion segment, and overlaying point-form review information from the computer. This requires no additional investment of disc real estate, and allows the creation of several remedial versions based on learner input.

Of course, this requires attention to consistent field dominance during post-production, and if movement is apparent in the sequence, it would be advisable to use motion picture film as the source medium to reduce movement.

In all, however, this provides a flexible and inexpensive method for creating several remedial branches within a program.

Blue Plate Special

As developers, we often arrogantly assume that we must predict a learner's remedial needs, and automatically activate remedial branches based upon their responses to questions. This is not very flattering to a learner, and indeed may be based on an incorrect assumption—that remediation is the responsibility of the producer (teacher). In many learning situations, learners are quite capable of assessing their own remedial needs, and as developers we can accommodate this level of intellectual freedom. How?

One method is to first judge a learner's response, and provide a brief description of why the answer was inadequate. Then the learner is given choices, such as:

- See the instruction one more time.
- See a different version of the same content.
- Receive another question.

This "advisement" approach places the responsibility for remediation on the learner, and lessens the developer's task of prophesying every possible type of remedial need.

Summary: Branching

- Branching refers to moving a user from place to place in a treatment.

- Multimedia programs permit a wide range of branching possibilities.

- Any treatment may combine several types of branches, including linear, user-directed, redundant-remedial, remedial-audio, single-remediation, or multiple-remediation branching.

- To avoid problems, extra attention should be given to segment placement and looped portions of instruction.

- A variety of creative approaches can be used to develop efficient, flexible, and user-directed remedial paths.

References for Chapter 10

Alessi, S. M., and Trollip, S. R. (1985). *Computer-based instruction: Methods and development.* Englewood Cliffs, NJ: Prentice-Hall.

Arwady, J. W., and Gayeski, D. M. (1989). *Using video: Interactive and linear designs.* Englewood Cliffs, NJ: Educational Technology Publications.

Bergman, R. E., and Moore, T. V. (1990). *Managing interactive video/multimedia projects.* Englewood Cliffs, NJ: Educational Technology Publications.

DeBloois, M. L. (1982). *Videodisc/microcomputer courseware design.* Englewood Cliffs, NJ: Educational Technology Publications.

Hannafin, M. J., and Peck, K. L. (1988). *The design, development, and evaluation of instructional software.* New York: Macmillan.

Heinich, R., Molenda, M., and Russell, J. (1989). *Instructional media and the new technologies of instruction* (3rd ed.). New York: Macmillan.

Iuppa, N. V. (1984). *A practical guide to interactive video design.* White Plains, NY: Knowledge Industry Publications, Inc.

Jonassen, D. H. (1988). *Instructional designs for microcomputer courseware.* Hillsdale, NJ: Lawrence Erlbaum Associates.

Kemp, J. E., and Smellie, D. C. (1989). *Planning, producing and using instructional media* (6th ed.). New York: Harper and Row.

Romiszowski, A. J. (1986). *Developing auto-instructional materials.* New York: Nichols Publishing.

Chapter 11

Designing Screen Displays

Hannafin and Hooper (1989) identify five functions of screen design:

- focusing attention,
- developing and maintaining interest,
- promoting deep processing,
- promoting engagement, and
- facilitating navigation through the lesson.

Most of the effort expended on achieving those functions appears to be based on art, rather than science. Although a fair amount of research on screen design has been done, the number of studies extant pales in comparison to the amount left to do.

Screen design encompasses a multitude of concerns. The first ones that spring to the minds of most people are primarily technical concerns: What font should be used? How large should the characters be? How long should a line of text be? Should color be used? Reverse video? Blinking text? How much text should be displayed on each screen? How much "white space?" In other words, how can I make my screen displays look good and be maximally legible?

There are also structural concerns: What style should be applied to the writing? What about textual structure? Topical relatedness? Superordination? Cohesion? Although a substantial amount of guidance exists to help designers write more appropriately for print-based instruction (e.g., Felker, Pickering, Charrow, Holland, and Redish, 1981; Jonassen, 1982, 1985b; Noble, 1989; Race, 1989), there is somewhat less help available for those writing for the screen. Some recent works, however (e.g., Gillingham, 1988; Hartley, 1987; Isaacs, 1987; Reynolds, 1982), have provided glimpses into the uniqueness of screen displays, even while focusing primarily on other considerations. Since there is likely to be considerable overlap between the two literatures—writing for the screen and writing for paper—and because their combined volume is sizable and space here is limited, structural concerns will not be dealt with in this section.

Nor will concerns like avoiding sexism, racism, and stereotyping, which are dealt with adequately elsewhere (e.g., American Psychological Association, 1983; Semrau and Boyer, 1991). Primarily, then, we will deal with those we identified as springing first to mind. Consideration of those concerns will not likely make a badly-designed or -written presentation good, but advice on good design and writing is available elsewhere. Extending the argument made by Hooper and Hannafin (1986), it is reasonable to expect that screens that are pleasant to look at may contribute in a cumulative series of small ways to the efficacy of learning.

The whole area of writing for the screen as opposed to writing for paper has yet to be researched in depth. Reinking (1992) notes that there are two separate branches of research literature related to the use of electronic text: studies in which the electronic text simply emulates printed text; and studies in which the electronic text capitalizes on the unique capabilities of the computer (e.g., hypertext, on-line help, control of access to portions of the text, control of timing of presentation of the text, perceived structure of the text, iconic symbols intermingled with text, capability of interaction). We anticipate much research activity in this area in the near future.

Generalizing Print-Based Research to Screen Design

Most reviews of the literature on screen design variables tend to intermix findings from research on both printed and screen-based materials, presumably on the assumption that the results are generalizable across the two media (e.g., Gillingham, 1988; Hartley, 1987; Hartley and Jonassen, 1985; Hooper and Hannafin, 1986; Isaacs, 1987). However, it may not be safe to abstract screen-based guidelines from print-based studies. Indeed, there is some reason to believe that such generalizations may not be safely made, at least with respect to some characteristics. As will be detailed below, discrepancies appear in recommendations for optimum line length between printed and screen text. Also, some of our own (unpublished) research shows similar discrepancies for leading (vertical spacing between lines). Kolers, Duchnicky, and Ferguson (1981) conclude that "uncritical extrapolation from printed page to electronic page may not be justified" (p. 526), and that "...classical sources that discuss the printed page...cannot be extrapolated wholesale to [CRTs]" (p. 527).

It would appear that there is a need for research on variables affecting screen-based learning which parallels that on print-based learning. Furthermore, not only such things as reading speed, comprehension, and retention should be used as dependent variables; cognitive processes, learner preferences, and satisfaction with the instruction should also be considered.

Without meaning to imply that print-based research results can be applied directly to screen design, we do present below some generalizations derived from the former, on the assumption that a fully-informed reader can derive hypotheses from a broad knowledge base. Furthermore, we don't know at this point which characteristics generalize and which do not. We recommend caution, but offer many of the following suggestions based on the best available information.

Generalizations about display characteristics such as line length, font selection, leading, etc., should be viewed with some suspicion unless the generalization also includes information about the exact equipment used. Tinker (1963,1965) showed clearly that for print materials, line length, font size, and leading are inter-related. Even if print-based findings don't generalize to screen-based findings in this instance, it is important for researchers to report exactly the characteristics of the screen size and resolution, fonts, line lengths, etc., they used. Findings on an Apple II CBI system may not apply to similar CBI on a Macintosh. To discuss line length in terms of number of characters per line may be misleading unless the proportion of the screen that is filled is taken into account, as well as the distance between the viewer and the screen (since the angle subtended by the eye takes in an increasingly wider field as the screen is moved away from the viewer, a longer line length can be accommodated when the screen is separated from the learner). Kolers, Duchnicky, and Ferguson (1981) are exemplary in this regard. The description of their study includes this information:

> Texts appeared on a screen approximately 120 cm from the reader's eye. The effective field of the screen measured 38 × 28 cm, or approximately 17.5 × 13 deg visual angle. The letter M, the usual standard, measured 5 and 10 mm in width, or 0.25 and 0.5 deg visual angle at the eye, and 10 mm in height, in the two character sizes. Line length was 35 or 70 characters (p. 519).

Armed with this amount of detail, a researcher can calculate that the font size used was roughly equivalent to 11-point on paper, or 14-point on a Macintosh screen, and use that information in planning future research. Far too few research reports provide this amount of detail, however.

General Design Principles

The purpose of interactive multimedia instruction is not to dazzle, to impress, to amaze, or to delight, but to communicate. Let that not be forgotten when it comes time to design the screens that form the presentation. While getting attention (and holding it) are important concerns for any communication process, there is a fine line between doing that and failing to do it by trying too hard and creating distraction instead.

You may experience a tendency to want to apply all the bells and whistles that multimedia environments make available to you, and end up using too many different fonts and styles in your text, too much or inappropriate color or sound, too many graphics, and/or too many zooms, fades, and dissolves. Graphic designers have special skills in design, and should, if possible, form part of your design team. They too are human, and therefore subject to the temptation of bells and whistles, but the really good ones know that the most effective communication comes with very restrained use of the "gee-whiz" effects.

Indeed, some of the most powerful concepts in screen design (as in other kinds of design) come about by the application of a few basic principles: simplicity, consistency, clarity, and aesthetic considerations such as balance, harmony, and unity.

Simplicity

KISS.

Keep It Simple and Straightforward.

Present your message, and only your message. Don't confound it with superfluous graphics, animations, sounds, colors, or activities.

Be minimalist in your approach. Think "lean." Make it a challenge to present your message with as few textual and audiovisual stimuli as possible. If you make it too lean, and your learners have trouble understanding the communication, you will find that out during your formative evaluation, and take steps to correct it. (You *will* be doing formative evaluation, won't you?) If you make your message too "fat" or too flowery, you will probably never find out. All it will do is take up time—yours and the learners'—and disk space.

You may have to fight hard to follow this principle diligently: The siren song of multimedia is powerful. Resist it. Tie yourself to the nearest handy mast, and KISS.

Consistency

People expect certain things, and the unexpected often upsets them. As a multimedia designer, you may occasionally want to use the unexpected to generate excitement. But by and large, you should reserve that strategy for very occasional use. After all, when the unexpected becomes what people expect, it's no longer exciting; merely annoying. And even when the unexpected occurs, it is only useful—instructionally speaking—when it is completely surrounded by the expected.

Thus, one of the most fundamental dictates of good screen design is consistency—consistency in:

- level of discourse and style of presentation from one section of the sequence to another;
- placement of various items (e.g., orientation information, navigation devices, student input, feedback, operating instructions);
- use of color (including "grays" in black and white presentations);
- access structure (e.g., use of headings);
- use of cues (font, including size and style; bolding, italics, and color);
- style of graphics;
- screen density and white space;
- terminology (directions, prompts, menus, and help screens);

- names of commands and manner of evoking them;

- interaction behavior required in similar situations (e.g., don't require a learner to click on a button one time and to type a character another time, if the situations are highly similar. This doesn't mean, however, that you cannot vary the type of learner response required when the situations change).

Clarity

Clarity of communication comes with knowing what you want to say, and that of course, implies the nebulous activity variously known as task analysis, content analysis, instructional analysis, and a host of other names. All of them refer to the process of figuring out what it is that we need to teach or communicate.

A simple, yet effective, approach to the problem involves separating content into three categories: what the learner must know, what it would be nice for the learner to know, and what the learner doesn't really need to know. If you can do this with the content of your multimedia presentation, the battle is half-won. Ignore the stuff the learner doesn't need to know, make sure you include everything the learner needs to know, and put in as much of the "nice-to-know" stuff as you have room for, making it accessible at the learner's option.

Note that last phrase; it's important. The "nice-to-know" material should always be offered as an option, if it is offered at all. If you include it with the "must know" materials, clarity of communication is almost sure to suffer.

Clarity of communication also speaks to the kind of language used. Writing for instruction is different from academic writing, so writing for interactive multimedia is different from writing term papers or scholarly articles. Furthermore, writing for the screen is different from writing for print. Applying the following rules of thumb to your writing for screen displays will likely improve your presentations:

- Keep the instruction at a language level compatible with the intended learners.

- Avoid jargon and overly-scholarly language.

- Present ideas succinctly; keep your prose lean.

- Keep sentences short.

- Avoid compound constructions.

- Use "point form" (bulleted lists, like this one) whenever possible.

- Use the active, rather than the passive, voice.

- Stay away from negative statements if possible; avoid double negatives entirely.

- Use informal language. Write the way you would speak to a learner, rather than the way you would describe it in a journal article. Contractions and abbreviations are OK.

- Use personal pronouns: Call yourself "I," call the learner "you."

- Use examples that learners will find familiar. And do use lots of examples.

- Use inclusive (i.e., non-sexist, non-racist) language.

Aesthetic Considerations

There are certain long-standing aesthetic concepts that apply equally to screen design and the other forms of artistic expression. Some of these concepts are inter-related, making it difficult to describe one without reference to another. For convenience, a few of the most important ones are described below as separate entities.

These aesthetic considerations should be applied to screen design, but with a second level of priority; first and foremost should come instructional considerations. If, after satisfying them, aesthetic considerations can be applied without doing violence to the instructional considerations, then that should be done. (Often, those priorities are reversed, and aesthetic considerations are allowed to dominate. We reject that approach.)

Balance

Balance, in graphic design terms, is achieved by ensuring that for every graphic object on the screen (including blocks of text), there is one or more visually complementary objects.

Balance in screen design evokes a feeling of stability—things don't look like they're about to slide off the screen; the screen doesn't look likely to tip over to one side (Figures 11-1, 11-2, and 11-3).

Figure 11-1.   A screen lacking balance. The mass of the instruments along the right edge make it appear the screen wants to tip to the right.

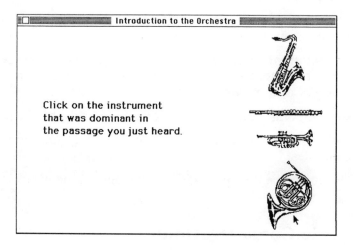

Figure 11-2.   A balanced screen. Placing the instruments in a row along the bottom of the screen, with the two largest ones placed symmetrically, gives a sense of stability.

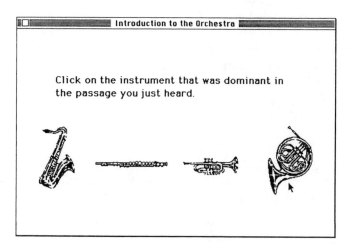

Figure 11-3. Another balanced screen. Moving the instruments slightly to the left, increasing the font size of the instructions slightly, and adding the header—the name of the sequence—in a black surround provides a balanced screen that is less staid than the one in Figure 11-2.

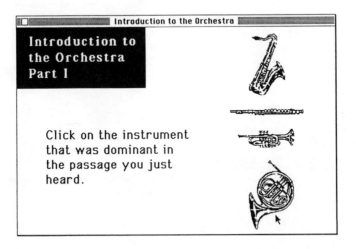

Balance can be formal or informal, symmetric or asymmetric (Figure 11-4). There is no strong reason for one type of balance to be preferred over another, as long as balance is achieved. However, formal, symmetric balance is often perceived as being less exciting than informal and/or asymmetric balance.

Figure 11-4. Balance can be formal or informal, symmetric or asymmetric. The arrangement in (a) is symmetric and formal, while the arrangement in (b) is asymmetric and informal.

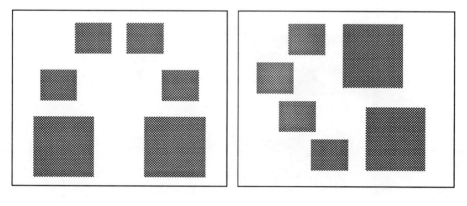

(a)   (b)

Harmony

Harmony is achieved in large part by consistency, which has already been addressed as a topic in its own right, and by repetition. Using similar text fonts, or colors, within a screen display and across successive screen displays creates harmony. So does using a consistent graphic style.

Lack of harmony can result when an inappropriate style of graphic is used among a number whose styles match one another, when a font is suddenly injected that is incompatible with the other fonts used, or when a sound is presented that is inappropriate to the rest of the display (e.g., a high-tech sound accompanying text and graphics depicting life in the 17th century).

Harmony can be achieved or destroyed through good or bad choices of font (Figure 11-5) or of graphic style (Figure 11-6).

Figure 11-5. Harmony is absent in Screen (a), because the font used is not consistent with the topic being presented. Screen (b) is more harmonious.

(a)

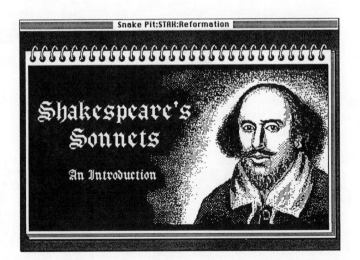

(b)

Figure 11-6.   Harmony is absent in Screen (a), because the two graphics used are of very different style. Screen (b) is more harmonious.

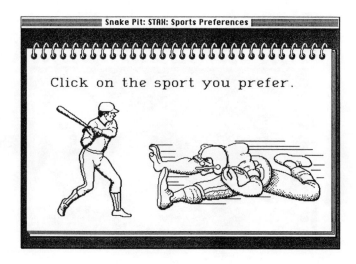

(a)

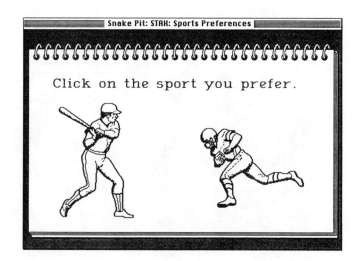

(b)

Unity

Unity refers to the singularity and wholeness of the display. A screen display should look as though all the elements forming it belong together. Every element should "fit in"; none should be missing and none should be superfluous. A learner looking at a display feels his or her eyes being attracted first to a focal point or center of interest, then drawn around the various components making up the display, with inter-relationships between and among those components becoming evident all the while. Although the focal point immediately attracts your attention, no element "sticks out like a sore thumb." Furthermore, achieving unity first requires ensuring both harmony and balance.

Perhaps the best way to illustrate unity is to give an example of when unity is lacking. If, when looking at a screen display, you find several points of interest competing for your attention—or conversely, when you are unable to find a focal point—you are experiencing a lack of unity (Figure 11-7).

Figure 11-7. This screen exhibits a distinct lack of unity.

White Space

White space refers to space (on a printed page or on a CRT) that is not devoted to text or graphics. It is not merely a left-over, something that remains when the text and graphics have been placed; it can and should be used as a tool for achieving certain ends. White space can:

- bring together or separate ideas;
- create a lightness to the screen display; (i.e., make it less overpowering and crammed with information); and
- illustrate relationships through use of space. Text with effectively-used white space can border on being a diagram.

The appropriate use of white space does not necessarily come naturally. Many of our habits regarding the placement of text on the screen have their origins in the way we place text on the printed page. Those habits, in turn, appear to have derived from the production of the earliest books, by monks scribing them by hand. Because paper (perhaps papyrus) was expensive in those days, the scribes made every effort to use all the available space by crowding the text together as much as possible. We have continued to this day to put as much on a page as is physically possible, and that habit has too often transferred to the screen.

It is true that we permit borders (margins) on most printed pages, and that we often insert some space between lines of text (e.g., double-spaced typewritten material), but by and large we tend to run our words to the end of every line, and our lines to the end of every page (or screen). There is no longer a need to do that today, and that habitual practice may be counter-productive from an instructional point of view, both on paper and on computer screens.

> Blank space on computer screens is "free" .... Unlike paper-based media, the presence of large amounts of blank space does not increase printing and reproduction costs. Information that should be logically separated for either conceptual or aesthetic reasons can easily be presented on two different displays, because it is no more expensive to use two displays than it is to use one. (Heines, 1984, p. 4)

This means that information should be grouped onto screens in "chunks" that make sense instructionally, without regard for whether or not there is white space left over. Thus the basis for deciding what material should appear on one screen display and what should appear on another ought to be the content, not the margin.

Extrapolating that idea, it makes sense that what appears on one line as opposed to the following one should also be determined by the content of the sentence, rather than by the margin. Frase and Schwartz (1979), for example applied a process they called segmentation—dividing text into "meaningful components"—and determined that such text resulted in response times that were 14%–18% faster than those for normally-presented text. Thus, this very paragraph might look something like this when segmented:

> Extrapolating that idea,
> it makes sense that what appears on one line
> as opposed to the following one
> should also be determined by the content of the sentence,
> rather than by the margin.
> Frase and Schwartz (1979), for example,
> applied a process they called segmentation—
> dividing text into "meaningful components"—
> and determined that such text resulted in response times
> that were 14%–18% faster
> than those for normally-presented text.

Several writers recommend the application of this type of segmentation to screen displays, most often without reference to any research on the matter. The research does present a mixed picture: Morrison, Ross, Schultz, and O'Dell (1989) suggest that there is no research evidence to support the notion of chunking. However, when some of the background studies leading to that conclusion are examined carefully, there is reason to believe that chunking may, in fact, be a worthwhile procedure. Carver (1970), for example, based his conclusion that there was not likely to be any merit in chunking upon three small studies, all of which have shortcomings. O'Shea and Sindelar (1983) suggest that some of the earlier studies may have found segmentation to be unhelpful because they failed to take into account developmental differences (most of the earlier studies were done on adults, and reading ability has not been well controlled).

O'Shea and Sindelar (1983) noted that Cromer (1970) found that segmentation helped poor readers' performance, and that Mason and Kendall (1979) found that low-ability learners were aided by segmentation. O'Shea and Sindelar's own study found clear evidence that segmenting sentences helped both high- and low-performance readers. Brozo, Schmelzer, and Spires (1983) also found chunking to be a significant benefit, although they used a somewhat different method of displaying the chunks than that suggested above.

Time

Screen displays have a potentially-controllable attribute that print-based displays do not: time. Whereas a reader is solely and completely in control of progress from one page to the next (and back again), the computer can (optionally) take total control of timing or share the control with the learner. This permits such things as sequential displays of information at a teacher-determined rate, in the manner of a slide/tape show.

Generally, control of time should be used sparingly and with caution. It is very easy to present information either too quickly or too slowly for some students. A momentary distraction may cause a learner to miss an important point if it is presented in a controlled-time manner. Unless there is good reason to control the time of display, you should permit the learner to do it.

Another aspect of the control of time is that the designer can make text or graphics (or sound, for that matter) appear and disappear at any time. Printed text, of course, just lies there on the page; there is no way for the designer/author to make it appear or disappear under any circumstances. Only the reader can do that, by opening or closing the book, or by covering portions of the page. Placing that control in the hands of the designer/author creates certain opportunities:

- a hint may be made to flash briefly on the screen;

- lengthy bodies of text that might appear forbidding if presented all together, yet which fit together logically and/or will be used as a unit, can be presented a passage at a time, in a sequentially-revealed single page;

- speed-test-like situations, with the learner given only a certain amount of time to provide the response, can be used where appropriate;

- a sequence can be made to refuse to proceed unless and until the learner inputs a response.

The control of time also permits animation. Presenting a number of related images in quick succession causes the images to blend into one another to form a continuous motion, thanks to the phenomenon known as persistence of vision.

Minimal Memory Load

A cardinal principle of good screen design is to impose a minimal memory load on the learner with respect to operation of the interactive multimedia environment. That is, while it may be reasonable to expect the learner to remember the content being learned, he or she should not have to remember very much about how to operate the system delivering the content. Computers are good at "remembering"—let them do so, and allow the learner to capitalize on that strength. Rather than expect learners to remember and type commands, provide them with the opportunity to recognize and select commands. Options should be presented to the learner at appropriate times, rather than expecting learners to generate commands to exercise choices. When options are presented, they should be succinctly worded in language understandable to the learner (i.e., avoid jargon). Learners must be able to clearly perceive the differences between the choices being offered, without having to rely on arcane terminology, cryptic commands, or Boolean operators.

Command line interfaces are examples of systems which require a high memory load. Users must recall exactly what commands to type in to get certain responses from the system. Fortunately, command line interfaces are rapidly becoming a thing of the past; most modern interfaces use some combination of menus, icons, and buttons that can be clicked or touched. Also looming on the horizon is voice actuation. When it arrives, one hopes that it can be made flexible enough that it does not simply become an auditory command line interface, or else it should not be used for multimedia instruction.

Standard Screen Components

According to Heines (1984), there are five standard screen components:

- orientation information,
- directions,
- student responses,
- error messages, and
- student options.

Heines suggests that displays should be divided up into functional areas, with each component consistently occupying one area of the screen. We concur with Heines' classification scheme generally, but have combined some elements of Heines' first and last categories, so we use slightly different terminology below to describe the screen components: orientation and navigation information, instructions, learner responses, and feedback and error messages.

Orientation and Navigation Information

Where am I? Where can I go next? How much have I completed, and how much more is there to do before I'm finished? These are the kinds of learners' questions that are addressed by orientation and navigation information.

Orientation information lets the learner know where he or she is, relative to the sequence of instruction. It is equivalent to page numbers, chapter names, and headings in print-based instruction. Navigation devices are those that permit a learner to traverse the instructional sequence.

Keeping orientation information in the same place on every display helps it blend into the background, making it less obtrusive to learners, while still keeping it available for when they need it. Heines suggests putting the current module and lesson name on the top of every display comprising the lesson, similar to running headers in a book. Hypertext environments make orientation information more difficult to provide—maps or outlines of the content may be necessary. It might become a useful convention to permit learners simply to click on headings to bring up a map or outline of the content.

Page numbers can be considered part of orientation information, but they may also be considered part of navigation information. With a book, a reader can flip pages forward and back to preview or review, or can go directly to a selected spot with the aid of a page number. CBI and IMI sequences may not permit exactly the same kind of traversal freedom, but insofar as is possible, authors/producers should provide learners with the opportunity to move about through the sequence at their discretion.

This means that, at minimum, page numbers or some equivalent marking device should be provided on each screen display. Provision must also be made for the learner to go back one or more screenfuls, perhaps to travel forward one or more screenfuls (although there may be reasons, at times, not to permit forward motion over material not already covered), and perhaps to jump back entire sections, or to selected spots, for review. In addition, there may be hypertext-like jump-out capabilities, whereby the learner can leave the current sequence to explore another one, to look up the meaning of a word, or to pursue some other activity, then return to the original sequence.

In the days when the range of fonts and methods of learner input was limited, Heines' advice to reserve a special section of the screen for orientation and navigational information was sound. Today, however, navigation devices can take the form of buttons or icons to be clicked, menus to be pulled down or popped up, or key commands. (Note that key commands, other than arrow keys, may require considerable memory load.) Whatever devices are used, instruction should be given regarding their use. Given the increased range of possibilities, it seems less important than it once was to set aside a certain section of the screen for orientation and navigational information. Rather, a consistent method of accessing this information should be explained to the learner early in the sequence, with obvious on-screen reminders of how to access the information (e.g., a question-mark icon, a compass icon, arrows to represent the direction of navigation, etc.).

Instructions

Instructions tell the learner what to do at any given point (although the word *directions* implies more or less the same thing, we eschew it because it may be confused with navigational actions, such as moving forward or back through a sequence of displays). Instructions may be simple, such as "Click on the square next to what you consider to be the best answer," or they may be complex, describing a whole series of steps in a lengthy procedure that must be executed in a specified way.

If they are simple, presenting them once at the beginning of the sequence is probably enough, especially if the directions refer to acts that are more or less intuitive (e.g., selecting the correct answer) or if there are continuing external cues as to what type of response is required (e.g., a standard cursor indicating a keyboard response is required, or buttons to be clicked with the mouse). However, if the directions are lengthy, complex, or for some other reason likely to be referred to again and again, they should be accessible after they are first given, for as long as they might be needed. Thus it may be necessary to provide a pull-down or pop-up menu or an *Instructions* button that remains operational throughout the sequence.

In the days of limited font selection, it was important to keep instructions to the learner in a distinct location on the screen, so that they would not be confused with other kinds of information. Hence, screen design advice given by some experts noted that instructions should be a separate entity (e.g., Heines, 1984). With the greater flexibility in screen display afforded by modern microcomputers, perhaps it is somewhat less important to keep instructions in a separate screen area than it once was. Use of different fonts for instructions and for content, for example, may be an equally effective substitute for special screen areas. Still, learners depend on certain cues to help them make appropriate response decisions (e.g., the existence of a statement or a cue indicating "Press Return to continue"), and it is wise to keep at least the most common elements of instructions in a consistent location on the screen.

Learner Responses

Interactivity implies learner responses, which may be of several types:

- typing in text;
- clicking (with a mouse) or touching (on a touch screen) a particular area of the screen;
- moving an object on the screen;
- selecting an item from a menu on the screen by
    - clicking on it, or
    - pressing a corresponding key;
- pulling down or popping up a menu and making a selection from it;
- clicking on a "push-button" on the screen;
- uttering a sound (this option is not yet widespread commercially, but is possible).

Care should be taken to ensure that learners understand how they are to respond in every instance. While it may not be necessary to place elaborate instructions on every screen, at least some guidance should be given the first few times a particular learner response method is employed. That is, the first time or two you expect learners to click on a button, tell them so, explicitly. If a whole series of screens employ the same response mode, the cue can gradually be faded over three or four displays. (Perhaps it can be re-activated as a reminder if the learner takes an inordinately long time to respond.) If another learner response mode is introduced, full explanation should then be given about it. If the original response mode is then re-employed, a brief reminder should probably accompany at least the initial screenful of the reiterated response mode.

Don't assume that the learner knows what is expected. We wish we had a nickel for every CBI sequence we've seen where learners are instructed to type in their names—which they dutifully do—then wait, and wait, and wait, because the author either forgot to tell the learners, or assumed they already knew, that they had to press the *Return* key when they were finished.

As with the other categories Heines suggests, while there may be some advantage to reserving a certain portion of the screen for learners to input text, doing so may be less crucial than it was when computer displays were more limited in their modes of accepting learner responses.

Feedback and Error Messages

Feedback is the name normally given to information about the quality of the learner's response. An error message is a different type of feedback, usually dealing with the way in which the learner is responding.

Feedback and error messages should be presented in plain language—that of the learner, not the author/producer or programmer. Although feedback messages should be concise, they should not be so terse that they are unhelpful. This is particularly true when the feedback is really an error message. "Error ID = 42" tells most people nothing; such a message should never appear on the screen once the instruction is undertaken by students.

Simple, straightforward messages form the most useful and appreciated feedback. Flowery or overly-enthusiastic statements begin to wear thin on learners after a while. Keep the feedback relatively subdued. Use common sense: If you were teaching a class and someone correctly added two numbers, would you likely say "Wow! That's terrific!"? More likely, you would say something like "Yes, that's correct," or just plain "Right." Try to vary the responses, however. Receiving exactly the same feedback to a string of responses is likely to become tedious to the learner.

Feedback can also be aural: A pleasant sound can be presented to indicate acceptance, while a less pleasant sound can be used to indicate non-acceptance. (Keep it only moderately unpleasant, however!) Similarly, musical notes can be used. An ascending portion of a scale would indicate positive feedback, while a descending portion would indicate negative feedback. Once again, keep the feedback reasonable and restrained. The opening bars of Beethoven's Fifth Symphony may have a certain amount of dramatic appeal as positive feedback the first time they are used, but will become very tiresome after five correct answers.

Feedback should be virtually instantaneous; if it must be delayed, that fact should be indicated to the learner. Switching from a practice mode, where feedback is provided for every response, to testing mode, where feedback is withheld, at least until the end of the test, can be disconcerting to learners, who may wonder why the feedback suddenly stopped. If your sequence involves this type of transition, make it explicit that feedback will henceforth be withheld. An explanation of why that is happening would also be wise.

The learner should always be kept informed of what is happening. Whenever the computer is busy doing things, so that it is not available to respond to the learner's input, some standard way of notifying the learner of that fact should be employed (e.g., on a Macintosh, a wrist-watch cursor or a spinning globe or ball indicates that the computer is otherwise employed, and not hung up or waiting for a learner action).

Learner interaction interfaces should be designed to be forgiving, so that learners making errors simply get no response, or, at worst, activate a message that tells them what they are trying to do is not a viable option. The wording is important here, too: "Illegal action" or a similar message is unhelpful and intimidating. A more diagnostic message is preferred; at minimum, it should remind the learner how to access an on-line help file. Even a "beep" sound can be employed effectively to act as an error message; if so, it should not sound pleasant (lest it be mistaken for positive feedback), but neither should it be too obtrusive or harsh.

Building in forgiveness includes making errors reversible whenever possible. If it is not possible, learners should be forewarned that the action they are about to undertake is irreversible, and they should be required to give explicit permission before the action is taken.

Other Options

Given the power and capabilities of current machines, learners may be given other opportunities over which they exercise discretionary control. For example, they may use a pull-down menu to bring up a calculator, a spelling checker, or a grammar-checker. Perhaps a paint program may be at their beck and call; or a note-pad on which they can type notes or copy portions of the lesson, to be printed out subsequently to take home; or the capability of "photographing" the screen and saving it as a graphic image. Whenever these options are presented, of course, learners must not only be told they exist, but explanations should be offered regarding their use.

Note that because it is difficult to know exactly how much a given learner already knows about some of the available options (perhaps he or she has run into some of them in other instructional sequences, or used them with other programs), it is wise to offer instruction on the options, but not to insist on it.

Technical Aspects of Screen Design

In addition to general design principles and concerns, several specific and technical issues surface. Seemingly simple decisions such as which font to use or how much information should appear on a screen can have an impact on the learner.

Screen Grids and Layout

A concept transferred from design and layout on paper to screen design is the grid, an invisible structure that underlies each display and organizes it. A grid establishes certain areas of the screen as being reserved for certain kinds of information. On a printed page, the margins define the area within which the text and illustrations are placed. Page numbers are always located in a certain place. Columns may exist as differentiable entities.

On a screen display, some contend, all similar elements should appear in exactly the same place. That is, the orientation and navigation information, the instructions, the learner responses, the feedback and error messages, and the other options available to the learner should remain consistently placed (Heines, 1984). Advocates of the use of a screen grid suggest partitioning the screen into such areas early in the design stage, adjusting their size marginally if necessary, but generally keeping the same grid operative throughout the sequence (Figure 11-8). Within limits, of course, this is good advice, but there may be times that grids have to be violated due to differences in the manner in which learners input their responses or make use of the material presented. (That is, now that learners have more methods of inputting responses than just the keyboard, some variation from the grid may be either necessary or desirable.) Too, some variation may be desirable from the point of view of motivation (i.e., alleviating boredom), but care should be taken to ensure that the learner is not left confused: The consistency provided by a screen grid is useful for most instruction.

Figure 11-8.   Examples of screen grids.

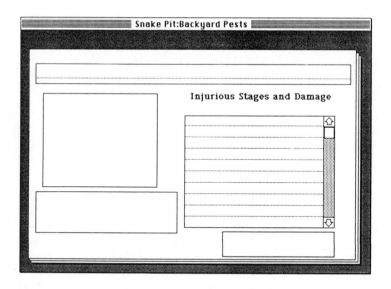

Figure 11-8.   (continued)

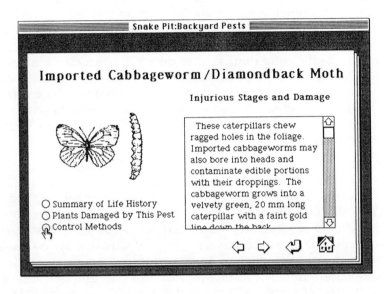

Line Length

Advice on screen design is often predicated upon rules of thumb from the print medium. Whether or not that is a valid method of deriving guidelines was deliberated earlier. Additionally, in the case of line length, there seems to be little unanimity about what is optimum. For print materials, some writers suggest that a line should be 35–40 characters long (West, 1987). Others suggest that it should not be more than about 1 $1/2$ lower-case alphabets long (i.e., the space occupied by typing the lower-case characters *a* through *z* followed by *a* through *m*) —roughly 40 characters (*Printing layout and design*, 1968; Walker, 1990); others say 50 (Parker, 1988); still others say up to 60 characters (Burns, Venit, and Hansen, 1988). One expert says that 60–65 characters is the most comfortable line length for reading (Miles, 1987), while another will permit as many as 75 characters in a line (*Publish!*, 1989). Research has shown that readers tend to dislike both very short and very long line lengths (Tinker, 1965, p. 147). How is one to abstract a meaningful guideline from such conflicting advice?

Such respected authorities on computer-based instruction as Bork (1984) and Heines (1984) recommend short lines, noting that a CRT's width forms no mandate that line length correspond to the full width. Whether this advice is based on generalizations from research or merely an intuitive generalization based on extensive personal experience with CBI is not clear. However, Duchnicky and Kolers (1983) found that longer lines (52 characters and 78 characters) were read more efficiently than shorter ones (26 characters), albeit not in an instructional setting. Grabinger (1985) also found that longer lines (60 characters) were preferred over shorter lines (40 characters), although the preference was not strong. Some writers advise that CBI should use lines of 40–60 characters or double columns of 30–35 characters (Garner, 1991).

As noted earlier, Frase and Schwartz (1979) adopt a different view on the question of line length, suggesting that there is no such thing as an optimum line length for all material. Rather, they suggest, line length should be based on the natural breaks in the thoughts being expressed, a process they called text segmentation. Their research showed faster response times in job-like activities when text on paper was segmented rather than presented in conventional fashion. Although a number of authors allude to Frase and Schwartz's work in discussions of screen design, we did not find any empirical studies testing their procedures on screen displays.

Hooper and Hannafin (1986) described the need for additional research on the topic of line length (which does not seem to have been addressed since their call) and conclude that until such research is completed, a rule of thumb to use is that "...text is read more efficiently when presented in a dense manner" (p. 26).

As already noted, Tinker (1963, 1965) established empirically that optimum line lengths for printed material are related to the size of the font used and the leading. However, there seems to be no research on this question for CRT-based text.

Screen Density

How much instruction should be put onto a single screen display? There seems to be no easy answer to the question. A number of authorities in computer-based instruction recommend providing minimal amounts of text, with lots of white space and double-spaced lines (Alessi and Trollip, 1985; Bork, 1984; Grabinger, 1984; Heines, 1984; Hooper and Hannafin, 1986; Tullis, 1983). Gillingham (1988), on the other hand, says "Display as many legible double-spaced lines as the screen will comfortably hold" (p. 1).

Morrison, Ross, Schultz, and O'Dell (1989) distinguish between text density ("...the length of the materials, redundancy of explanations, and depth of contextual support for main ideas" [p. 53]) and screen density ("...how much information...the expository frame should contain" [p. 54]), and offer some evidence that learners prefer high-screen-density displays to low-screen-density ones. On the other hand, some of their earlier research showed that low-text-density instruction produced equivalent achievement to high-text-density instruction, while taking less time to complete (Morrison, Ross, and O'Dell, 1988). It also showed that low-text-density instruction was more popular among students than high-text-density instruction, while being as effective (Ross, Morrison, and O'Dell, 1988).

Clear guidelines with respect to screen density have not yet emerged from the research. We suspect that the lack may have to do with one or more of the following:

- Confounding of constructs—although Morrison, Ross, Schultz, and O'Dell explicated the difference between text density and screen density, there has been insufficient empirical work to date that takes the difference into account. Changing the display characteristics can be accomplished by changing either or both of the text density and the screen density, and researchers must be more assiduous in documenting what has been done, and how. Researchers varying text density will have to tread carefully to ensure that they are not simply starting with "fat" instruction (i.e., containing superfluous information), and making it "lean," a step which should be part of good instructional design in any event (Markle, 1983).

- Methodological differences in display content—in reviews of research in published reports, studies of two very different kinds of activities have been summarized as though they were the same: information retrieval and instruction. Studies investigating videotex and instrumentation displays are cited as though they had relevance for instructional materials. In fact, however, there is no reason to believe that displays that NASA employees find useful in their work are the same ones that will prove effective in teaching third-graders (or tenth-graders, for that matter) mathematics or history. Yet the distinction is rarely made when a generalization such as "double-spaced text should be used" is derived from a synthesis of prior and current research.

Furthermore, stimulus materials have varied from screenfuls of Xs and Os representing text (Grabinger, 1984, 1985; Twyman, 1981), to "dummy" text ("...nonsensical text that resembled real text in syntactic structure and in word and sentence length" [Misanchuk, 1989c, p. 197]), to actual instructional materials (Morrison, Ross, Schultz, and O'Dell, 1989). The obvious advantage of using displays that are content-free is that possible effects of the content are obviated (Misanchuk, 1989c); the advantage of using "real" instructional materials lies in their face validity (Morrison, Ross, Schultz, and O'Dell, 1989). There seems to be no concrete evidence that there even is a difference between the two approaches, let alone which one is the better for researchers to use.

- Methodological differences in equipment—more care should be taken by researchers to document exactly what equipment was used in the research—including brand names and model numbers (Misanchuk, 1989b). Furthermore, more care must be taken by reviewers of earlier research to factor equipment differences into the generalizations they derive. There is some evidence that these differences are sometimes glossed over (Misanchuk, 1989b), and the resulting generalizations are therefore questionable. For example, Morrison, Ross, Schultz, and O'Dell (1989) are exemplary in documenting precisely their equipment configuration (basically Apple IIe systems). However, one wonders how long it will be before one sees generalization of their research findings built into the literature review leading to a study employing Macintosh technology. How useful will Morrison, Ross, Schultz, and O'Dell's generalizations that the "...optimum [screen] density appears to be between 31% and 53%" (p. 59), derived on an Apple IIe monochrome screen, be when applied to a multiple-font, multiple-font-size, multiple-font-style screen that offers variable spacing and justification of text?

This is not to say that research conducted on various types of hardware cannot be generalized; indeed, some such generalizations are made here. Rather, it means that careful thought must be applied while the generalization is being made, to determine whether or not the generalization is applicable to a wide range of hardware configurations.

Obviously, a good deal more research is needed in this area.

Font Selection

The font, or typeface, is the name given to a collection of characters with a distinctive shape to the characters comprising it. Figure 11-9 contains some examples of different fonts (in a couple of different sizes) commonly used on a Macintosh, for example.

Figure 11-9.   Some different fonts.

This font is Geneva.

This font is New York.

This font is Boston.

This font is London.

Тьис фонт ис Киев.

Although in typography, whence the term originated, *font* has a somewhat more limited meaning, in computer-user circles it generally includes not only the "normal" or plain characters (i.e., roman), but also the italics, boldface, and combinations thereof. The names of fonts therefore may be modified by those descriptors (e.g., Geneva bold, New York italic, etc.) (Figure 11-10).

Figure 11-10. Fonts, in computer parlance, consist of families of typefaces, including bold and italic versions, as well as the plain, or roman, version.

This font is Geneva plain (roman).

This font is Geneva bold.

This font is Geneva italic.

This font is Geneva bold italic.

This font is New York plain (roman).

This font is New York bold.

This font is New York italic.

This font is New York bold italic.

Furthermore, fonts may assume different styles—outline, shadow, small caps, reverse, and combinations thereof (Figure 11-11).

Figure 11-11.   Different styles of the same font.

Variations	plain (roman)
Variations	bold
Variations	italic
Variations	bold italic
Variations	outline
Variations	bold outline
Variations	shadow
Variations	shadow italic
VARIATIONS	all caps
Variations	small caps
Variations	reverse

Some fonts have serifs—small perpendicular finishing strokes that
mark the end of a line forming the character (Figure 11-12).

Figure 11-12.   The font on the left has serifs; the one on the right is sans-serif.

Choosing the Font Size

Until recently, questions of font size on a CRT were irrelevant—a
particular computer came with a certain font, and that was the end of

the matter. Since the advent of the Macintosh in 1984, however, choice of font size has not only become possible, but widespread. Despite the increasing prevalence, there still seems to be a dearth of research on font size on CRTs. At best, the advice is to make sure that it is large enough to be read comfortably, but not so large as to interfere. Considerable personal experience indicates that reading very small text on a screen for extended periods can result in very tired eyes. On the other hand, simply increasing the size of text arbitrarily may not be the best idea, either: Kolers, Duchnicky, and Ferguson (1981) say that

> ...one might think that large, widely spaced characters would be read more easily...[however, their research showed the opposite]. Reading smaller, more densely packed characters requires less ocular (and presumably less cognitive) work. People expend more fixations on large characters, but they do not achieve any greater comprehension of the text in doing so. Large characters require more screen space and more time to be read but with no measurable gain in reading. (p. 525)

(Although these researchers were not investigating instructional materials, their findings may well generalize.)

The size of print required is influenced in part by the screen definition (i.e., the number of pixels per inch): The higher the definition, the more likely it is that small print can be read comfortably. Even on relatively high-definition screens (e.g., Macintosh monochrome; NeXT), however, print that is smaller than about 12-point should be used only when absolutely necessary. Twelve- to 14-point text appears to be comfortable for most people.

Choosing the Font

Heines (1984) suggests that CRT fonts should have lowercase letters and true descenders, as well as variable character widths (proportional spacing). (Although these features are pretty well standard on modern computer systems, there may still be some older systems in use where these features are lacking.)

Tinker (1963; 1965) has shown quite conclusively that the use of upper- and lower-case letters, rather than all upper-case letters, promotes legibility for printed text. Although no similar research seems to have been done based on CRTs, some think it likely that this finding will generalize, at least if the lower-case letters have true descenders (Isaacs, 1987).

Some writers contend that serif fonts are slightly more legible than sans-serif fonts (Garner, 1991). Perhaps this generalization is based on the findings of printed text (where that generalization is supported by research findings). There is some indication, however, that user preferences for fonts on CRT-based text don't necessarily follow font preferences for paper-based text (Misanchuk, 1989a, 1989b). While seriffed fonts such as Bookman and New Century Schoolbook were preferred over sans-serif fonts such as Helvetica in printed materials, Geneva (a sans-serif font) was preferred over other fonts with serifs when the text was displayed on a Macintosh screen. Boston was a relatively close second to Geneva. It was followed by Monaco, New York, Courier, and Chicago (least preferred). While clearly user preference may include things other than legibility, there appears to be sufficient discrepancy between the findings of print-based and CRT-based text to cast doubt on the generalizability of print-based research to CRT-based text.

Aesthetics suggest that no more than two different fonts should appear on a single screen display. If more distinction is required, style variations (e.g., **bold**, *italic*) may be used to create differentiation.

Choosing the Font Style

Good writing style of instructional materials dictates that the use of unusual type styles (e.g., italic, bold, reverse, shadowed text, etc.) be strictly limited (Misanchuk, 1992). Basically, it is safest to stick to plain (roman) text, with occasional use of italic or bold for specific purposes. Although different disciplines may subscribe to different style manuals, that of the American Psychological Association (1983) serves as a good model. The APA style manual recommends the use of italics only for:

- introducing technical terms (the first time they are used);

- titles of books, periodicals, films, etc.;

- characters, words, or phrases that are cited as linguistic examples;

- specialized applications (like genera and species in biology; statistical symbols, etc.);

- distinguishing different types of material (e.g., two individuals in a dialogue; editorial comment in main body of text).

Note that the use of italics for mere emphasis, or for foreign words, is specifically discouraged.

On paper, research has shown that italic text causes reading to be slower, and is less preferred by readers than plain text (Paterson and Tinker, 1940; Tinker, 1955; Tinker and Paterson, 1928). Although we are unaware of similar research on CRT text, it seems (subjectively) likely to be generalizable, since italic type for most fonts appears harder to read. Thus its use for substantial bodies of text should be discouraged.

The use of bold type for emphasis and cuing may be useful, provided that it is not used too frequently. Simply put, to act as a cue, a stimulus must be unusual. If it is overused, it loses its effectiveness as a cue (Glynn, Britton, and Tillman, 1985).

On paper, research shows that bold text can be read as quickly as plain text, although most readers prefer the latter (Paterson and Tinker, 1940; Tinker, 1963, 1965). Once again, there seems to be no comparable research on CRT text.

The following tips regarding fonts and style are a synthesis of advice from various sources (primarily Heines, 1984, and Isaacs, 1987), leavened with some personal opinions:

- If reverse video is used to highlight text, leave one reverse video space before and after the text in question, to provide a border around the characters.

- Underlining text, on paper, indicates to a typesetter that the text should be set in italic. Since many computers now provide italic fonts, and since underlining can make the following line of text difficult to read, italic or boldface should be used instead of underlining.

- Blinking and flashing text should be used very rarely and cautiously. They are very powerful attention-getters—perhaps too much so; they can easily function as distractors and produce exactly the opposite effect of the one intended. Blinking or flashing should never be used in two places on the same screen display.

- Color is perhaps the most abused text characteristic extant. Far too many courseware authors rationalize the use of several different colors of text on a single screen display, on the basis that they are attention-getting and motivational, or that they function as cues of some sort. These same authors would not likely use the same number of different "highlighter" felt pens on a single page of printed text, yet they run amok when authoring courseware.

Our personal bias is that the overwhelmingly large proportion of computer-based courseware, like its print-based relative, could be done in black and white (or equivalent monochrome). Extrapolating from considerable evidence from research on print materials, the use of color is likely to make a difference only when it is truly salient. It seems unlikely to have a powerful effect when applied to text.

Leading

Leading (rhymes with *wedding*) is the vertical spacing between successive lines of text. In many computers, especially aging models, increased leading could only be accomplished by double spacing text. Several studies showed that double-spaced text was either preferred to or more effective than single-spaced text for CRT displays (Grabinger, 1984, 1985; Grabinger and Amedeo, 1985; Hathaway, 1984; Kolers, Duchnicky, and Ferguson, 1981; Kruk and Muter, 1984). The International Reading Association (cited by Gillingham, 1988) recommended that screen text be double-spaced.

However, more recent computers provide for considerable flexibility in adjusting leading. This begs the question: Is there an optimum inter-line spacing for CRT displays? If so, is it single- or double-spacing, or perhaps somewhere in between?

An attempt to address this question empirically led to some ambiguous results. One study compared leading roughly equivalent to single-spacing (a 13-point line with 12-point text) through roughly double-spacing (a 25-point line), with intermediate values in 3-point increments (Misanchuk, 1989b). The results showed that a 25-point line (double-spaced) was preferred to all others; however, the possibility of a ceiling effect could not be discarded. An attempted replication of the study, with more "headroom" (i.e., leadings varying from 19-point—roughly line and one-half spacing—through 37-point—roughly triple-spacing—in 3-point increments) showed something of a reversal of preferences: Most preferred was 19-point spacing, and 25-point spacing was the third most preferred (Misanchuk, 1990). As a result of these ambiguous results, the strongest conclusion possible—and a relatively weak one at that—is that until further evidence is gathered, designers should keep leading on screen displays somewhere in the 19–25-point range when displaying full pages of 12-point text.

Justification of Text

Heines (1984) advocates against using right-justified text, on the strength of Gregory and Poulton's (1970) research. Isaacs (1987) agrees, citing the same research plus some done by Zachrisson (1965). Trollip and Sales (1986) and Muncer, Gorman, Gorman, and Bibel (1986) also found right justification detrimental to reading, albeit on paper. However, the manner in which they generated their text passages yielded text that more closely resembled screen displays than typical justified paper-based text (i.e., their text was not proportionally spaced), so their results are likely to be generalizable to the screen.

Right-justified text typically creates "rivers of white" (which can be distracting as well as aesthetically bothersome) unless some words in a paragraph are hyphenated, further inhibiting comprehension. Hyphenation can require readers to skip back and forth between the end of one line and the beginning of the next, since reading hyphenated words appears to involve hypothesis-making (and possibly revision when initial hypotheses are proved incorrect).

The bottom line seems to be: Don't right-justify text on the screen.

Color

Color is a difficult subject to address in the context of multimedia instruction; our inclination is to go against much of the advice in the literature, and to downplay the importance of color in screen displays. For one thing, video segments will almost always contain color despite instructional requirements or Peter Bogdanovich "wannabees." Choice about color therefore will largely be exercised in the development of accompanying CBI components.

In the CBI literature, it is quite common to find a variety of attestations to the value of color in screen displays, but almost always without supporting evidence from research. Claims that color is essential for motivation are among the most frequent. While there is some evidence that color is motivating with respect to computer games (Shneiderman, 1987), there seems to be a dearth of evidence that it really makes much of a difference for most instructional applications. A number of speculations about the effectiveness of color in screen displays appear to be based on early work with videotex, when only a limited palette of highly-saturated colors was available. Today, of course, much more control over color saturation and value is available, at least on some systems.

Our cautious approach to the use of color is predicated on the fact that we have seen many examples of bad use of color (e.g., three or four garish colors per screen display). Furthermore, color monitors frequently vary widely in their representation of color, so it is difficult for the designer to predict what individual learners will actually see on their screens. We feel it is safer to suggest avoiding color unless you have a good reason to use it. Generally, screen displays should be designed in monochrome, then color added later, if it must be. That approach ensures that, at minimum, an adequate monochrome version exists.

There may be some situations where color can help, of course, particularly where color is germane to what is being taught. In a fifteen year retrospective of research on visuals, Berry (1991) concluded that all colors facilitate recognition equally, and both realistic and non-realistic color materials are superior to monochrome materials for cuing. Of course, recognition is not considered a significant instructional outcome in many learning camps. Cuing is important; however, one of the problems we have encountered is the over-use of color, thus cuing learners to several items, many of which might be irrelevant to the learning task at hand. The potential for confusing the learner through over-cuing was documented by Glynn, Britton, and Tillman (1985).

Berry (1991) further concluded that for recall tasks, realistic color was superior to both monochrome pictures and line drawings. Non-realistic color was least effective, and in fact, may inhibit encoding. These studies are based on print media, so as with earlier discussions, we suggest caution before generalizing them to screen displays.

When color is deemed necessary, you should be aware that attractive color displays are the product of discriminating and restrained use of color. Two approaches that can bolster attractiveness are the reduction of saturation (intensity) of the colors used, and the restriction of the number of colors (hues) employed. Adjusting the saturation of colors, where possible, helps produce less garish displays; pastel tones can be much more pleasing to the eye than the default color palettes many computer systems provide. Also, attractive displays can usually be made by using several different shades of the same basic color (artists refer to such displays as monochromatic, but we eschew that word here due to the potential for confusion with the more common interpretation of *monochrome* in computers—i.e., black and white).

The use of color in instructional screen displays is another area in which additional research would be welcome.

Combining Graphics and Text

The value of graphics and pictorial material in instruction has been extensively researched and widely reported (e.g., Alesandrini, 1984; Anglin, 1985, 1986a, 1986b, 1987; Anglin and Kwak, 1991; Brody, 1982; Duchastel, 1978; Duchastel and Waller, 1979; Dwyer, 1978; Levie, 1987; Levie and Lentz, 1982; Levin, 1981; Levin and Lesgold, 1978; Levin, Anglin, and Carney, 1987; Merrill and Bunderson, 1981; Peeck, 1987; Schallert, 1980). There remains little doubt that graphics, properly chosen and appropriately presented, can add substantially to learning from text. By far the majority of research on graphics has, however, been done in the medium of print. Below, we offer some reasoned speculation, based on the above-mentioned research, about the combination of graphics and print on computer screens. While considering it, bear in mind our cautions at the beginning of this chapter, about the safety of generalizing print-based research to screen design.

At the outset, we must state that we believe graphics *should* be used on screens. Their effectiveness for communication is not likely to be limited to only the print medium. But, as in print, it is likely that there is a fine line between appropriate use of graphics and inappropriate use.

What you must keep in mind as you design interactive multimedia instruction screens is that in order for graphics to be more helpful than harmful, they must, first and foremost, be germane. That is, they must support the message being presented by the text, and not be merely decorative. To add graphics as decoration is to invite learner distraction from the communication.

The availability of current computer graphics (either drawn on-screen, scanned in, or selected from electronic clip-art collections) makes it easy for the screen designer to place a wide variety of pictorial material on the screen—perhaps too easy, in some cases.

The result is sometimes an overabundance of graphics intermingled with text on screen displays, which can be distracting.

> Although instructional software routinely incorporates graphics with text, research suggests that this practice often distracts from learning or results in unrelated processing which reduces learning efficiency. Combined text and graphics, and other multi-channel communication, should be avoided unless high redundancy exists between the information....(Hannafin and Hooper, 1989, p. 157)

An appropriate amount of pictorial material can be effective, however. Just as much content cannot be communicated solely by illustrations in other teaching environments, so it is possible for graphics to augment the message in multimediated instruction.

Not only must graphics accompanying text be germane to the communication, and present in reasonable quantities, but it is probable that learners will have to be given explicit instructions on how and when to make use of the graphical information if it is to add significantly to learning.

Use graphics if and when they provide message redundancy. Use graphic elements such as rules (lines), boxes, and icons in a minimalist manner to help organize text presentation, but avoid allowing them to become overbearing. Graphics can be used as focal points, attracting the eye, and, if properly placed, leading the eye to appropriate text. Good taste in using graphics is as important in screen design as it is in page design.

Icons

The advent of Macintosh microcomputers and subsequently, its imitators, brought to public attention the value of icons for representing certain activities. Icons can depict choices succinctly, thereby reducing the learner's memory load. To be effective, icons must be

- unambiguous,
- relatively small,
- simple line drawings.

The first point is crucial, and often the most difficult to achieve. Developing an effective icon is usually a process that requires considerable formative evaluation; take care that the formative evaluation is done with typical learners, not with individuals who are already conversant with a particular computer system's operation.

Icons have become particularly popular for indicating highly repetitive activities, such as traversal through a sequence via arrows such as those shown in Figure 11-13.

Figure 11-13.   Examples of icons and their usual meanings.

Go to next card/display

Go to previous card/display

Go to first card/display

Go to last card/display

Return from jump-out

Go home (i.e., to main menu)

Help

Content map ("Where am I?")

Keyboard Input

Far and away the most common method of inputting learner responses is through the keyboard. Despite glowing prognostications about voice input and other sophisticated means of capturing information in the human-machine interface, the keyboard is likely to remain an important input device for some time to come. Even young children are now being taught keyboarding skills.

Following are some heuristics about designing screen displays to accommodate keyboard input.

Learner Response Area

As already noted, it is usually advisable to keep the learner response area in the same place on the screen, so that the learner knows where to look for it. If this is not possible, due to the design of the remainder of the screen, some overt prompt should be placed in the body of the text being presented that refers the learner to the appropriate area.

It might be useful to have a consistent means of indicating to the learner how long an answer you anticipate: a blank might be used to indicate you expect one or a few words; a window might indicate the expectation of a lengthier answer. If a scrolling window is used to contain the learner's response, make sure appropriate instruction is provided on how to bring about the scrolling.

Remember the Return Key!

Don't forget that learners new to multimediated instruction or computer-based instruction may not already know that any text they enter must be followed by a carriage return before the computer can act on it. An optional explanation, perhaps followed by a few reminders, will often suffice to get learners into the right habit.

If some other action is required to progress, provide appropriate instruction. For example, if a lengthy answer is expected, a scrolling window may be provided to hold the learner's response. In that case, some action other than a carriage return would be necessary to indicate that the learner has completed the task of responding.

Dealing with Synonyms

Sometimes a question can be answered correctly with more than one answer. Most authoring environments permit the specification of synonyms. Usually the formative evaluation phase will generate a list of synonyms that you should subsequently include. However, be prepared for the possibility that novel ones will emerge later. Recording incorrect responses in a file which is reviewed periodically may help identify those synonyms; they can then be incorporated into the pool of answers considered correct.

Is Spelling Important?

Sometimes exactly-correct spelling isn't one of your expectations; an approximation may do. In that case, you may have to include a wide variety of "correct" answers in your pool. Alternatively, your authoring environment may allow for variations in spelling, and provide a "close-is-good-enough" facility with a single click or command.

Close-is-good-enough spelling may also be used to provide remedial instruction. If, in the initial stages of instruction, you don't want to overly emphasize exact spelling, you might be able to provide one message for an exactly-correct answer, and a slightly different message for a "close" answer.

Using Keys as Alternatives to Buttons

Sometimes, especially when developing and debugging instruction, it is useful to provide keyboard equivalents for buttons or other mouse-based responses (i.e., depressing a selected key brings about the same condition as clicking a particular button); some authoring environments permit this facility.

If you use this option in your instruction, make sure that learners are notified that it is operative. Otherwise, you may have confused learners who will wonder why the screen display changed (by virtue of a finger accidentally brushing a key) before they had a chance to click the appropriate response.

"Draggable" Objects

The recent—and growing—emphasis on object-oriented programming environments brings the prospect of having learners move objects around the screen by clicking and dragging them. While this mode of response is a reasonable one to use, and provides some much-needed variety to keyboard response, remember that learners may have to develop considerable facility with a mouse before dragging becomes a reasonable response option. That is, inexperienced users should be given an opportunity to develop the necessary eye-hand coordination required by a mouse before being confronted with dragging responses.

Buttons

Buttons are areas of the screen which, when clicked upon with the mouse, or when touched on a touch screen, constitute a response and cause certain actions to occur.

Types of Buttons

Screen buttons can be of several types. Most common is the simple Macintosh button, pictured in Figure 11-14. When using buttons like this, you should not assume that all users will know how to deal with them: some instruction may be in order. Assuming that learners know how to deal with a button is equivalent to assuming that learners know that they have to press *Return* after typing in a response. Even experienced Macintosh users, for example, may not know that default buttons (those ringed by a heavier-than-normal border) can be selected from the keyboard simply by pressing the *Return* key, especially if they are disinclined to read manuals.

Figure 11-14. Macintosh screen buttons, one of which (Quiz) is a default button.

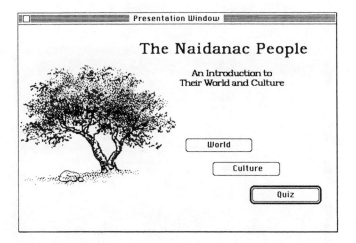

Other types of buttons are possible, as well. Radio buttons (Figure 11-15) are useful for indicating mutually exclusive choices (the name reflects the analogy: you can only listen to one radio station at a time, by pressing the appropriate button). Check boxes (Figure 11-16) are also useful for selecting one or more of a number of possible choices. They act like toggle switches, and can therefore be either on or off. By causing the boxes to become checked, it is possible to use a list of check boxes as a "score card," indicating which selections have been made previously. This makes them especially useful for menus where alternative paths are offered.

Figure 11-15.   Macintosh screen with radio buttons.

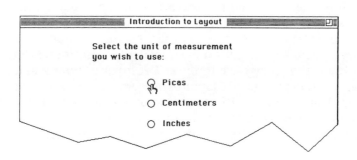

Figure 11-16.   Macintosh screen with check-box buttons.

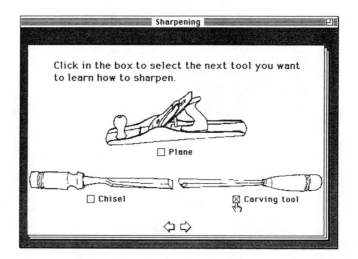

Still another variation is the invisible button, popular in hypertext-like environments. Either text or graphics may be fitted with invisible buttons so that merely clicking on the text or the appropriate part of the graphic causes some action, such as a jump to another screen display. Figure 11-17 shows a screenful of text on which the invisible buttons are outlined with dotted lines (for authoring and for illustration purposes only—the dotted lines disappear in normal use). Clicking on a word enclosed by one of the buttons causes movement to some other screen display. Figure 11-18 illustrates a similar situation with graphics. Clicking on the blossom might bring forth a close-up view of it, while clicking on the developed root may bring up additional text information about root development.

Figure 11-17.   Invisible buttons on text.

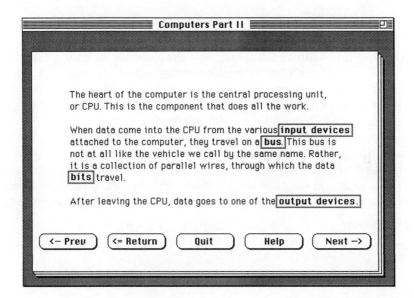

Figure 11-18.   Invisible buttons on graphic.

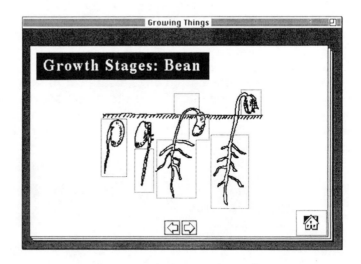

When using any kind of a button, you should always let the learner know when the button has actually been selected. For radio buttons, for example, the circle should become filled in when clicked; for check boxes, an X or a check-mark should appear. For regular Macintosh-like buttons, and especially for invisible buttons, a momentary change in color at the moment it is clicked (e.g., white to black) will act as sufficient indication. Without this indication, a user may be left wondering whether the machine actually accepted the response and is doing something about it, or whether the attempted response just missed the mark (i.e., the click was outside the limits of the button).

Labels on buttons must be unambiguous. As with icons, only formative evaluation with typical learners (not computer-literate ones) can be used to evaluate ambiguity.

Placement

Navigation buttons—those that move the learner through the instruction—should typically be placed around the edges of the screen. If navigation is intended within the screen, the buttons should be placed near the object to be controlled, and the placement should reflect the action to be caused by the button. Insofar as is possible, navigation buttons should be located consistently across all screens. Thus, the screen grid decisions with respect to navigation button placement should be made very early.

With other types of buttons, the same general principle of consistency applies: Buttons serving similar functions should be similarly placed through the instructional sequence. Changes in placement, when necessary, should be brought to learners' attention.

Speed of Presentation/Display

Although a good deal of research has been done on non-static displays of information on CRTs (e.g., see Kang and Muter, 1989; Muter, Kruk, Buttigieg, and Kang, 1988), the general consensus seems to be that moving text on the screen is less appropriate and effective for most instructional applications than static text (i.e., a screenful of information delivered as quickly as possible) (Gillingham, 1988). Text should be delivered onto the screen a minimum of a paragraph at a time, rather than a sentence or a line at a time.

References for Chapter 11

Alesandrini, K. L. (1984). Pictures and adult learning. *Instructional Science*, *13*, 63–77.

Alessi, S. M., and Trollip, S. R. (1985). *Computer-based instruction: Methods and development.* Englewood Cliffs, NJ: Prentice-Hall.

American Psychological Association. (1983). *Publication manual of the American Psychological Association* (3rd ed.). Washington, DC: The Association.

Anglin, G. J. (1985, January). *Prose-relevant pictures and older learners' recall of written prose.* Paper presented at the Annual Convention of the Association for Educational Communications and Technology, Anaheim, CA. (ERIC Document Reproduction Service No. ED 256 305)

Anglin, G. J. (1986a, January). *Effect of pictures on recall of written prose: How durable are picture effects?* Paper presented at the Annual Convention of the Association for Educational Communications and Technology, Las Vegas, NV. (ERIC Document Reproduction Service No. ED 267 755)

Anglin, G. J. (1986b). Prose-relevant pictures and older learners' recall of written prose. *Educational Communications and Technology Journal, 34,* 131–136.

Anglin, G. J. (1987). Effect of pictures on recall of written prose: How durable are picture effects? *Educational Communications and Technology Journal, 35,* 25–30.

Anglin, G. J., and Kwak, E. (1991, February). *Research on pictures: Knowledge acquisition, visual thinking, and cognitive skill acquisition: A guide to the literature, 1986–1990.* Paper presented at the Annual Convention of the Association for Educational Communications and Technology, Orlando, FL.

Aspillaga, M. (1991a). Implications of screen design upon learning. *Journal of Educational Technology Systems, 20*(1), 53–58.

Aspillaga, M. (1991b). Screen design: Location of information and its effects on learning. *Journal of Computer-Based Instruction, 18*(3), 89–92.

Berry, L. (1991). Visual complexity and pictorial memory: A fifteen year research perspective. In M. R. Simonson and M. Treimer (Eds.), *Proceedings of selected research paper presentations at the 1985 Annual Convention of the Association for Educational Communications and Technology*(pp. 92–102). Ames, IA: Iowa State University Press.

Bork, A. (1984). Computers in composition instruction. In R. Shostak (Ed.), *Courseware design: Design considerations.* Eugene, OR: ICCE Publications.

Brody, P. J. (1982). Affecting instructional textbooks through pictures. In D. H. Jonassen (Ed.), *The technology of text: Principles for structuring, designing, and displaying text* (pp. 301–316). Englewood Cliffs, NJ: Educational Technology Publications.

Brozo, W. G., Schmelzer, R. V., and Spires, H. A. (1983). The beneficial effect of chunking on good readers' comprehension of expository prose. *Journal of Reading, 26,* 442–445.

Burns, D., Venit, S., and Hansen, R. (1988). *The electronic publisher.* New York: Brady.

Carver, R. P. (1970). Effect of "chunked" typography on reading rate and comprehension. *Journal of Applied Psychology, 54,* 288–296.

Cromer, W. (1970). The difference model: A new explanation for some reading difficulties. *Journal of Educational Psychology, 61,* 471–483. Cited by O'Shea, L. J., and Sindelar, P. T. (1983). The effects of segmenting written discourse on the reading comprehension of low- and high-performance readers. *Reading Research Quarterly, 18,* 458–465.

Duchastel, P. C. (1978). Illustrating instructional texts. *Educational Technology, 18*(11), 36–39.

Duchastel, P., and Waller, R. (1979). Pictorial illustration in instructional texts. *Educational Technology, 19*(11), 20–25.

Duchnicky, R. L., and Kolers, P. A. (1983). Readability of text scrolled on visual display terminals as a function of window size. *Human Factors, 25*(6), 683–692.

Dwyer, F. M. (1978). *Strategies for improving visual learning.* State College, PA: Learning Services.

Felker, D. B., Pickering, F., Charrow, V. R., Holland, V. M., and Redish, J. C. (1981). *Guidelines for document designers.* Washington, DC: American Institutes for Research.

Frase, L. T., and Schwartz, B. J. (1979). Typographical cues that facilitate comprehension. *Journal of Educational Psychology, 71,* 197–206.

Garner, K. H. (1991). 20 rules for arranging text on a screen. In R. B. Frantzreb (Ed.), *Training and development yearbook, 1991 edition* (pp. 4.16–4.18). Englewood Cliffs, NJ: Prentice-Hall.

Gillingham, M. G. (1988). Text in computer-based instruction: What the research says. *Journal of Computer-Based Instruction, 15*(1),1–6.

Glynn, S. M., Britton, B. K., and Tillman, M. H. (1985). Typographical cues in text: Management of the reader's attention. In D. H. Jonassen (Ed.), *The technology of text (volume two): Principles for structuring, designing, and displaying text* (pp. 192–209). Englewood Cliffs, NJ: Educational Technology Publications.

Grabinger, R. S. (1984). CRT text design: Psychological attributes underlying the evaluation of models of CRT text displays. *Journal of Visual Verbal Languaging, 4*(1), 17–39.

Grabinger, R. S. (1985, January). *Relationships among text format variables in computer-generated text.* Paper presented at the Annual Conference of the Association for Educational Communications and Technology, Research and Theory Division, Las Vegas, NV.

Grabinger, R. S. (1989). Screen layout design: Research into the overall appearance of the screen. *Computers in Human Behavior, 5,* 175–183.

Grabinger, R. S., and Amedeo, D. (1985). CRT text layout: Prominent layout variables. In M. R. Simonson and M. Treimer (Eds.), *Proceedings of selected research paper presentations at the 1985 Annual Convention of the Association for Educational Communications and Technology.* Ames, IA: Iowa State University Press.

Grabinger, R. S. (1992). *Model vs. real screen perceptions: Viewer preferences.* Manuscript submitted for publication.

Gregory, M., and Poulton, E. C. (1970). Even versus uneven right-hand margins and the rate of comprehension in reading. *Ergonomics, 13*(4), 427–434.

Hannafin, M. J., and Hooper, S. (1989). An integrated framework for CBI screen design and layout. *Computers in Human Behavior, 5,* 155–165.

Hartley, J. (1987). Designing electronic text: The role of print-based research. *Educational Communications and Technology Journal, 35*(1), 3–17.

Hartley, J., and Jonassen, D. H. (1985). The role of headings in printed and electronic text. In D. H. Jonassen (Ed.), *The technology of text (volume two): Principles for structuring, designing, and displaying text* (pp. 237–263). Englewood Cliffs, NJ: Educational Technology Publications.

Hathaway, M. D. (1984). Variables of computer screen design and how they affect learning. *Educational Technology, 24*(1), 7–11.

Heines, J. M. (1984). *Screen design strategies for computer-assisted instruction.* Bedford, MA: Digital Press.

Hooper, S., and Hannafin, M. J. (1986). Variables affecting the legibility of computer-generated text. *Journal of Instructional Development, 9*(4), 22–28.

Isaacs, G. (1987). Text screen design for computer-assisted learning. *British Journal of Educational Technology, 1*(18), 41–51.

Jonassen, D. H. (Ed.) (1982). *The technology of text: Principles for structuring, designing, and displaying text.* Englewood Cliffs, NJ: Educational Technology Publications.

Jonassen, D. H. (Ed.) (1985b). *The technology of text (volume two): Principles for structuring, designing, and displaying text.* Englewood Cliffs, NJ: Educational Technology Publications.

Kang, T. J., and Muter, P. (1989). Reading dynamically displayed text. *Behavior and Information Technology, 8*(1), 33–42.

Kolers, P. A., Duchnicky, R. L., and Ferguson, D. C. (1981). Eye movement measurement of readability of C.R.T. displays. *Human Factors, 23*(5), 517–527.

Kruk, R. S., and Muter, P. (1984). Reading of continuous text on video screen. *Human Factors, 26*(3), 339–345.

Levie, W. H. (1987). Research on pictures: A guide to the literature. In D. M. Willows and H. A. Houghton (Eds.), *The psychology of illustration, volume 1* (pp. 1–50). New York: Springer-Verlag.

Levie, W. H., and Lentz, R. (1982). Effects of text illustrations: A review of research. *Educational Communications and Technology Journal, 30,* 195–232.

Levin, J. R. (1981). On functions of pictures in prose. In F. J. Pirozzolo and M. C. Wittrock (Eds.), *Neuropsychological and cognitive processes in reading* (pp. 203–228). New York: Academic Press.

Levin, J. R., Anglin, G. J., and Carney, R. N. (1987). On empirically validating functions of pictures in prose. In D. M. Willows and H. A. Houghton (Eds.), *The psychology of illustration, volume 1* (pp. 51–86). New York: Springer-Verlag.

Levin, J. R., and Lesgold, A. M. (1978). On pictures in prose. *Educational Communications and Technology Journal, 26,* 233–243.

Lockheed Missile and Space Company. (1981). *Human factors review of electric power dispatch control centers: Volume 2: Detailed survey results.* Prepared for Electric Power Research Institute, 3412 Hillview Avenue, Palo Alto, CA 94304. Cited by Shneiderman, B. (1987). *Designing the user interface: Strategies for effective human-computer interaction.* Reading, MA: Addison-Wesley Publishing.

Lucas, L. (1991). Visually designing the computer-learner interface. *Educational Technology, July,* 56–58.

Markle, S. M. (1983). *Designs for instructional designers* (2nd ed.). Champaign, IL: Stipes Publishing.

Mason, J. M., and Kendall, J. R. (1979). Facilitating reading comprehension through text structure manipulation. *The Alberta Journal of Educational Research, 25,* 68–76. Cited by O'Shea, L. J., and Sindelar, P. T. (1983). The effects of segmenting written discourse on the reading comprehension of low- and high-performance readers. *Reading Research Quarterly, 18,* 458–465.

Merrill, P. F., and Bunderson, C. V. (1981). Preliminary guidelines for employing graphics in instruction. *Journal of Instructional Development, 4*(4), 2–9.

Miles, J. (1987). *Design for desktop publishing.* San Francisco, CA: Chronicle Books.

Misanchuk, E. R. (1989a). *Learner preferences for typeface (font) and leading in print materials.* Saskatoon, SK: Division of Extension and Community Relations, The University of Saskatchewan. (ERIC Document Reproduction Service No. ED 307 854)

Misanchuk, E. R. (1989b). Learner preferences for screen text attributes in a Macintosh microcomputer learning environment. In *Transitions:*

Proceedings of the AMTEC '89 Conference . Edmonton, AB: Association for Media and Technology in Education in Canada.

Misanchuk, E. R. (1989c). Learner/user preferences for fonts in microcomputer screen displays. *Canadian Journal of Educational Communication, 18*(3), 193–205.

Misanchuk, E. R. (1990). *Learner/user preferences for leading (vertical spacing) in microcomputer screen displays.* Unpublished manuscript, University of Saskatchewan, Extension Division, Saskatoon, SK.

Misanchuk, E. R. (1992). *Preparing instructional text: Document design using desktop publishing.* Englewood Cliffs, NJ: Educational Technology Publications.

Morrison, G. R., Ross, S. M., and O'Dell, J. K. (1988). Text density level as a design variable in instructional displays. *Educational Communications and Technology Journal, 36*(1), 103–115.

Morrison, G. R., Ross, S. M., Schultz, C. W., and O'Dell, J. K. (1989). Learner preferences for varying screen densities using realistic stimulus materials with single and multiple designs. *Educational Technology Research and Development, 37*(3), 53–60.

Muncer, S. J., Gorman, B. S., Gorman, S., and Bibel, D. (1986). Right is wrong: An examination of the effect of right justification on reading. *British Journal of Educational Technology, 17*, 5–10.

Muter, P., Kruk, R. S., Buttigieg, M. A., and Kang, T. J. (1988). Reader-controlled computerized presentation of text. *Human Factors, 30*(4), 473–486.

Noble, K. A. (1989). Good writing: What role for the educator? *British Journal of Educational Technology, 20*, 142–144.

O'Shea, L. J., and Sindelar, P. T. (1983). The effects of segmenting written discourse on the reading comprehension of low- and high-performance readers. *Reading Research Quarterly, 18*, 458–465.

Parker, R. C. (1988). *The Aldus guide to basic design* (2nd ed.). Seattle, WA: Aldus Corporation.

Paterson, D. G., and Tinker, M. A. (1940). *How to make type readable.* New York: Harper and Row. Cited by Tinker, M. A. (1965). *Bases for effective reading.* Minneapolis, MN: University of Minnesota Press.

Peeck, J. (1987) The role of illustrations in processing and remembering illustrated text. In D. M. Willows and H. A. Houghton (Eds.), *The psychology of illustration, volume 1* (pp. 115–151). New York: Springer-Verlag.

Printing layout and design. (1968). Albany, NY: Delmar Publishers.

Publish! (1989). *101 best desktop publishing tips, vol. 2*. San Francisco, CA: PCW Communications.

Race, P. (1989). Writing to promote learning. *British Journal of Educational Technology, 20*, 215.

Reinking, D. (1992). Differences between electronic and printed texts: An agenda for research. *Journal of Educational Multimedia and Hypermedia, 1*, 11–24.

Reynolds, L. (1982). Display problems for teletext. In D. H. Jonassen (Ed.), *The technology of text: Principles for structuring, designing, and displaying text* (pp. 415–437). Englewood Cliffs, NJ: Educational Technology Publications.

Ross, S. M., Morrison, G. R., and O'Dell, J. K. (1988). Obtaining more out of less text in CBI: Effects of varied text density levels as a function of learner characteristics and control strategy. *Educational Communications and Technology Journal, 36*(3), 131–142.

Schallert, D. L. (1980). The role of illustrations in reading comprehension. In R. J. Spiro, B. C. Bruce, and W. F. Brewer (Eds.), *Theoretical issues in reading comprehension: Perspectives from cognitive psychology, linguistics, artificial intelligence, and education* (pp. 503–524). Hillsdale, NJ: Lawrence Erlbaum Associates.

Semrau, P., and Boyer, A. (1991). Examining educational software from both an aesthetic and cultural perspective. *Journal of Hypermedia and Multimedia Studies, 2*(1), 25–29.

Shneiderman, B. (1987). *Designing the user interface: Strategies for effective human-computer interaction*. Reading, MA: Addison-Wesley Publishing.

Smith, S. L., and Mosier, J. N. (1984). *Design guidelines for the user interface for computer-based information systems*. The MITRE Corporation, Bedford, MA 01730, Electronic Systems Division. (Available from the National Technical Information Service, Springfield VA.) Cited by Shneiderman, B. (1987). *Designing the user interface: Strategies for effective human-computer interaction*. Reading, MA: Addison-Wesley Publishing.

Tinker, M. A. (1955). Prolonged reading tasks in visual research. *Journal of Applied Psychology, 39*, 444–446.

Tinker, M. A. (1963). *Legibility of print*. Ames, IA: Iowa State University Press.

Tinker, M. A. (1965). *Bases for effective reading*. Minneapolis, MN: University of Minnesota Press.

Tinker, M. A., and Paterson, D. G. (1928). Influence of type form on speed of reading. *Journal of Applied Psychology, 12*, 359–368.

Trollip, S. R., and Sales, G. (1986, January). *Readability of computer-generated fill-justified text.* Paper presented at the Annual Convention of the Association for Educational Communications and Technology, Las Vegas, NV.

Tullis, T. S. (1983). The formatting of alphanumeric displays: A review and analysis. *Human Factors, 25*(6), 657–682.

Twyman, M. (1981). Typography without words. *Visible Language, 15,* 5–12.

Walker, P. (1990). A lesson in leading. *Aldus Magazine, March/April,* 45–47.

West, S. (1987). Design for desktop publishing. In The Waite Group (J. Stockford, Ed.), *Desktop publishing bible* (pp. 53–72). Indianapolis, IN: Howard W. Sams.

Zachrisson, B. (1965). *Studies in the legibility of printed text.* Stockholm: Almqvist and Wiskell. Cited by Isaacs, G. (1987). Text screen design for computer-assisted learning. *British Journal of Educational Technology, 1*(18), 41–51.

Chapter 12

Designing Components of Interactive Multimedia Instruction

Regardless of the system used to deliver instruction, a designer still needs to be concerned with the design of audio, video, print, and computer-based components. A well-designed treatment will attend carefully to each component, and it will blend them seamlessly into a fluid unit. In this chapter we consider designing audio, video, and print materials for IMI.

Designing Audio Segments

The very word *audio* conjures up images of studios with sound-proof double doors and egg-carton-like baffles on the wall, of spaghetti-like strands of microphone cables running every which way, and of entire crews of technicians hovering over control boards sufficiently complex-looking to put the space shuttle to shame. High-tech electronics are everywhere, and specialists populate the studio, mysteriously making coconut shells sound like horses' hooves and sheets of tin sound like thunder.

Yet sound has always been a fundamental medium of communication, hence education: It preceded written language by thousands of years. We use it daily. Why is recording not as accessible as print?

Part of the reason for the mystique surrounding audio may be that spoken audio segments usually consist of two separate acts—creating a script and delivering (i.e., reading) it—which are normally carried out by different people. Too, local production of audio has been relatively limited until recently, because sophisticated audio equipment and studios have been required, and they are expensive; most educators have limited their audio work to simple tape recordings. Finally, the production of audio has always been much more an arcane art than a science. That recording artists (or politicians, or anyone else) could be made to sound better or worse through judicious use of the right microphone or recording venue has long been recognized, but there seems to be a huge gap of widespread understanding between the principles of acoustics—the science of sound—and their practical application. Knowledge of two sets of principles—composition and optics—underlies the making of a good photograph, for example, and both domains of knowledge are quite accessible, even to the non-professional. With audio, however, while the principles of acoustics are well-enough known to engineers, the "composition" of audio is more evanescent. (Musical composition, on the other hand, is reasonably well understood and documented, and therefore accessible.)

Not very much longer will the old constraints apply, however. During the next few years we are likely to see a boom in computer-based local production of audio, and its incorporation into multimedia instruction, that is unprecedented. Sound—and particularly non-speech and non-musical sound—is beginning to be examined in a formal and systematic way (e.g., see Blattner, Sumikawa, and Greenberg, 1989; Buxton, 1989; Gaver, 1989; Mann, 1992) with the intent of applying it to computer-based and multimedia applications. Larry Katz suggests that "...one of the three fundamental differences in future interactive treatments will be the sophistication of the sound" (personal communication, February, 1991). It will all be top-quality, too; much better than even the best studio recording of only a decade ago. Hollywood has already discovered the potential (note how many blockbuster movies in the last decade have made powerful use of sound systems), as has the home entertainment industry (with integrated audio/video home systems).

As with any new capability, there will be much experimentation, and some resultant misuse of audio. Loud bleeps and blats will emanate from interactive multimedia stations, frightening or annoying learners, until a level of sophistication and comfort with this "new" medium becomes established. To help short-cut the trial-and-error learning process, Lynch (1991) provides the following guidelines for using audio effectively:

- Be subtle and restrained. Audio can be overpowering; don't use it in that manner unless you mean to.

- Beware of excessive repetition. A sound bite that is cute or amusing the first time you hear it soon loses its appeal.

- Do not use sound as a punishment. If a sound is necessary to indicate an error, make it inoffensive and subdued. Avoid rude or insensitive language or other sounds.

- Do not attempt to "jazz up" a presentation with sound. If the presentation itself is inadequate, adding audio won't save it.

- Allow the learner to control the audio as much as possible. Volume, pause, repeat, and similar controls will help alleviate learners' falling behind, or suffering uncomfortable situations.

- Remember that some learners may be hearing impaired; provide alternatives for them.

The use of sound (especially non-musical sound) has not yet been sufficiently studied to yield much beyond these few brief guidelines. We encourage you, however, to look into such thought-provoking sources as Gaver (1989) and Blattner, Sumikawa, and Greenberg (1989) for ideas on designing audio segments.

Audio Sources

There are several different sources of audio available for interactive multimedia instruction, including recorded speech, synthesized speech, music, and natural sounds.

Recorded Speech

As noted earlier, the spoken word is a prime source of audio. It is now no more difficult for a designer to produce a high-quality spoken recording than to produce a high-quality printed page. Often, all that is required is speaking into a microphone, and since even extremely high-quality microphones are now available in unobtrusively small sizes, there is less intimidation in that process, and it can be done in a natural setting. Not all of us have adequately "golden tonsils," however, and once we hear our own voices recorded, may feel shy or embarrassed. Sometimes, it is just unfamiliarity with how we actually sound (we hear ourselves differently than others do), but there are some voices that really do record badly; if you have one of them, you may want to follow the more traditional model of writing a script for someone else to read.

Synthesized Speech

Spoken audio sources are virtually a necessity in some cases (e.g., teaching a foreign language). At other times, other options may be viable, like synthesized speech. The computer can be programmed to "speak" reasonably clearly, and depending on make and model, may actually allow the learner to choose the gender and sometimes even the regional accent of the voice. A phonetically-based, near-English language may be used to program the speech. For example, this is how you would express the phrase *an otherwise ordinary bridge* in Macintosh's HyperTalk:

```
AEN AH5DHERWAY4Z OHRDIH1NEH4RIY BRIH1DJ
```

The numbers indicate emphasis. The vowels appear strange because the same letter can have different sounds; it is therefore necessary to use two vowels in combination to represent the different sounds:

made	EY
bat	AE
about	AX
talk	AO

Computer-generated speech is still not as natural-sounding as human speech; this may or may not be a concern in any given situation. On the other hand, digitized human speech requires much more disk space to store than computer-generated speech, so the trade-off of naturalness against space may be a consideration.

Music

Music, of course, can be used to augment the spoken word, and to add emotional texture to the presentation. A variety of audio sources exist here: LP record, audio cassette, CD, videocassette, traditional instruments recorded onto one of the aforementioned media, or MIDI instruments connected directly to the computer.

The decision regarding source of audio to use may have some quality and cost considerations. Amount of digital storage space may be a concern, as may portability from one platform to another. Many of these notions were discussed in Chapter 4, and should be reviewed when audio source decisions are encountered.

Remember that unless you are using original music and musicians in your project, copyright restrictions probably apply, and you must obtain formal clearance for using the music and/or its performance.

Natural Sounds

Sound effects of various kinds can be recorded and incorporated into instructional sequences. Beware that they are not used gratuitously, however, or they may simply become annoying.

Localization

In an increasingly international marketplace, computer manufacturers speak in terms of *localization*, the development of parallel versions of operating system software for different cultures (Apple Computer, Inc., 1987). Education has always been a relatively local concern, governed by state and provincial authority, rather than federal (let alone international!). However, many producers of educational courseware are becoming increasingly aware of the opportunities for developing educational packages accessible to audiences of many different cultures, which may differ in various ways. Often only the spoken language needs to be changed to make a multimedia sequence accessible to learners from another culture. (Other times, of course, the differences may be greater.)

Consideration of whether or not a localized (parallel) version of a multimedia segment will be prepared for another culture should be done early in the planning process. While at times the accommodation may be made as simply as putting one language or dialect on one track of a videodisc and another language on the other, it may be possible to incorporate substantially larger differences between the versions as well. Giving the learner the option of what language to receive subsequent instruction in can be as simple as providing an appropriate menu, or as complex as parsing the learner's answers to determine the existence of words or phrases from another language.

End-Use Considerations

As noted by Lynch (1991), audio segments should permit learner control over volume, pauses, and repetition. Where the audio segment is not essential (e.g., when it is used as a signal indicating correct or incorrect answers, or as an accompaniment), the learner should be given the option of turning it off entirely. Alternative signals should be provided for the hearing-impaired.

As a matter of course, designing audio segments should include the possibility that the sound will be played back through amplified speakers (if a group is the intended audience) or through headphones (if the sequence is intended for individuals in a multi-station lab situation).

If stereo is important, of course, both channels must be devoted to the same sound source. However, if monaural sound is adequate, the possibility of assigning different sources to each track becomes an option.

Designing Video Segments

Video is primarily a realistic visual medium with audio and some text or graphics. Animation and special effects can be easily added to any material produced, given the need and resources for these types of special treatment. Video is best employed in multimedia learning systems where dynamic processes or motion are needed, or where a treatment requires realistic still pictures. All other things being equal (and they seldom are), video is the preferred medium for content which requires motion, a presentation of actual events, realism, historical re-enactment, compressed or expanded time, drama, micro- or macro-photography, and a simulation of hazardous events in a safe environment. Outside a multimedia environment, video is often limited by a linear presentation capability, inflexibility, and a lack of learner control.

Some Characteristics of Video

Video is:

- primarily a visual medium with audio and some text/graphics;
- best for dynamic processes/motion, but adequate for presentation of static content with optical formats;
- usually in a linear order of presentation controlled by the producer, but data bases of images and segments are popular for multimedia;

- a preferred medium for content which requires:
  - motion;
  - presentation of actual events;
  - historical re-enactment;
  - compressed or expanded time;
  - dramatic representation;
  - micro or macro photography;
  - simulation of hazardous events in a safe environment; or
  - a high degree of realism.

Two families of video production concerns encompass most decisions you must make: What type(s) of treatments to use as a structure for the video program; and, how to deal with the elements within that structure.

Video Treatments

Probably the best metaphor we have found for designing interactive video segments was by Arwady and Gayeski (1989). They stated:

> Designing a good interactive video program is more like
> planning an interview than writing a speech. You must not
> only concentrate on what you'll say, but on what to ask,
> what the person is likely to say in response, and what you'll
> say for each category of possible response. (pp. 106–107)

When planning an interactive multimedia treatment, it is useful to think specifically about how the video can be treated to become part of an interactive system. Linear video design issues still pervade the production, to be sure, but what are some strategies which are more specifically interactive by nature? How can these strategies contribute to an interactive multimedia instruction system? Arwady and Gayeski (1989) describe 18 linear and 22 interactive techniques an instructional designer can use for video. We have selected (and in some cases adapted) 15 of our favorites from their list to whet your appetite. We recommend their book, should you be interested in finding out more about any of these techniques, or encountering several others.

- *Introductory menu:* This approach divides a disc or other video source into content chapters which are selected by users.

- *Intelligent manual:* This technique, based on expert systems approaches for diagnosing problems, asks the user to identify several salient characteristics, and the program branches to the appropriate, or likely, video material.

- *Visual data base:* This organization uses the videodisc as a storehouse of visual images and segments, with access provided through an interface.

- *Selecting relevant examples:* Structurally similar to the Introductory Menu technique, this approach divides the video content according to the job roles or needs of the user.

- *Vicarious travel:* The user can explore a geographic area by moving around with a joystick, mouse, or keyboard.

- *Third person "directed" simulation:* The user directs a person in a video program to do something, then watches the consequences of the action.

- *First person simulation:* The user interacts with people on screen, makes decisions, and vicariously experiences the consequences. The difference between a first person and third person simulation is that with a first person simulation, the user is the protagonist; with a third person simulation, the user is directing an on-screen protagonist.

- *Simulation with feedback:* This is a simulation which provides informed commentary on decisions made by the user while they are being made, or provides analysis following the consequences of actions. This feedback is given either in specific video segments or on a separate audio track.

- *Gaming:* Interactive competition between the user and system or other users is part of a gaming strategy (see discussion of prescriptive environments in Chapter 2). Using full motion video can create some very realistic and involving gaming contexts.

- *Tutorial:* Instruction contains questions or test-like events, the answers to which result in different subsequent instruction for learners.

- *Opinion question:* This type of instruction is characterized by a series of introductory questions aimed at determining a learner's attitudes toward the content. The learner is then branched into content which is appropriate for the expressed attitudes.

- *Auditory-visual test:* This technique recognizes that audio stimuli can be used to present test questions. This is particularly true for multimedia systems, where the range of audio sources includes videodisc, CD, and computers.

- *User comment file:* This technique employs the notion of generative strategies in a democratic multimedia environment. The learner can interrupt the instruction and make notes for later use or leave comments for the instructor. Beyond instruction, this is a very useful feature for automated formative evaluation.

- *Learning style diagnosis and branching:* From learner responses, learning styles or preferences are diagnosed, and the program branches to alternatives which accommodate the diagnosed characteristics.

- *Hidden programming:* Secret passwords are used to restrict access to specific versions of instruction or special content aimed at specific groups or individuals.

Specific Video Design Ideas

If you can afford to devote disc real estate to production value, having major video segments fade to black, and fade up from black looks better than hard cuts. A videodisc treatment will typically contain many snippets of material—long motion segments, short motion segments, stills with audio, menu frames, and the like. The user will encounter an array of these, jumping among the pieces. If segments are clipped and then replaced with the next image, the result can appear rather abrupt. The learner is jolted from one hard cut to another, without any of the easy transitions we have learned to expect from video. "Landing pads" of black are convenient places to hide jumps from one segment to another, and it gives the product a much smoother, refined look. Remember, however, that a fade to black in television lingo is roughly equivalent to a period in a sentence, signaling the finish of a complete thought. So use it only in places where that would be an appropriate assumption.

A fade to black and fade up from black are also useful at main menus. Picture it: The learner makes a selection, the menu fades to black (jump), and the selected segment then fades in. When the segment is finished, it fades to black (jump) and then fades up on the menu. The problem with this is the amount of disc real estate which must be devoted to the fades. A menu which once occupied only a single frame in the production may now occupy 30 frames. One way to ease the burden is to produce only a fade to black on menus, and not a fade up from black. Most videodisc players can be programmed to jump to the black frame (at the end of a fade to black) and then play in reverse to the menu. Since the menu is static, the reversed fade to black is indistinguishable from a fade up from black to the viewer. We use menu frames as an example, but this technique will work with any still frames where you can afford the production luxury.

Targets come in many varieties, and can be generated in a number of ways. Target size will depend on the use of the program, the hardware, and the audience. Use common sense. A mouse target can be much smaller than a touch screen target, as users often point with more than one finger at the screen (we have seen individuals slapping at the screen with an open palm). As much as possible, generate targets and other textual and graphic overlays from computer, so you can change them without remastering a videodisc or compact disc. Think of videodisc or CD-ROM as carrying stable information, while the computer handles volatile information. This approach, while reasonable from a production perspective, reduces the portability of the product. A user must have a compatible system to play the program. Including targets and graphic material in the video production increases the portability of the material.

Frame placement, or the sequence in which you lay out the still frames and motion segments on a videodisc, can be important. Several points need to be made. Still frames should be placed in the middle zones of a videodisc wherever possible, rather than at the beginning or end of a disc. This cuts access time in half from any other position on the disc. On a CAV videodisc, the physical space devoted to each frame is smaller at the beginning of the disc, resulting in poorer image resolution. At the exterior edges of the disc, although the frame space is larger, access is slower. In any case, this may be considered splitting technological hairs, as image quality is reasonably good everywhere on the disc, and edge-to-edge access times are very rapid with newer videodisc players.

For your particular production, it may be a better idea to intersperse still frames throughout the disc, and place them near related segments, rather than clump them together in a single location.

Again, this will shorten access times between components. The drawback is that it is more convenient, and probably less expensive, to insert stills in a single location during post-production. It is easier to set up procedures for single frame recording and then pace through the frames until completed, than it is to assemble motion segments and stills according to their usage. But for instruction to run smoothly, the extra effort may be desirable.

Main menu or other frames which act as "crossroads" to other parts of the disc should be placed in the middle regions of the disc. Not only does this give good resolution to heavily used frames, but it also cuts the maximum branching time to most other locations in half. Submenu frames should be located in the middle of their respective clusters of content for the same reasons.

Increased searching speed and frame-grabbing capabilities of newer technology reduce the number of times a screen is likely to go blank during execution. Seamless searching is a prevalent, if not yet universal, feature of videodisc equipment. Blank screens still happen. Some users are very nervous around technology, and a blank screen may imply something is wrong. If possible, place something on the screen for the user to read or do while the program is accessing segments, or the computer is loading programs.

If you are using a multimedia system with two screens (which even violates the definition of multimedia for some), use only one at a time for display. Place a "Watch other screen" direction on the computer screen when the videodisc is playing, and "park" the videodisc on a "Watch other screen" still frame while the computer is presenting information. Of course, this means you will need to produce some direction frames for the videodisc, and scatter them at accessible locations throughout the videodisc.

Video may, of course, include graphic and textual overlays and captions. Generally speaking, place graphic or textual overlays in positions which will attract attention, but will not interfere with the video presentation. Common sense should prevail. Plan "dead spaces" to hold text for visuals. Avoid plastering titles across someone's forehead. Include dark areas for light colored graphics or text. Much more information is included in the chapter on screen design, but at this stage, remember to plan for the combination of graphic, textual and visual elements in video.

Interactive multimedia often take on a conversational tone with the learner. This can be done well, but may introduce some problems. We have noticed that a number of instructional programs attempt to include cute, clever, or even mildly sarcastic comments to the learner. As mentioned elsewhere, the outcome of humor is unpredictable, and can interfere with the effectiveness or credibility of instruction. Use a light touch on negative feedback. Learners can be easily intimidated or offended, and kicking the computer is probably more interactivity than you want to promote. Watch out for sexist, racist, and stereo-typical content—it can sneak in very subtly, and sometimes overtly. After answering a question incorrectly on a CAI treatment, one of our colleagues was rewarded with "Nice try, for a girl!" That computer still leans a little to the left.

Summary: Video Design Ideas

- Fade to black and fade up from black to make smooth transitions between video elements.

- Use only fade to black from menus and other still frames, and program the player to search to black and play backwards to simulate a fade up from black.

- Where possible, generate targets and graphic overlays from a computer.

- Carefully consider the type of interface in the system when determining target size.

- Avoid placing significant still frames at the beginning or end of a videodisc.

- Place the main menu or any frames which act as crossroads to other parts of the disc in the middle of the disc.

- Place submenu frames at the center of their associated clusters.

- Intersperse still frames on the disc near their usage, rather than clump them together at the end.

- If possible, place something on the screen for the user to read or do while the program is accessing segments, or the computer is loading programs.

- If you are using a multimedia system with two screens, use only one at a time for display.

- When using two screen displays, place directions on the inactive screen to watch the active screen.

- Place material that has a long shelf-life on the videodisc, and use the computer to present volatile content.

- Place graphic or textual overlays in positions which will attract attention, but will not interfere with the video presentation.

- Use a light touch on negative feedback.

- Watch out for sexist, racist, and stereotypical content.

Designing Printed Materials

Amidst the shimmer and glow of high-tech multimedia, we tend to forget about that low-cost, time-tested, flexible instructional medium: print. Although we think of interactive multimedia as necessarily involving a computer, not every component needs to be computer-driven. In other words, printed materials can effectively be used as adjuncts to computers in interactive multimedia instruction. They are more efficient and cost-effective than computers for providing quantities of text in large chunks, and can constitute effective resource and reference materials for learners to consult in the course of interacting with the computer-mediated materials.

Desktop publishing has provided educators with the potential for producing professional-looking instructional materials. Heretofore, educators had few choices to make in designing print materials; perhaps the most complex decision had to do with which "golf ball" to use on the electric typewriter. Now, however, decisions need to be made about the font and font style to use, the font size, the length of printed line (and, consequently, margin size), the vertical distance between lines, whether or not to use columns, whether to use justified right margins, and a host of others. Some of these decisions are more important than others, from the point of view of instructional efficacy. Some decisions are made by default by the word processing or desktop publishing software; sometimes the default decisions are good, but sometimes they are not so good, and should be over-ridden.

While the design and layout of print materials is too broad a topic to be treated comprehensively here (but has been elsewhere; see Misanchuk, 1992, from which most of the following material was drawn), we present below some fundamental notions about the design of printed materials.

Choice of Font

There are many thousands of different fonts available to the professional graphic designer or typographer. Even educators now have some choice: A typical word processing or desktop publishing system will offer the choice of a dozen or two different fonts. Some of these are suitable for use as instructional text, while others are suitable only for occasional use as attention-getters or for special purposes and should not be used to present sizable bodies of text (Figure 12-1).

Figure 12-1.   Fonts such as Bookman, New Century Schoolbook, Courier, Times, and Helvetica are suitable for use as body text, but fonts such as London and Zapf Chancery should be reserved for specialized uses such as announcements and invitations.

Bookman

New Century Schoolbook

Courier

Times

Helvetica

London

Zapf Chancery

Recall from Chapter 11 that typefaces can be classified into two general categories: those that have serifs and those that do not (sans-serif fonts) (Figure 12-2).

Figure 12-2.   The typeface on the left has serifs; the one on the right does not.

SCM   SCM

Research on printed materials has shown that while most readers are able to comprehend a wide variety of typefaces with equal ease and rapidity, they exhibit strong preferences for fonts with serifs. That is, while readers may learn just about as well regardless of the font used (within limits, of course: fancy typefaces, such as Old English, and script typefaces are excluded from this generalization), they generally show strong preferences for seriffed fonts. A recent study (Misanchuk, 1989a) concurred with earlier findings in showing that Times and Helvetica were least preferred, Courier was in the middle, and Bookman and New Century Schoolbook (Figure 12-1) were most preferred. We suggest, as do Hooper and Hannafin (1986), that providing text that learners find pleasant to look at may have positive transfer to learning, and that even though the effects may be small, several such effects may cumulate. To that end, especially since there is little or no cost involved in using a preferred font over a non-preferred one, we recommend preparing text materials in typefaces like Bookman or New Century Schoolbook (or their equivalents, since different computer systems use different names for similar fonts). The sans-serif Helvetica, and the seriffed but relatively compact Times, should be avoided.

In general, research findings suggest that readers prefer text with

- a serif,
- a heavy stroke (bordering on boldface),
- clearly distinguishing characteristics between letters,
- considerable white space within letters, and
- substantial width to the letters.

Font Size

Discussing font size without simultaneously discussing line length and leading (the vertical distance between lines) is almost impossible, because the three variables are intimately related. In keeping with the spirit of providing rules of thumb, however, we venture the following, and refer you to Misanchuk (1992) for additional detail.

Considerable research a number of years ago by Tinker and his associates (Tinker, 1963, 1965; Paterson and Tinker, 1940) has shown that optimal legibility is achieved with text that is 9–12 points in size (a point is equal to about $^1/_{72}$ inch) (Figure 12-3). Note that, as a consequence of the way in which type is measured, not all type of a given size is actually the same height (Figure 12-4).

Figure 12-3. Commonly-used sizes of text: 9-point, 10-point, 11-point, and 12-point.

This is 9-point Bookman. This is 9-point Helvetica.

This is 10-point Bookman. This is 10-point Helvetica.

This is 11-point Bookman. This is 11-point Helvetica.

This is 12-point Bookman. This is 12-point Helvetica.

Figure 12-4.   24-point Bookman, Avant Garde, and Times. Note that the characters in the Times and Avant Garde fonts are smaller and larger, respectively, than the corresponding characters in the Bookman font.

Hajk   Hajk   Hajk

Although sizes as small as 8-point (or even 7-point in unusual circumstances) can be used in figures and tables, they are too small for comfortable reading of extensive portions of text. (Such very small text is more legible in a sans-serif font than in a seriffed font.) On the other hand, text larger than 12-point is unnecessarily large under normal circumstances (young children or learners with vision problems are exceptions), and simply wastes space. Typefaces larger than 12-point should be reserved for use as headings and titles. The most reasonable choices for body text appear to be 10- or 11-point.

Font Style

The use of the various styles available for each font (e.g., italic, bold, outline, shadow, etc.) has been discussed earlier in the section "Choosing the Font Style" in Chapter 11. The comments made there apply equally to print materials.

Line Length and Margins

Line lengths (or column widths) and margins are inter-related, too; changing one affects the other. Although research by Tinker (1963) showed that the lack of margins does not affect legibility, most learners prefer to have them, presumably for aesthetic reasons or because of habit. Their precise size does not seem to be a significant factor; however, there exist some rules of thumb for designing aesthetically pleasing margins (see Misanchuk, 1992).

Line lengths are a different story, however: Very short lines (i.e., very narrow columns) can be dysfunctional inasmuch as the text becomes choppy and difficult to read. As lines are made longer, however, the leading must be increased in order to maintain legibility. The general advice derived from both researchers and practitioners is that line lengths for normal-sized body text (9–12 point) should be no longer than about 5 $^1/_2$ inches, and ideally should be about an inch shorter than that.

Columns

Of course, line length and the number of columns that can be placed on a page are also inter-related. Although word processing and page layout programs have made it easier to create text in multiple columns, there are some disadvantages to using multiple columns (Misanchuk, 1992), especially if the materials are likely to be revised frequently (as instructional materials often are). For this reason, sticking to a single-column format may be wise.

Right (or Full) Justification

Desktop publishing programs have also made it easy to cause the right margins of text to be fully justified (i.e., the right margin forms a straight line down the page). However, a number of educators and desktop publishers recommend against the practice, on the grounds that even if right-justification doesn't involves extra work in hyphenating (which it usually does, despite the best efforts of software writers), right-justified text probably has a negative effect on legibility (Davis, Barry, and Wiesenberg, 1986; Hartley and Burnhill, 1977; Kleper, 1987; Lichty, 1989; Misanchuk, 1992; Muncer, Gorman, Gorman, and Bibel, 1986; Spiegelman, 1987; Trollip and Sales, 1986; White, 1983).

Headings

There has been a fair amount of research done on headings (Brooks, Danserau, Spurlin, and Holley, 1983; Hartley and Jonassen, 1985; Hartley and Trueman, 1983; 1985). Headings are valuable devices for communicating the structure of the subject-matter, but only for learners older than about 13 years. Furthermore, learners of any age may need to be taught to make use of them. Whether the headings are placed in the margins or embedded in the body of the text does not seem to matter, nor does whether they are formulated as statements or as questions. Separating headings from the body text with white space appears to be both aesthetically pleasing and effective in identifying the heading as such. The amount of white space preceding the heading should reflect the order of the heading: Major headings should have more white space around them than minor headings. The use of all capital letters has been shown to be counter-productive in terms of legibility (Tinker, 1963), hence headings should be printed with upper- and lower-case letters rather than upper-case only.

References for Chapter 12

Apple Computer, Inc. (1987). *Human interface guidelines: The Apple desktop interface.* Reading, MA: Addison-Wesley Publishing Co.

Arwady, J., and Gayeski, D. (1989). *Using video: Interactive and linear designs.* Englewood Cliffs, NJ: Educational Technology Publications.

Blattner, M. M., Sumikawa, D. A., and Greenberg, R. M. (1989). Earcons and icons: Their structure and common design principles. *Human-Computer Interaction, 4,* 11–44.

Brooks, L. W., Danserau, D. F., Spurlin, J. E., and Holley, C. D. (1983). Effects of headings on text processing. *Journal of Educational Psychology, 75,* 292–302.

Buxton, W. (1989). Introduction to this special issue on nonspeech audio. *Human-Computer Interaction, 4,* 1–9.

Davis, F. E., Barry, J., and Wiesenberg, M. (1986). *Desktop publishing.* Homewood, IL: Dow Jones-Irwin.

Gaver, W. W. (1989). The SonicFinder: An interface that uses auditory icons. *Human-Computer Interaction, 4,* 67–94.

Hannafin, M. J., Garhart, C., Rieber, L. P., and Phillips, T. L. (1985). Keeping interactive video in perspective: Tentative guidelines and cautions in the design of interactive video. In E. Miller and M. Mosley (Eds.), *Educational media and technology yearbook*. Denver, CO: Libraries Unlimited.

Hartley, J., and Burnhill, P. (1977). Fifty guidelines for improving instructional text. *Programmed Learning and Educational Technology, 14,* 65–73.

Hartley, J., and Jonassen, D. H. (1985). The role of headings in printed and electronic text. In D. H. Jonassen (Ed.), *The technology of text (volume two): Principles for structuring, designing, and displaying text* (pp. 237–263). Englewood Cliffs, NJ: Educational Technology Publications.

Hartley, J., and Trueman, M. (1983). The effects of headings in text on recall, search and retrieval. *British Journal of Educational Psychology, 53,* 205–214.

Hooper, S., and Hannafin, M. J. (1986). Variables affecting the legibility of computer-generated text. *Journal of Instructional Development, 9*(4), 22–28.

Kleper, M. L. (1987). *The illustrated handbook of desktop publishing and typesetting*. Blue Ridge Summit, PA: Tab Books.

Lichty, T. (1989). *Design principles for desktop publishers*. Glenview, IL: Scott, Foresman and Co.

Lynch, P. (1991). *Multimedia: Getting started*. Sunnyvale, CA: PUBLIX Information Products, Inc. for Apple Computer, Inc.

Mann, B. L. (1992). The SSF model: Structuring the functions of the sound attribute. *Canadian Journal of Educational Communication, 21,* 45–65.

Misanchuk, E. R. (1989a). *Learner preferences for typeface (font) and leading in print materials*. Saskatoon, SK: Division of Extension and Community Relations, The University of Saskatchewan. (ERIC Document Reproduction Service No. ED 307 854)

Misanchuk, E. R. (1992). *Preparing instructional text: Document design using desktop publishing*. Englewood Cliffs, NJ: Educational Technology Publications.

Muncer, S. J., Gorman, B. S., Gorman, S., and Bibel, D. (1986). Right is wrong: An examination of the effect of right justification on reading. *British Journal of Educational Technology, 17,* 5–10.

Paterson, D. G., and Tinker, M. A. (1940). *How to make type readable*. New York: Harper and Row. Cited by Tinker, M. A. (1965). *Bases for effective reading*. Minneapolis, MN: University of Minnesota Press.

Schwier, R. A. (1991). Current issues in interactive design. In G. J. Anglin (Ed.), *Instructional technology: Past, present, and future.* (pp. 195–201). Englewood, CO: Libraries Unlimited.

Spiegelman, M. (1987). Interior design for documents. *PC World, March,* 178–185.

Tinker, M. A. (1963). *Legibility of print.* Ames, IA: Iowa State University Press.

Tinker, M. A. (1965). *Bases for effective reading.* Minneapolis, MN: University of Minnesota Press.

Trollip, S. R., and Sales, G. (1986, January). *Readability of computer-generated fill-justified text.* Paper presented at the Annual Convention of the Association for Educational Communications and Technology, Las Vegas, NV.

White, J. V. (1983). *Mastering graphics.* New York: Bowker.

Chapter 13

Miscellaneous Design Considerations

This chapter is a potpourri. It addresses a number of issues and presents a number of ideas that did not seem to fit logically into earlier chapters, but were important enough, in our estimation, to be included in the book. The topics addressed include audit trails, repurposing source material, constructing storyboards, caring for optical and magnetic media, and copyright.

Audit Trails in Interactive Multimedia Instruction

In any independent learning experience, the learner strikes a path through the instruction. In linear media, such as audiotaped instruction, that path is fixed and predetermined by the producer; learners share essentially similar instructional experiences.

Interactive multimedia, on the other hand, provides the learner with the opportunity to shape the program, and consequently the learning experience. Two learners, even in pursuit of the same objectives, may strike radically different paths through the instruction. A host of questions arise about various instructional paths which require ways of recording and analyzing the instructional path taken by each learner. We refer to that record of the path as the audit trail (after M. W. Petruk, personal communication, February 7, 1990).

To date, we have identified four purposes for audit trails:

- for formative evaluation in instructional design,
- for basic research into instructional multimedia design,
- for auditing program usage, and
- for advising learners as they use a program.

Audit Trails and Formative Evaluation

Audit trails have historically been used for formative evaluation of instructional materials. It is useful to be able to determine which paths are perceived as attractive or significant by learners, and to learn where and how they make errors. If particular paths or segments of instruction receive less traffic than others, this may indicate a need for revision. In some cases, no traffic along particular paths may allow the instructional designer to eliminate those options from the system, perhaps improving the efficiency of the program or liberating space for other options.

The primary purpose of formative evaluation is to optimize the performance of the product. This aspect of formative evaluation becomes less significant in the context of hypermedia structures, however, especially in democratic or cybernetic environments. When designer influence is reduced, and learner influence is increased, what does it mean to attempt to optimize the learner's path through multimedia, where the learner is the only arbiter of the "correct" path? In hypermedia, the purpose is not always to optimize the treatment, but rather to open up the number of possibilities available to the learner. In such cases, formative evaluation concerns will likely emphasize issues such as ease of navigation and meaningful transitions among elements of instruction learners encounter, and certainly de-emphasize issues such as efficiency.

Audit Trails and Basic Research

Audit trails can also be used to track learner performance in research settings. Individuals, and indeed groups of individuals, can approach instruction differently, and this has traditionally been of theoretical interest. For example, consider individual differences or cognitive style constructs, such as locus of control. How might internalizers and externalizers differ in their approaches to highly organized interactive treatments? Would they react differently to, and take different paths through, very linear treatments and hypermedia treatments? One learner may select the shortest path available; another may select every available remedial segment in the same treatment. Resultant paths would be very different from one another, but, short of actually watching both individuals progress through the materials, how can these differences be expressed? As interest grows in the effectiveness of learner control of instruction (e.g., see Higginbotham-Wheat, 1990; López, 1990; Ross, Morrison, and O'Dell,

1990; Steinberg, 1977), and especially as it broadens into learner control of interactive and hypermediated instruction, these kinds of questions will command increasing interest. For example, using very liberal confidence levels (75%, 92%), Beasley and Vila (1992) found that males and individuals with lower ACT scores in English used more exploratory and non-linear strategies in a hypermedia program than did females or those with higher ACT-English scores.

Research on linear structures, as on many branching structures, is necessarily quantitative in nature. As we progress into multimedia/hypermedia structures, however, the research mode takes on a decidedly qualitative bent. On the surface, this may sound like a curious statement, but consider the following. There are relatively few questions one can ask about the use of linear media beyond achievement/efficiency, performance, and interactions with designs and learner variables. Meaning is imposed on the designs studied, usually by the producer or designer. For example, we could examine the effectiveness of a particular cuing strategy on different types of learners in linear media. We can ask questions like "Did the cuing strategies help one group more than another?" But the treatment is fixed, so we are largely restricted to quasi-experimental designs unless parallel treatments are developed for comparison and control.

Audit trails in hypermedia fit the increasingly popular paradigm of naturalistic observation in that they are collected unobtrusively, in a natural setting. The instructional developer, given this orientation, is charged with designing a rich context within which learning can occur. Rather than being concerned about the direction and substance each learner encounters in instruction, the instructional developer is more concerned about the landscape of the instruction—the contours, breadth, and depth of the terrain—and the ease with which learners can maneuver through the materials. The learner is viewed as part of an instructional ecosystem, simultaneously shaping and being shaped by the instruction encountered.

Audit Trails and Usage Audits

Sometimes multimedia packages are produced for use by a rather vaguely-defined audience (e.g., visitors to a museum or tourist site). Producers of such packages can only speculate about what content or paths in them will be most of interest and in demand, and observation of viewer/users is the only means of validating the producers' initial estimates.

A third use of audit trails therefore is to determine which paths of existing interactive media packages are of most interest to certain classes of viewers/users. The use of audit trails forms an unobtrusive way of effectively peering over the shoulders of groups of users to determine how they are traversing the interactive media package. This approach is similar to the classic unobtrusive measure of determining the popularity of various museum displays by measuring the amount of wear on floor tiles in front of them (Webb, Campbell, Schwartz, and Sechrest, 1966).

In most cases, audit trail data for unstructured or public environments will include relatively simple census data. The question of primary interest of most designers is "Who is using this, and for what purpose?" The audit trail data offer information about who was exposed to which portions of a treatment, tracking user preferences rather than user performance.

Audit Trails and Advising

Perhaps the most potent instructional use for audit trail data is counseling and advising the learner, "on the fly," about how choices made and paths taken may bear on future choices or outcomes. For example, the audit trail could not only be stored by the computer, but also interpreted by it: The computer could construct a data bank from which inferences could be made. Coupled with appropriate rules, the data bank could form the basis for a comparison of the learner's path choices with data collected from prior learners, to provide suggestions about what other paths might interest the learner, what paths are most likely to be rewarding in terms of learning accomplishment, or what difficulties the learner might be expected to face if particular paths are chosen.

This counseling and advising use of audit trail data differs from the traditional use of adaptive decision logic for routing learners through sequences, in that it makes the learner a full partner in the decision-making. For example, it is common to find decision logic that says, in effect, "If the learner achieved a score of less than 14 on the quiz, send him or her through the remedial sequence; if the learner achieved a score of 25 or more on the quiz, skip the next five frames; otherwise proceed." Similarly, adaptive computer-based testing (Frick, 1990a, 1991; Kingsbury and Weiss, 1983; Luk, 1991; Novick and Lewis, 1974; Tennyson and Park, 1984; Tennyson, Christensen, and Park, 1984; Weiss and Kingsbury, 1984) makes decisions on how many test questions must be presented to the learner before a decision of mastery or non-mastery can be made with a certain degree of confidence. However, the kind of counseling and advising we are talking about here involves the learner as an informed decision-maker: The function of the audit trail data base is to provide information about what consequences occurred to previous learners who made similar decisions under similar circumstances. Armed with that information, the learner is left free to make the choice.

We believe this application of audit trail data is the most exciting and promising of all the uses we have identified, but much work remains to be done before the tools are available to implement fully the strategies described above.

Description of the Audit Trail

In our search for meaningful ways to represent the audit trail, we investigated and considered several formats. The list we offer below is not exhaustive, but merely a point of departure.

Raw Data Matrix

The most basic way of representing audit trail data is to simply record the responses of each learner (as a vector), one above the other (Figure 13-1). Matrices like these have the advantage of being easily constructed and relatively easily interpreted for each individual. The interpretation, however, can only be relatively limited, and context-bound. For crude formative evaluation purposes, the data are useful. An instructional designer can see which choices are attracting individual learners, and speculate about design decisions. But there is a serious limitation with this type of approach: raw data, by definition, aren't summarized and therefore conclusions based on the group are difficult to derive.

Figure 13-1.　Sample raw data matrix for a small group of learners. Numbers in the vectors represent the ordinal number of paths chosen by learners.

Subject	1	2	2	2	1	1	1	1	3	
Subject	2	2	2	2	2	1	1	1	1	
Subject	3	2	2	2	2	1	1	2	1	
Subject	4	2	2	1	2	1	2	2	3	
Subject	5	2	1	2	2	1	1	1	1	
Subject	6	1	3	2	1	2	1	1	1	
Subject	7	2	2	2	2	2	1	1	1	
Subject	8	2	1	2	2	2	1	1	1	
Subject	9	2	3	3	2	1	1	2	2	
Subject	10	2	1	3	2	1	2	2	2	
Subject	11	2	3	2	2	1	1			
Subject	12	2	3	3	3	1	2			
Subject	13	1	3	3	3	1	1			
Subject	14	2	3	3	3	1	1			
Subject	15	2	2	2	2	1	1	1		

Nodal Frequencies and Proportions

Another approach is to present data associated with each decision point (node) in the treatment. Data can be presented in at least two forms, as raw data (Figure 13-2) or as proportions (Figure 13-3).

Raw nodal frequencies, like raw data matrices, are easy to create. They are perhaps easier to interpret, since the data are now summarized. Magnitudes of differences are obvious, and at any node, comparisons have high precision and are intuitively satisfying. At the same time, relationships across nodes, or among variables, are difficult to interpret. For example, how should four choices of A at one node be compared with 103 choices of A at another node, if they occupy different locations in the treatment? Perhaps only eight individuals encountered the first node, whereas several hundred encountered the second. Looping problems surface here to cause difficulties in interpretation. If an individual loops through a node several times, frequency data become distorted. Either the same choice is made several times, thereby inflating the frequencies at that node, or several different choices are made, thereby leveling the data at that decision point.

Figure 13-2. Tabular representation of raw frequencies of paths chosen in sample data. Although the sample data actually have eight decision nodes, only three are presented here, for simplicity. Note how quickly the size and complexity of the table grows as the number of decision nodes and/or the number of choices increases

Node 1	Resp.	1			2		
	Freq.	2			13		

Node 2	Resp.	1	2	3	1	2	3
	Freq.	0	0	2	3	6	4

Node 3	Resp.	1	2	3	1	2	3	1	2	3	1	2	3
	Freq.	0	1	1	2	1	0	0	5	1	0	1	3

Figure 13-3. Tabular representation of proportions of paths chosen in sample data for first three decision nodes. Note how, as one progresses through more decision nodes, smaller frequencies of responses produce deceptively larger proportions.

Node 1	Resp.	1			2		
	Freq.	.13			.87		

Node 2	Resp.	1	2	3	1	2	3
	Freq.	0	0	1.0	.23	.46	.31

Node 3	Resp.	1	2	3	1	2	3	1	2	3	1	2	3
	Freq.	0	.50	.50	.67	.33	0	0	.83	.17	0	.25	.75

Nodal data can also be presented proportionally. Again, this type of format is easy to create and precision is retained at a high level. Proportions allow easier comparisons across nodes or among variables at different positions in the treatment. Of course some calculation is necessary, and the user must struggle with the question of what to use as a denominator. For example, is the denominator consistently the total number of learners encountering the treatment, or is the denominator the total number of learners who pass a particular decision point? Perhaps obviously, the denominator of any proportion will be determined by the comparisons the user chooses to make—yet another type of context dependence. As with raw nodal data, proportional data are also sensitive to looping problems. An individual looping several times through a particular node can inflate its proportion of the total. Different kinds of distortions will occur, depending on which denominator is used. In addition, as one descends deeper into the data matrix, smaller raw numbers translate into larger proportions.

When considering nodal data (either frequencies or proportions), individual differences are lost in the compression of data. Any design decisions based on these data are limited to conclusions about the group as a homogeneous entity, and we sacrifice any more subtle interpretations. Furthermore, data spread across several tables, each representing a single node (or, alternatively one large table showing multiple crossbreaks), are difficult to assimilate. Patterns that exist within them are difficult to detect.

Audit Trail Tree

The audit trail tree (Figure 13-4) presents the data in a more intuitively powerful way.

The audit trail tree is drawn so that the thickness of the line depicts the number of learners who chose the path represented. Of course, if large numbers of learners are involved, the line width could be scaled. Too, numbers (either frequencies or proportions) could be attached to each node to provide greater detail. It is clear, it is graphical, it is intuitive, and it is grounded in reality. Comparisons are easy to make; flow can be read into the diagram as learners progress from the beginning to the end of instruction. Although the drawing process is not difficult to do manually, it is somewhat tedious, and automation of the process on a graphic-interface microcomputer would be desirable.

Figure 13-4.   Audit trail tree of example data. The width of the line represents the number of learners taking any given path. A dashed line indicates no learners took the path.

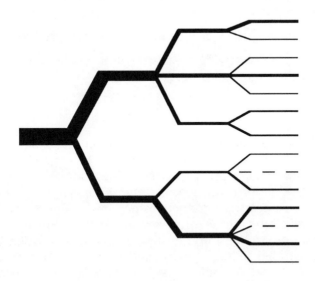

On the other hand, unless numbers are attached (as suggested above), the precision of the display is fairly low (i.e., it is difficult sometimes to tell the difference between 3 learners and 4, or between 11 and 13). The problem of conceptual distance and the problem of how to represent the loops remain in the audit trail tree approach.

Content or Document Analysis

In one sense, an instructional product can be treated as a document, and a thorough examination of that document and related documentary sources can provide useful data for analysis. The usual purpose of document analysis is to explain the "status of some phenomenon at a particular time or its development over a period of time" (Best and Kahn, 1989, p. 90). Any documents related to the development of an instructional product could be used in this type of analysis, and might include such things as client/developer contracts, outlines, storyboards, usage data, production schedules, other related instructional products, drafts of material, formative evaluations, and the like.

Some examples of audit trail studies which could employ this approach might include:

- to analyze the instructional design preferences of a producer of interactive media;
- to evaluate prejudice or bias in instructional products; or
- to reveal the underlying structures or levels of difficulty inherent in a particular product.

Case Study

Often used for longitudinal study of development of social phenomena and change, case study methods can probably be extended to instructional products or processes. The case under study would not be a specific product or process, but rather an exemplar of, or prototype for, a category of products or processes. For example, a researcher conducting a case study would not be interested in a CD-ROM treatment on architectural design as an entity. Rather, in a case study, the researcher might be interested in the development process and instructional design employed as an example of other products which might fall into a similar category.

Data are typically gathered from a number of sources, including direct observation, interviews, formal instruments and inventories, or recorded data. The emphasis in conducting a case study is depth of analysis, not broad generalization. Generalizations would only be drawn from a series of cases which reveal consistent observations.

Repurposing Source Material

An adage in instructional development is that first you attempt to find and adopt existing material to suit your needs, adapt existing material if what you find is not quite right, and only produce your own as a last resort. It applies somewhat uneasily to interactive video, but applies nonetheless. Videodiscs and CD-ROM discs are not abundant, but their numbers are growing dramatically, and it is likely that at some time you will encounter a videodisc containing programming you would like to adapt by writing your own computer program to drive the program. Some argue that this will result in "video-enhanced computer-assisted instruction," rather than truly interactive multimedia. Perhaps, but the point is moot. Designing treatments from existing programs is cheaper—much cheaper—than designing your own material from scratch, and going through the rigors of production. Sure, you need to fill in some gaps in the treatments with computer text screens and graphics, and indeed you must rely on computer-generated feedback, menus, and animation more than you may like. Videophiles are somewhat snobbish about the quality of computer-generated frames. But face it, you also save yourself a great deal of time and expense in the bargain.

The initial steps are the same as any other development effort. A need analysis, a learner analysis, and task analysis are completed and objectives written. As content is outlined, discs which contain appropriate material are reviewed, and finally selected.

The process then diverges from designing your own program. Instead of creation, dissection is the approach used. With the frame display activated so you can read the frame numbers on the screen, you will carefully review the treatment several times, and note the segment locations. Useful segments can be added to your content outline in the *Treatment* column next to the content satisfied. Note the frame numbers of question and feedback segments as well, and include them on the outline with the associated instructional segments. It is a good idea to view the videodisc in a linear fashion at some point, to ensure that you have not overlooked any segments buried in the resident program's algorithm. Otherwise, your path choices will influence which segments you miss, and even attempting to run every possible path can lead to omissions. If the content you are reviewing is a Level II treatment, remember to turn off Audio Channel 2 if you want to assume control of the player.

Once all segments have been identified, and the useful ones added to your content outline, the blanks in the *Treatment* column will represent content which requires computer-based instruction to fill the gaps. Other components will also be missing. Some questions, problems, feedback segments, and menus will need to be added to existing instructional segments, and entire sections of content will require computer-based treatment.

Arguments for and against this approach aside, there is a secondary use for the process which is attractive. Training developers to write programs for existing videodisc treatments requires time and opportunities to practice skills. Level II interactive videodisc treatments can be used to hone authoring skills. It can be an interesting challenge to try to write a program which mimics the function of a Level II treatment. Various levels of sophistication can be selected from a variety of treatments to develop specific procedures, such as menus, multiple or random feedback, timed responses, and counters. The resident Level II program provides a template for development, and a model for comparison. Students receive almost immediate feedback by comparing their products to the Level II counterpart. This approach to training lowers expense by eliminating video production costs. Still, it primarily develops mechanical skills for programming, and sacrifices some of the creativity and writing practice inherent in full-scale treatment development.

Constructing Storyboards

Storyboards are useful for visualizing the overall multimedia production. Although some developers can maintain a mental map of what a whole production looks like, most of us require some help. Some developers prefer to work from outlines or shooting scripts. We do not have a strong opinion on which approach might work for your application, but suggest you will want to have a method of clearly communicating the specific compositions comprising the multimedia treatment. Storyboards provide that. They are also very useful for communicating that information to others (perhaps outside the immediate work group).

Work on storyboards can be started after the general design parameters are established, specifications selected, content defined, and flowcharts designed. Storyboarding for an interactive multimedia treatment can be tricky. For one thing, the treatment is not linear, so the pages of a storyboard cannot be sequenced in any predictable fashion. The compromise is usually to identify clusters of activities or events from the flowchart, and design example frames for them. For instance, a designer might select one branch from the flowchart, then storyboard a video segment, and sample frames which include navigation control, questions, graphics, and animation.

Another problem with storyboarding multimedia treatments is how to handle the multiple sources and levels of input. A single presentation frame may be comprised of information from several sources. How can the individual sources be represented visually without interfering with the integrity of the composition? If everything is included, will the format become complex and unwieldy?

One excellent solution was achieved by Bergman and Moore (1990). They designed a "Super Story Board" which includes ample space for video production details, and separate visual displays for composite video, graphics and control information. We recommend it, particularly if you are working on a large scale project.

Many IMI development projects don't require the level of detail in this, and similar, storyboard formats. Space devoted to administrative documentation can often be handled elsewhere, and preserve the primary purpose of the storyboard—to communicate the visual and aural constructions of program segments.

So for the purposes of most IMI projects, we offer our own version (Figure 13-5). This is a simplified storyboard format, one which includes few frills but contains useful features. For one thing, it does not assume a single monitor display. It can accommodate single or dual screen productions. Monitor 1 is usually devoted to video, regardless of format. The second screen is devoted to a second source, and it is identified as an overlay, window, or second monitor, depending on the application. Source and production information is included for each screen. Audio information usually includes an identification of the source(s), and the actual text of narration and sound.

If you like it, use it. We grant full permission to reproduce it or adapt it with impunity.

Figure 13-5. IMI storyboard.

Production Title: _____ Date: _____

Reference: _____

Monitor 1

Production Notes, Monitor 1

Overlay-Window-Monitor 2

Production Notes, Source 2

Audio Production Notes

Caring for Optical and Magnetic Media

Sure, they're resilient. Yes, videodiscs and CDs are durable. Still, for longest life and quality replay, you should do a few simple things, such as:

- Handle discs like a good LP record. Avoid getting fingerprints on the surface of the disc. For one-sided discs, the player "reads" the bottom side, opposite the label.

- Store discs vertically—not in a stack or in the disc player.

- Store in a temperate climate (40°F–95°F; 4°C–35°C is a safe temperature range).

- Discs may be washed in warm water and mild detergent. Use a soft, lint-free cloth to dry.

- Skipping during playback may be caused by foreign objects (sometimes even fingerprints) on the surface of an optical disc. Brush foreign objects off with a soft cloth, moving from center to edge.

- Skipping during disc playback may also be caused by dirty player optics. Smoke residue is a common culprit. It and other airborne contaminants can build up on the laser. The focusing lens can be reached on most players. Cleaning the focusing lens and the disc will cure most problems.

- Discard badly scratched discs. They won't harm the machine, but there is nothing you can do to repair them.

- Avoid placing magnetic media in a magnetic field. Television sets, monitors, electric motors, and airport X-ray machines are common producers of magnetic fields. So are refrigerator magnets and magnetized paper-clip dispensers. Even power cords have a magnetic field around them.

- Floppy disks and videotapes should be handled carefully. Avoid touching the emulsion of a disk or tape.

- Protect magnetic media from heat and dirt. Store them in protective sleeves.

- Mark magnetic disk labels with soft felt-tipped pens only. Do not use paper clips on them.

Copyright

Copyright is essentially a property right, that is, the legal protection afforded intellectual property. Subtleties shift its legal application from country to country and from time to time, but generally speaking, the intention of copyright is to protect the creator's moral and financial rights to use material. If you create something, you alone have the right to say how it is used. It is not possible to protect ideas, so copyright protects only the tangible expression of the idea (a book, painting, photograph). Again, generally speaking, copyright includes the right to:

- reproduce the work, including changing the work into a different form (e.g., language or medium);
- perform a work in public;
- publish;
- adapt;
- broadcast;
- authorize others to exercise your rights.

Copyright, of course, has important implications for the design and production of interactive multimedia. Many projects include amassing data from a variety of sources. It is important that developers realize permission must be obtained from the person or entity holding the copyright on any component prior to including it in a new product.

This holds true for "all or a substantial part" of anything you wish to use which is derived from another source. What comprises "a substantial part?" A substantial part of any material can be interpreted quantitatively or qualitatively. Some libraries and individuals have attempted to set "rules of thumb" to guide routine business, such as "not more than 10% of the original work" or "not more than 60 consecutive words," but these are arbitrary guidelines of little worth to an instructional developer. You may want to use only three bars from the song "I Did It My Way." The composer can argue, perhaps successfully, that those three bars represent a substantial part of the song. The point is, there is no trustworthy method—short of a court ruling—of measuring "a substantial part." If contested, the definition would be subject to legal argument and interpretation—not a comfortable circumstance. It is wise to obtain permission to use anything created by someone else, in a product you are developing.

It is a common misconception that changing a graphic or photograph slightly is enough to circumvent copyright. For example, some people think that merely tracing a line drawing, possibly embellishing it, or leaving out some parts, is enough to obviate the original copyright. Although we don't presume to give legal advice, we are reasonably confident that such activity doesn't change the copyright status. As long as the derivative work is substantially the same as the original, the copyright holds.

Our experience has been that permission may be very easy and inexpensive, or very difficult and expensive, to obtain. Copyright holders' reactions and responses vary all over the map. Some internationally-known creators of original material are very generous, granting permission for educational use of their material almost as a matter of course. On the other hand, sometimes obscure, local creators demand exorbitant fees before permitting you to use their works. (When that happens, we usually don't use them.)

There are two things you should be aware of when seeking copyright clearance:

- Obtaining permission can be very time-consuming: It is no longer surprising to us to find that eight months or a year can go by between the time of initial contact and receipt of the final written agreement. Plan for those kinds of possible delays if you can. One way to shorten them is to seek permission by telephone, and confirm it in writing. Fax machines have helped speed the process somewhat.

- Sometimes copyright holders require you to provide them with a copy of your finished work for their files. This can create a substantial drain on a tight production budget if you haven't contemplated producing extra copies.

We recommend you use a form letter which specifies the material to be used, states the purpose it will serve, and describes the form it will take. As a matter of courtesy, you should provide a duplicate copy for the owner's files and a self-addressed, stamped envelope for the return of the signed permission form. Samples of two copyright permission forms (one for print, one for non-print media) are offered in Figures 13-6 and 13-7. We make no claims about their legal status, but offer them as examples of formats we have used without incident. To be on the safe side, you should have any form you use approved by a lawyer.

Figure 13-6.   Sample copyright release form for print materials.

Date, etc.

Permissions Editor
Etc_etc_etc

Dear Person;

We would appreciate receiving permission to reprint the article
"ARTICLE_NAME," by AUTHOR_NAME, from volume NN, no. NN of
JOURNAL_OR_BOOK_NAME.

The reprints will be distributed as part of a package of readings for a
distance education course entitled COURSE_NAME. We will not sell
the copies in the normal sense of the word; students will be charged a
very modest fee to cover the cost of duplicating and handling.

We cannot predict with any degree of accuracy how many copies we
will eventually require, but there will not likely be more than about
250 copies made. Our operating procedure is to print up only as many
copies as we need for the upcoming year; if we were to exceed 100
copies in any given year, we would contact you to validate our
permission.

If, at the time of revision of the course, the materials are identified for
inclusion in the revised version, we will contact you again for
permission.

We would, of course, include with the materials an appropriate credit
to the holder of the copyright. If you have a preferred specification,
please let us know.

If you require any further information, you may call me at (306) 966-
XXXX.

Sincerely,

YOUR_NAME
YOUR_TITLE

Figure 13-7. Sample copyright release form for visual materials.

Date

I grant permission to YOUR NAME OR COMPANY to use the following material in their videodisc production entitled "PROJECT NAME." The material will be used for non-profit, educational purposes in public displays, schools and promotions.

Photograph: View of Saskatoon skyline at night

Videotape: 38 second clip of Louis Riel Day festivities

_____

COPYRIGHT OWNER'S NAME
TITLE

References for Chapter 13

Beasley, R. E., and Vila, J. A. (1992). The identification of navigation patterns in a multimedia environment: A case study. *Journal of Educational Multimedia and Hypermedia, 1*(2), 209–222.

Best, J. W., and Kahn, J. W. (1989). *Research in education* (6th ed.). Englewood Cliffs, NJ: Prentice-Hall.

Dede, C. (1990). Knowledge processing: Navigating the sea of information. *Authorware, 3*(1), 17–22.

Frick, T. W. (1988, August). *Non-metric temporal path analysis: A method by which tutorial systems can learn through inquiry.* Paper presented at the 4th Annual International Conference on Systems Research, Cybernetics and Informatics, Baden-Baden, West Germany.

Frick, T. W. (1990a). A comparison of three decision models for adapting the length of computer-based mastery tests. *Journal of Educational Computing Research, 6*(4), 479–513.

Frick, T. W. (1990b). Analysis of patterns in time: A method of recording and quantifying temporal relations in education. *American Educational Research Journal, 27*(1), 180–204.

Frick, T. W. (1991, February). *A comparison of an expert systems approach to computerized adaptive testing and an item response theory model.* Paper presented at the Annual Conference of the Association for Educational Communications and Technology, Orlando, FL.

Grabinger, R. S. (1989). Screen layout design: Research into the overall appearance of the screen. *Computers in Human Behavior, 5,* 175–183.

Higginbotham-Wheat, N. (1990). Learner control: When does it work? In M. R. Simonson and C. Hargrave (Eds.), *Proceedings of the 1990 Convention of the Association for Educational Communications and Technology.* Anaheim, CA: Association for Educational Communications and Technology. (ERIC Document Reproduction Service No. ED 323 930)

Kingsbury, G. G., and Weiss, D. J. (1983). A comparison of IRT-based adaptive mastery testing and a sequential mastery testing procedure. In D. Weiss (Ed.), *New horizons in testing* (pp. 257–283). New York: Academic Press.

López, C. L. (1990, February). *Personalizing math word problems.* Paper presented at the Annual Meeting of the Association of Educational Communications and Technology, Anaheim, CA.

Luk, HK. (1991, April). *An empirical comparison of an expert systems approach and an IRT approach to computer-based adaptive mastery testing.* Paper presented at the Annual Meeting of the American Educational Research Association, Chicago, IL.

Misanchuk, E. R., and Schwier, R. A. (1991). Interactive media audit trails: Approaches and issues. In M. R. Simonson & C. Hargrave (Eds.), *13th annual proceedings of selected research presentations at the 1991 annual convention of the Association for Educational Communications and Technology* (pp. 499–520). Ames, IA: Research and Theory Division, Association for Educational Communications and Technology.

Misanchuk, E. R., and Schwier, R. A. (1992). Representing interactive multimedia and hypermedia audit trails. *Journal of Educational Multimedia and Hypermedia, 1*(3), 1–18.

Novick, M. R., and Lewis, C. (1974). *Prescribing test length for criterion-referenced measurement* (Tech. Bull. No. 18). Iowa City, IA: American College Testing Program.

Ross, S., Morrison, G., and O'Dell, J. (1990, February). *Uses and effects of learner control of context and instructional support in computer-based instruction.* Paper presented at the Annual Meeting of the Association of Educational Communications and Technology, Anaheim, CA.

Steinberg, E. R. (1977). Review of student control in computer-assisted instruction. *Journal of Computer-Based Instruction, 3*(3), 84–90.

Tennyson, R. D., Christensen, D. L., and Park, S. (1984). The Minnesota adaptive instructional system: An intelligent CBI system. *Journal of Computer-Based Instruction, 1 1*(1), 2–13.

Tennyson, R. D., and Park, O. (1984). Computer-based adaptive instructional systems: A review of empirically based models. *Machine-Mediated Learning, 1*(2), 129–153.

Webb, E. J., Campbell, D. T., Schwartz, R. D., and Sechrest, L. (1966). *Unobtrusive measures: Nonreacting research in the social sciences.* Chicago: Rand-McNally.

Weiss, D. J., and Kingsbury, G. G. (1984). Application of computerized adaptive testing to educational problems. *Journal of Educational Measurement, 21*(4), 361–375.

Section IV

Interactive Multimedia Resources

Chapter 14

Resources for Interactive Multimedia Instruction

Software Catalogues/Distributors

A-J Tech
R.R. 2
Morinville, Alberta
Canada T0G 1P0

Activision
3885 Bohannon Drive
Menlo Park, CA 90425

American Chemical Society
1155-16th St. N.W.
Washington, DC 20036

Brøderbund Software, Inc.
17 Paul Drive
San Rafael, CA 94903-2101

Bureau of Electronic Publishing
141 New Road
Parsippany, NJ 07054

Compact Publishing, Inc.
P.O. Box 40310
Washington, DC 20016

Discis Knowledge Research, Inc.
PO Box #45099
5150 Yonge Street
North York, Ontario
Canada M2N 6N2

EDUCORP Computer Services
7434 Trade Street
San Diego, CA 92121-2410

Emerging Technology
   Consultants , Inc.
P.O. Box 120444
St. Paul, MN 55112

Encyclopaedia Britannica
   Educational Corporation
310 South Michigan Avenue
Chicago, IL 60604

Grolier Electronic Publishing, Inc.
Sherman Turnpike
Danbury, CT 06816

Heartbeat Software Solutions
P.O. Box 4497
Cerritos, CA 90703-4497

Highlighted Data, Inc.
4350 N. Fairfax Dr.
Suite 450
Arlington, VA   22203-1620

Hyperglot
505 Forest Hills Blvd.
Knoxville, TN   37919

Image Entertainment
9333 Oso Avenue
Chatsworth, CA   91311

Jostens Learning Corp
6170 Cornerstone Court E.
San Diego, CA   92121

Lessoncard
P.O. Box 2778
220 Cypress Street
Abilene, TX   79704

Lumivision
1490 Lafayette Street
Suite 305
Denver, CO   80218

National Geographic Society
Educational Media Division
17th and M Sts. NW
Washington, DC   20036

Sierra On-Line, Inc.
P.O. Box 485
Coarsegold, CA   93614

The Software Toolworks
60 Leveroni Ct.
Novato, CA   94909

Videodisc Publishing
381 Park Avenue South
Suite 621
New York, NY   10016

Videodiscovery, Inc.
College Division
McGraw-Hill, Inc.
1221 Avenue of the Americas
New York, NY   10020

The Voyager Company
1352 Pacific Coast Highway
Santa Monica, CA   90401

VTAE, Inc
2564 Branch Street
Middleton, WI   53562

Wings for Learning
P.O. Box 3240
Station F
Scarborough, Ontario
Canada   M1W 9Z9

Xiphias
Helms Hall
8758 Venice Blvd.
Los Angeles, CA   90034

Selected Additional Readings

CD-ROM

Ali, S. N. (1989). Information on CD-ROM: A directory. 2: Factual data banks and full text files. *Information Development, 5*(1), 41–45.

Anonymous. (1988). Copyright, CD-ROM, and education. *TechTrends, 33*(3), 38–39.

Armento, G., and others. (1990). Maps and CD-ROM: A partnership for the future. *Laserdisk Professional, 3*(1), 65–71.

Barron, A., and Baumbach, D. (1990). A CD-ROM tutorial: Training for new technology. *Educational Technology, 30*(6), 20–23.

Baumbach, D. J. (1990). CD-ROM: Information at your fingertips. *School Library and Media Quarterly, 18*(3), 142–149.

Beiser, K. (1988). CD-ROM catalogs—the state of the art. *Wilson Library Bulletin, 63*(3), 25–26, 28, 30–32, 34.

Borman, S. (1989). Optical disc technology offers range of science, education uses. *Chemical and Engineering News, 67*(22), 22–25.

Brito, C. J. (1987). Pan-American Health Organization CD-ROM pilot project. *Information Development, 3*(4), 208–213.

Brueggeman, P. (1989). Software to monitor CD-ROM usage. *Laserdisk Professional, 2*(6), 44–48.

Campbell, B. (1989). CD-ROM publishing in Canada. *Laserdisk Professional, 2*(5), 31–34.

Cerva, J. R., and others. (1985). Selected conference proceedings from the 1985 videodisc, optical disk, and CD-ROM conference and exposition. *Optical Information Systems, 6*(2), 114–131.

Cooper, L. K. D., and Tharp, A. L. (1989). Inverted signature trees and text searching on CD-ROMs. *Information Processing and Management, 25*(2), 161–169.

Day, J. M. (1988). CD-ROM—an online training tool? *Education for Information, 6*(4), 403–410.

Desmarais, N. (1989). CD-ROM as a software distribution medium. *Optical Information Systems, 9*(4), 209–213.

Desmarais, N. (1989). CD-ROMs proliferate—part 2: Business/science/government CD-ROM disks. *Optical Information Systems, 9*(2), 98–105.

Dreiss, L. J., and Bashir, S. (1990). CD-ROM: Potential and pitfalls. *CD-ROM Professional*, 3(5), 70–73.

Editor. (1990). The keys to successful CD-ROM in-house publishing, part I: Cost estimation and hardware selection. *CD-ROM Professional*, 3(5), 74–80.

Gibbins, P. (1987). Pricing software and information on CD-ROM. *Electronic and Optical Publishing Review*, 7(4), 176–180.

Grant, M. A., and Stalker, J. C. (1989). The multiplatter CD-ROM network at Boston College. *Laserdisk Professional*, 2(5), 12–18.

Helsel, S. K. (1989). CD-ROM in general education. *Optical Information Systems*, 9(1), 30–37.

Hinds, T. H. (1990). CD-ROM development systems: A tutorial. *CD-ROM Professional*, 3(6), 56–61.

Hiscox, M. D., and Hiscox, S. B. (1986). The potential of CD–ROM in education. *TechTrends*, 31(3), 14–19.

Hlava, M. M. K., and others. (1987). CD-ROM vs online. *Bulletin of the American Society for Information Science*, 14(1), 14–27.

Kinyon, W. R. (1989). The NFAIS annual conference: A different perspective on CD-ROM technology. *Laserdisk Professional*, 2(5), 23–27.

Kuhn, C. (1987). Questions and answers about CD-ROM. *CALICO Journal*, 5(1), 73–76.

McQueen, H. (1990). Remote dial-in patron access to CD-ROM LANs. *CD-ROM Professional*, 3(4), 20–23.

Megarry, J. (1988). Hypertext and compact discs: The challenge of multi-media learning. *British Journal of Educational Technology*, 19(3), 172–183.

Moes, R. J. (1986). The CD-ROM puzzle: Where do the pieces fit? *Optical Information Systems*, 6(6), 509–511.

Moore, N. L. (1990). Integrated CD-ROM databases: The ideal solution for small and medium size publishers. *Laserdisk Professional*, 3(1), 42–49.

Nicholls, P. T. (1988). Statistical profile of currently available CD-ROM database products. *The Laserdisk Professional*, 1(4), 38–45.

Nicholls, P. T. (1990). A buyer's guide to CD-ROM selection: CD-ROM product directories and review tools. *CD-ROM Professional*, 3(3), 13–21.

Nicholls, P., and Majid, S. (1989). The potential for CD-ROM technology in less-developed countries. *Canadian Library Journal*, 46(4), 257–263.

Nicholls, P., and others. (1990). A framework for evaluating CD-ROM retrieval software. *Laserdisk Professional*, 3(2), 41–46.

Nicholls, P., and Van Den Elshout, R. (1990). Survey of databases available on CD-ROM: Types, availability, and content. *Database, 13*(1), 18–23.

Philbin, P., and Ryan J. (1988). ERIC and beyond: A survey of CD-ROMs for education collections. *The Laserdisk Professional, 1*(4), 17–27.

Phillipo, J. (1989). CD-ROM: A new research and study skills tool for the classroom. *Electronic Learning, 8*(8), 40–41.

Robinson, R., and others. (1990). Software for CD-ROM: A tutorial. *Laserdisk Professional, 3*(2), 47–52.

Rodgers, D. (1990). Step-by-step through the CD-ROM production process. *Laserdisk Professional, 3*(1), 36–39.

Rosen, D. (1986). History in the making: A report from Microsoft's first international conference on CD-ROM. *Educational Technology, 26*(7), 16–19.

Rutherford, J. (1990). Improving CD-ROM management through networking. *CD-ROM Professional, 3*(5), 20–27.

Schneider, E. (1987). The magic of optical memories. *CALICO Journal, 4*(4), 83–89.

Tanner, D.F., and Bane, R. K. (1988). CD-ROM: A new technology with promise for education. *Technological Horizons in Education, 16*(1), 57–60.

Tyckoson, D. (1989). Multi-media and the future of CD-ROM. *Technicalities, 9*(12), 6–9.

Urrows, H., and Urrows, E. (1990). Converting computer output microfiche (CDM) to CD-ROM. *Optical Information Systems, 10*(2), 93–98.

Woodbury, V. (1988). CD-ROM: Potential and practicalities. *CALICO Journal, 6*(1), 29–35.

Authoring

Barker, P. G. (1984). MUMEDALA—An approach to multi-media authoring. *British Journal of Educational Technology, 15*(1), 4–13.

Barker, P. G. (1984). MUMEDALA: An approach to multi-media authoring. *Computers and Education, 8*(4), 463–469.

Bork, A. (1990). Practical techniques useful in authoring technology-based learning material. *Journal of Computer-Based Instruction, 17*(2), 53–60.

McAleese, R. (1985). Some problems of knowledge representation in an authoring environment: Exteriorization, anomolous state metacognition and self-confrontation. *Programmed Learning and Educational Technology, 22*(4), 299–306.

Phillipo, J. (1989). An educator's guide to interfaces and authoring systems. *Electronic Learning, 8*(4), 44–45.

Robinson, D. (1989). Designing the TouchSource authoring program. *Optical Information Systems, 9*(2), 106–110.

Sales, G. C. (1989). Repurposing: Authoring tools for videodisc. *Computing Teacher, 16*(9), 12–14.

Hypermedia

Campbell, R. (1989). (I Learned It) through the grapevine: Hypermedia at work in the classroom. *American Libraries, 20*(3), 204–205.

Franklin, C. (1988). The hypermedia library. *Database, 11*(3), 43–48.

Goldman, E., and Barron, L. (1990). Using hypermedia to improve the preparation of elementary teachers. *Journal of Teacher Education, 41*(3), 21–31.

Hall, W., and others. (1989). Using HyperCard and interactive video in education: An application in cell biology. *Educational and Training Technology International, 26*(3), 207–214.

Hasselbring, T. S., and others. (1989). Making knowledge meaningful: Applications of hypermedia. *Journal of Special Education Technology, 10*(2), 61–72.

Jonassen, D. H. (1986). Hypertext principles for text and courseware design. *Educational Psychologist, 21*(4), 269–292.

Jonassen, D. H. (1988). Mindtools: Potential new liberating forces. *Educational Technology, 28*(12), 33–34.

Jonassen, D. H. (1988). Designing structured hypertext and structuring access to hypertext. *Educational Technology, 28*(11), 13–16.

Jonassen, D. H. (1989). *Hypertext/hypermedia.* Englewood Cliffs, NJ: Educational Technology Publications.

Jonassen, D. H. (1990). Semantic network elicitation: Tools for structuring hypertext. In R. McAleese and C. Green (Eds.), *Hypertext: The state of the art.* London: Intellect.

Jonassen, D.H., and Mandl, H. (1990). *Designing hypermedia for learning.* FRG: Springer-Verlag.

Locatis, C., Letourneau, G., and Banvard, R. (1989). Hypermedia and instruction. *Educational Technology Research and Development, 37*(4), 65–77.

Megarry, J. (1988). Hypertext and compact discs: The challenge of multi-media learning. *British Journal of Educational Technology, 19*(3), 172–183.

Trotter, A. (1989). Schools gear up for "hypermedia"—a quantum leap in electronic learning. *American School Board Journal, 176*(3), 35–37.

Underwood, J. (1989). HyperCard and interactive video. *CALICO Journal, 6*(3), 7–20.

Underwood, J. (1989). Hypermedia: Where we are and where we aren't. *CALICO Journal, 6*(4), 23–26.

Multimedia

Allen, B. S., and others. (1989). An educational technology curriculum for converging technologies. *Educational Technology Research and Development, 37*(4), 47–54.

Allen, B., and Carter, C. D. (1988). Expert systems and interactive video tutorials: Separating strategies from subject matter. *Journal of Computer-Based Instruction, 15*(4), 123–130.

Barker, P. G. (1984). MUMEDALA—An approach to multi-media authoring. *British Journal of Educational Technology, 15*(1), 4–13.

Barker, P. G. (1984). MUMEDALA: An approach to multi-media authoring. *Computers and Education, 8*(4), 463–469.

D'Ignazio, F. (1987). Setting up a multi-media classroom: A quickstart card. *Computers in the Schools, 4*(2), 5–29.

Friedlander, L. (1988). The Shakespeare project: Experiments in multimedia education. *Academic Computing, 2*(7), 26–29, 66–68.

Garrigues, M., and Monnerie, A. (1985). Exploration de "champs notionnels" par E.A.D. multi-medias (An exploration of "notional fields" by multi-media computer-assisted instruction). *Francais dans le Monde, 195*, 67–69.

Gayeski, D. M. (1989). Why information technologies fail. *Educational Technology, 29*(2), 9–17.

Gustafson, K. L., and Reeves, T. C. (1990). IDIOM: A platform for a course development expert system. *Educational Technology, 30*(3), 19–25.

Kozma, R. B., and others. (1989). New media for more classrooms: The 1989 EDUCOM/NCRIPTAL software awards winners. *EDUCOM Review, 24*(3), 44–49.

Litchfield, B. C., and Mattson, S. A. (1989). The interactive media science project: An inquiry-based multimedia science curriculum. *Journal of Computers in Mathematics and Science Teaching, 9*(1), 37–43.

Locatis, C., and others. (1990). Hypervideo. *Educational Technology Research and Development, 38*(2), 41–49.

Matts, K. F., and Kern, G. M. (1989). A framework for research in computer-aided instruction: Challenges and opportunities. *Computers and Education, 13*(1), 77–84.

Megarry, J. (1988). Hypertext and compact discs: The challenge of multi-media learning. *British Journal of Educational Technology, 19*(3), 172–183.

Midoro, V., and others. (1988). Interactive video and artificial intelligence: A convenient marriage. *Programmed Learning and Educational Technology, 25*(4), 299–309.

Miller, S. W., and Jackson, R. A. (1985). A comparison of multi-media instructional module with a traditional lecture format for geriatric pharmacy training. *American Journal of Pharmaceutical Education, 49*(2), 173–176.

Phillipo, J. (1989). An educator's guide to interfaces and authoring systems. *Electronic Learning, 8*(4), 44–45.

Pirolli, Peter, and Russell, D. M. (1990). The instructional design environment: Technology to support design problem solving. *Instructional Science, 19*(2), 121–144.

Rogers, R., and Rieff, J. (1989). Developing computer-based interactive video simulations on questioning strategies. *Action in Teacher Education, 11*(3), 33–36.

Underwood, J. (1989). HyperCard and interactive video. *CALICO Journal, 6*(3), 7–20.

Willams, B. F. (1990). Computer applications in behavior analysis: A review of the literature. *Educational Technology, 30*(5), 34–38.

Interactive Video and Videodisc

Alessi, S. M. (1988). Learning interactive videodisc development: A case study. *Journal of Instructional Development, 11*(2), 2–7.

Allen, B. S. (1986). A theoretical framework for interactivating linear video. *Journal of Computer-Based Instruction, 13*, 107–112.

Allen, B., and Erickson, D. (1986). Training interactive videodisc designers. *Journal of Instructional Development, 9*(2), 19–28.

Atkins, M., and Blissett, G. (1989). Learning activities and interactive videodisc: An exploratory study. *British Journal of Educational Technology, 20*(1), 47–56.

Bailey, H. J., and Klinsing, S. (1988). Employability skills: Using interactive video to keep students working. *Technological Horizons in Education, 15*(7), 79–81.

Beausey, M. M. (1988). Videodisc development: No lone rangers, please. *Training, 25*(2), 65–68.

Berry, J. (1988). Optical disc technology. *Technological Horizons in Education, 15*(6), 65–67.

Bijlstra, J. P. (1988). Some thoughts on interactive video as a training tool for process operators. *Programmed Learning and Educational Technology, 25*(1), 28–33.

Bolton, J. P. R., and others. (1990). The water videodisc: A problem-solving environment. *Computers and Education, 15*(1–3), 165–172.

Bosco, J., and Wagner, J. (1988). A comparison of the effectiveness of interactive laser disc and classroom videotape for safety instruction of General Motors workers. *Educational Technology, 28*(6), 15–22.

Braden, R. (1986). Visuals for interactive video: Images for a new technology. *Educational Technology, 26*(5), 18–23.

Brodeur, D. R. (1985). Interactive video: Fifty-one places to start. *Educational Technology, 25*(5), 42–47.

Brody, P. J. (1984, April). *Research on and research with interactive video.* Paper presented at the Annual Meeting of the American Educational Research Association, New Orleans, LA. (ERIC Document Reproduction Service No. ED 246 885)

Buttery, T. J., and Parks, D. (1988). Instructive innovation: Interactive videodisc systems. *Reading Improvement, 25*(1), 56–59.

Cantor, J. A. (1988-89). A systems approach to the design and development of interactive videodisc training. *Journal of Educational Technology Systems, 17*(4), 255–271.

Carlson, H. L., and Falk, D. R. (1989). Effective use of interactive videodisc instruction in understanding and implementing cooperative group learning with elementary pupils in social studies and social education. *Theory and Research in Social Education, 17*(3), 241–258.

Copeland, P. (1988). Interactive video: What the research says. *Media in Education and Development, 21*(2), 60–63.

Copra, E. R. (1990). Using interactive videodiscs for bilingual education. *Perspectives in Education and Deafness, 8*(5), 9–11.

Dalton, D. W. (1986). How effective is interactive video in improving performance and attitude? *Educational Technology, 26*(1), 27–30.

Dalton, D. W. (1990). The effects of cooperative learning strategies on achievement and attitudes during interactive video. *Journal of Computer-Based Instruction, 17*(1), 8–16.

Dalton, D. W., and Hannafin, M. J. (1987). The effects of knowledge- versus content-based design strategies on information and application learning from interactive video. *Journal of Computer-Based Instruction, 14,* 138–141.

Davis, G. (1988). Image learning: Higher education and interactive videodisc. *Teachers College Record, 89*(3), 352–359.

De Zonia, R. H. (1990). Interactive video. Learning with a difference. (and) Resources. Where to find information on interactive video. *Vocational Education Journal, 65*(5), 36–38.

Denee, J. (1988). Interactive videodisc: A new instructional technology. *Business Education Forum, 42*(6), 3–5.

Gayeski, D. M. (1985). Interactive video: Integrating design "levels" and hardware "levels." *Journal of Educational Technology Systems, 13*(3), 145–151.

Geber, B. (1989). Whither interactive videodisc? *Training, 26*(3), 47–49.

Glenn, A. D., and Gregory, C. (1990). Interactive video technology: Its status and future in the social sciences. *International Journal of Social Education, 5*(1), 74–84.

Hannafin, M. J. (1985). Empirical issues in the study of computer-assisted interactive video. *Educational Communications and Technology Journal, 33,* 235–247.

Hannaway, D. B., and others. (1988). An interactive videodisc module for forage quality and testing instruction. *Journal of Agronomic Education (JAE), 17*(2), 119–121.

Hansen, E. (1989). Interactive video for reflection: Learning theory and a new use of the medium. *Educational Technology, 29*(7), 7–15.

Hansen, E. (1990). The role of interactive video technology in higher education: Case study and a proposed framework. *Educational Technology, 30*(9), 13–21.

Harvard, G. R. (1990). Some exploratory uses of interactive video in teacher education: Designing and presenting interactive video sequences to primary student teachers. *Educational and Training Technology International, 37*(2), 155–173.

Hasselbring, T., and others. (1987-88). An evaluation of a level-one instructional videodisc program. *Journal of Educational Technology Systems, 16*(2), 151–169.

Hedden, S. K. (1989). Anne Winsor Miller, "Feasibility of instruction in instrumental music education with an interactive videodisc adapted from existing media." A review. *Bulletin of the Council for Research in Music Education, 100,* 27–30.

Helsel, S. (1988). Interactive videodisc and special education. *Optical Information Systems, 8*(4), 190–196.

Helsel, S. K. (1988). Videodisc in the public schools. *Optical Information Systems, 8*(1), 29–37.

Henderson, R. B., and Sales, G. C. (1988). A guide for the review of interactive videodisc instruction. *Performance and Instruction, 27*(6), 17–21.

Henderson, R. W., and Landesman, E. M. (1988-89). Interactive videodisc instruction in pre-calculus. *Journal of Educational Technology Systems, 17*(2), 91–101.

Hofmeister, A. M., and Thorkildsen, R. J. (1989). Videodisc levels: A case study in hardware obsession. *Journal of Special Education Technology, 19*(2), 73–79.

Hudson, B. (1990). Interactive video in the mathematics classroom. *Mathematics in School, 19*(1), 4–7.

Hughes, H. (1989). Conversion of a teacher-delivered course into an interactive videodisc-delivered program. *Foreign Language Annals, 22*(3), 283–294.

Iuppa, N. V. (1984). *A practical guide to interactive video design.* White Plains, NY: Knowledge Industry Publications, Inc.

Jonassen, D. H. (1984). The generic disc: Realizing the potential of adaptive, interactive videodiscs. *Educational Technology, 24*(1), 21–24.

Jonassen, D. H. (1985). Interactive lesson designs: A taxonomy. *Educational Technology, 25*(7), 7–17.

Jones, L. L., and Smith, S. G. (1989). [Lights, camera, reaction] The interactive videodisc: A tool for teaching chemistry. *Technological Horizons in Education, 16*(7), 78–85.

Jones, T. (1988). 'Dovetailing chunks': A technique for optimizing interactive videodisc design. *Technological Horizons in Education, 16*(2), 90–94.

Kelly, L. E., and others. (1988). Developing an interactive video disc application. *Journal of Physical Education, Recreation and Dance, 59*(4), 22–26.

King, J. M., and others. (1990). Optical disc technology: Education trend of the future? *Technology Teacher, 49*(8), 25–29.

Laurillard, M. (1984). Interactive video and the control of learning. *Educational Technology, 24*(6), 7–15.

Leonard, W. H. (1989). A comparison of student reactions to biology instruction by interactive videodisc or conventional laboratory. *Journal of Research in Science Teaching, 26*(2), 95–104.

Lindsey, J. (1984). The challenge of designing for interactive video. *Instructional Innovator, 29*(6), 17–20.

Litchfield, B. C. (1990). Criteria for evaluating videodisc interactivity. *Performance and Instruction, 29*(6), 23–26.

Lookatch, R. P. (1989). Options for interactive video. *Training and Development Journal, 43*(12), 65–67.

Lookatch, R. P. (1990). How to talk to a talking head. *Training and Development Journal, 44*(9), 63–65.

Maguire, D. J. (1989). The Domesday Interactive Videodisc System in geography teaching. *Journal of Georgraphy in Higher Education, 13*(1), 55–68.

Martin, R. J. (1987-88). Interactive video: Easier than you think. *Computing Teacher, 15*(4), 39–41.

Mashiter, J. (1988). Interactive video in science. *School Science Review, 69*, 446–450.

McHale, J., and Flegg, D. (1988). How to make the best of interactive video. *Transition from Education through Employment*, 21–22.

McInervney, M. (1989). Enlivening physics, a local video disc project. *Physics Teacher, 27*(3), 151–154.

Mercer, J., and others. (1989). The laser videodisc for interactive CAL in pathology. *Computers and Education, 13*(3), 245–250.

Miles, D. (1990). Videodiscs in community college education. *Community/Junior College Quarterly of Research and Practice, 14*(3), 251–257.

Milheim, W. D. (1990). The effects of pacing and sequence control in an interactive video lesson. *Educational and Training Technology International, 27*(1), 7–19.

Norris, N., and others. (1990). Evaluating new technology: The case of the interactive video in schools (IVIS) programme. *British Journal of Educational Technology, 21*(2), 84–94.

Nurminen, R., and others. (1988). An interactive videodisc project: A case study from the Technical Research Centre of Finland. *Electronic Library*, 6(3), 174–182.

O'Neill, P. N. (1990). Developing videodisc instruction for the health sciences: A consortium approach. *Academic Medicine*, 65(10), 624–627.

O'Sullivan, M., and others. (1989). Interactive video technology in teacher education. *Journal of Teacher Education*, 40(4), 20–25.

Parkinson, C. F. (1989). A comparative study between interactive television and traditional lecture course offerings for nursing students. *Nursing and Health Care*, 10(9), 498–502.

Pavlonnis, T. (1988). Interactive video—A spellbinding approach to solid learning. *Media and Methods*, 24(5), 21–22, 24, 27.

Peppard, H. (1989). Language learning with laser. *Journal of Reading*, 32(7), 628–633.

Phillips, T. L., and others. (1988). The effects of practice and orienting activities on learning from interactive video. *Educational Communications and Technology Journal*, 36(2), 93–102.

Reynolds, K. E. (1988). Videodisks serve up learning opportunities on a silvery platter. *American School Board Journal*, 175(3), 46–47.

Rickelman, R. J. (1988). The printout: Interactive video technology in reading. *Reading Teacher*, 41(8), 824–826.

Rubeck, R. F. (1990). The interactive videodisc in healthcare. *Academic Medicine*, 65(10), 624.

Sales, G. C. (1989). An introduction to videodisc III: Videodisc hardware. *Computing Teacher*, 16(7), 50–51.

Salpeter, J. (1987). The archival videodisc: A multi-media library you can hold in one hand. *Classroom Computer Learning*, 7(4), 49–55.

Schaffer, L. C., and Hannafin, M. J. (1986). The effects of progressive interactivity on learning from interactive video. *Educational Communications and Technology Journal*, 34, 89–96.

Schital, A. (1989). The design and development of an interactive videodisc for foreign language learning. *Educational Technology*, 29(7), 48–52.

Schmidt, H. (1989). Real conversation as a motivational factor through interactive video. *Canadian Modern Language Review*, 45(2), 329–338.

Schroeder, J. E. (1984). A pedagogical mode of instruction of interactive videodisc. *Journal of Educational Technology Systems*, 12(4), 311–317.

Schulz, R. A. (1988). The interactive videodisc and its potential for second-language acquisition. *Unterrichtspraxis, 21*(1), 55–59.

Schwartz, E. (1987). *The educators' handbook to interactive videodisc* (2nd ed.). Washington, DC: Association for Educational Communications and Technology.

Scott, T. M., and others. (1989). Interactive videodisc in computer-assisted language learning: A communicative project. *System, 17*(1), 49–60.

Seal-Wanner, C. (1988). Interactive video systems: Their promise and educational potential. *Teachers College Record, 89*(3), 373–383.

Slike, S. B., and others. (1989). The efficiency and effectiveness of an interactive videodisc system to teach sign language vocabulary. *American Annals of the Deaf, 134*(4), 288–290.

Smith, E. E., and Lehman, J. D.(1988). Interactive video: Implications of the literature for science education. *Journal of Computers in Mathematics and Science Teaching, 8*(1), 25–31.

Straker, N. (1988). Interactive video: A cost-effective model for mathematics and science classrooms. *British Journal of Educational Technology, 19*(3), 202–210.

Tovar, M. (1989). Effects of active vs. passive review strategies on recalling information from an interactive video instructional programme. *Canadian Journal of Educational Communication, 18*(3), 181–191.

Weigand, I. (1985). Videodisc players: Pasts and futures. *Video Manager, 8*(3), 14–15.

West, G. (1989). An interactive video program: TOPIC (training for oral proficiency interviewing competence). *CALICO Journal, 6*(3), 51–59.

White, B. M., and others. (1989). The cost-effectiveness of an interactive video system for science instruction. *Educational Technology, 29*(12), 19–23.

Wright, B., and Dillon, P. (1990). Some applications of interactive video in initial teacher training. *Education and Training Technology International, 27*(1), 43–50.

Zollman, D. (1984). Videodisc-computer interfaces. *Educational Technology, 24*(1), 25–27.

Glossary of Terms

ASCII—American Standard Code for Information Interchange. A standardized code for representing characters which is recognized by most computer systems.

Audit Trail—The record of a user's path taken through an interactive multimedia program.

Authoring Language—A computer language which is specifically designed for developing computer-assisted instruction. In order to be effective, the user requires some knowledge of computer programming.

Authoring System—A computer program which is designed for computer-assisted instruction development. Procedures are predefined, and require little or no programming knowledge on the part of the user.

Bar Code Reader—An infra-red scanning device which interprets bar coded commands for a videodisc player.

Bit-Mapped Graphics—Graphics composed of pixels which are individually addressed and accessed.

Branching—Moving the user from one sequence in a program to another, according to instructions in the program.

CAI—Computer-assisted instruction.

Capacitive Disc—An obsolete videodisc system that used capacitance signals embedded on the disc and a stylus which touched the surface of the disc to read encoded information.

CAV—Constant angular velocity. A CAV videodisc revolves continuously at 1800 rpm, one revolution per frame, making each frame of a CAV disc addressable, a basic requirement for interactive videodiscs.

CBI—Computer-based instruction.

CBT—Computer-based training.

CD—Compact disc. A format which records digital data on 12-cm optical discs.

CD-I—Compact disc–interactive. A compact disc format which includes audio, video, and program data.

CD-ROM—Compact disc–read only memory. A format for recording data on compact discs, permitting virtual storage of a large amount of information in a small format.

Chapter—A consecutive sequence of frames on a videodisc, usually identified as a coherent portion of a treatment.

Chapter Stop—A code embedded in the vertical blanking interval of a videodisc that enables certain videodisc players to locate the beginning of chapters.

Check Cassette—Either a $^1/_2$ inch or $^3/_4$ inch videocassette version of an encoded edit master used for review and approval before duplicating final copies of a videodisc.

Check Disc—A disc version of an encoded edit master which does not contain digital control programs, used for review and approval of a videodisc.

CLV—Constant linear velocity. A CLV or extended-play videodisc maintains a consistent length for each frame, thus enabling longer playing time per side, but sacrificing individual frame access in most players. Reference to locations on CLV discs is limited to time in minutes and seconds.

Conceptual Geography—The post-production process of determining that all video components exist, conforming them to the flowchart, and calculating disc space requirements.

Courseware—Instructional materials in a complete mediated format. May refer to a single instructional component, such as a computer-assisted instruction program, or a multiple instructional entity, such as guidebooks, videodiscs, and computer-assisted instruction.

Cue—A code recorded on one of the lines in the vertical-blanking interval (VBI) that results in frame numbers, picture codes, chapter codes, closed captions, white flags, etc., on a videodisc.

Digital Audio—Audio signals which have been encoded as a series of binary digits.

Digital Video—Video signals which have been encoded as a series of binary digits. In this format they can be accessed and manipulated in a computer program.

Disc—Optical storage medium from which data are read by a laser. Commonly includes CDs, CD-ROMs, and videodiscs.

Disk—Common abbreviation for *diskette*, which is a magnetic storage medium used with computers. Sometimes also called a floppy disk.

Driver—The portion of a computer program that controls peripherals, such as videodisc players, CD-ROM players, and disc drives.

DVI—Digital video interactive. A format for placing digital video on a compact disc. Compressed files can provide up to 72 minutes of full motion video on a CD.

Edit Master—The original final copy of an edited videotape. Videodiscs are copied from an edit master tape.

Field—A scan of 262 lines on the screen at $^1/_{60}$ second, constituting half of a complete video frame (see **Frame**).

Field Dominance—An indication of whether video frames begin with Field 1 or Field 2.

Flowchart—A diagram which illustrates the paths a user can follow through an instructional treatment.

Font—A collection of all characters making up a particular combination of typeface, typestyle, and size. In common computer usage, however, *font* has come to mean the family of a particular typeface (i.e., all typestyles and sizes of a typeface).

Frame—Two complete scans of the video screen at $^1/_{30}$ second. A frame is composed of two fields (each 262 lines). A single frame is a standard CAV videodisc reference point. There can be as many as 54,000 addressable frames on one side of a CAV videodisc.

Frame Accuracy—Editing videotape so that a single video frame is transferred for each intended still frame.

Frame Number—The number associated with each frame on a CAV format videodisc recorded in the vertical blanking interval.

Freeze Frame—A single frame from a motion sequence that is stopped.

Full Frame Time Code—Also known as on-drop frame time code. A SMPTE standard for addressing the time code for a videotape which preserves accurate frame counts instead of matching frames to real time. Edit masters for videodisc production must use this format.

Genlock—Synchronization generator lock. A method of matching the timing of a video system and outside signals, so as to overlay or combine one signal with another.

Graphics Tablet—A tablet on which freehand drawings can be created and input to a computer.

High Sierra—A name for a popular data format for CD-ROM.

Hypermedia—An approach to information storage and retrieval which provides multiple linkages among elements. In IMI, it allows the learner to navigate easily from one piece of information to another.

Icon—A graphic which identifies a function to be performed by a computer program. For example, an icon of a garbage can is used for disposing of unwanted files on a Macintosh computer.

Interaction—A reciprocal dialogue between the user and the system.

Interlace—In NTSC video, the scanning lines from one video field are laid down. After retrace, the scanning lines from the other video field are laid down so that they fall in between the previous lines. This "knitting together" of scan lines is called interlacing, and it results in one full frame of video.

ISO-9660 The most commonly used format for recording data on CD-ROM discs.

Landing Pad—A range of frames within which a videodisc player can locate a frame or frame sequence. Landing pad (LPD) is also a command that modifies the number of times a player attempts to locate a frame following an unsuccessful search.

Laser—Light amplification by stimulated emission of radiation. Lasers produce focussed beams of light which are used to read optical data on videodiscs, CDs, and CD-ROMs.

Leading—The vertical spacing between lines of text. Leading is commonly expressed in **points**.

Level of Interactivity—The potential for interaction prescribed by the capabilities of videodisc hardware and external intervention. Conventionally, Levels I, II, and III are labels used. (See discussion of a new taxonomy of interactivity based on the quality of interaction in Chapter 1.)

Level I—A level of interactivity in which the user can control a videodisc player with the keypad, but has no other method of influencing the order of presentation.

Level II—A videodisc presentation controlled by a digital program permanently recorded on the disc.

Level III—A videodisc presentation controlled externally, often by a computer. The computer controls the presentation, and the videodisc player acts as a peripheral device.

Mastering—A real-time process in which the premaster videotape is used to modulate a laser beam onto a photosensitive glass master disc.

Menu—A sequence or list of choices presented to the user in a program.

MIDI—Musical Instrument Digital Interface. MIDI is a set of standards for a common language, or protocol, for communication between synthesizers (and other electronic instruments) and computers manufactured by different companies.

Mouse—A computer interface with a button(s) mounted on a ball. It is rolled to position a cursor on the screen, and the button is depressed to initiate an action.

Multimedia—An instructional program which includes a variety of integrated sources in the instruction. The program is intentionally designed in segments, and viewer responses to structured opportunities (e.g., menus, problems, simulated crises, questions, virtual environments) influence the sequence, size, content, and shape of the program.

Non-Drop Frame Time Code—(See **Full-Frame Time Code**)

NTSC—The North American television standard based on 30 frames per second and 525 scan lines, specified by the National Television Standards Committee.

Optical Disc—A videodisc that uses a light beam to read information from the surface of the disc.

Optical Reflective Videodisc—Method by which the laser beam reads data encoded on an optical videodisc. In the case of a reflective disc, the beam is focused on information just below the surface of the disc, and reflected onto a photosensitive pick-up device.

PAL— A television standard used widely in Western Europe and some other countries based on 25 frames per second and 625 scan lines.

Picture Stop—An instruction encoded in the vertical blanking interval on the videodisc to stop the videodisc player on a predetermined frame.

Point—a measure of length used in typography, equal to approximately $1/72$ inch.

Post-production/Premastering—The process of editing, assembly, evaluation, revision, and coding of source media. A premaster or edit master is a fully coded videotape, with the exception of computer code.

Proof Disc—A final disc version of a master tape, including Level II digital control programs. The proof disc usually serves as the final approval copy before replication begins.

Remediation—A portion of instruction which is designed to correct a specific learning deficiency.

RGB—Video signals which use separate red, green, and blue signals to compose the picture.

RS-232C—A serial interface used to connect computers to peripheral devices.

Scan—A player option which allows the user to quickly cover the surface of the disc with the video displayed.

Search—To rapidly access a single frame or a sequence of frames on a disc without video displayed.

SECAM—A television standard used in France, Eastern Europe, the Commonwealth of Independent States, and several other countries based on 25 frames per second and 625 scan lines (but different from PALS).

Signal-To-Noise Ratio—The relative strength of a picture or audio signal to its residual background information. The higher the signal-to-noise ratio, the better the picture or sound.

Slow Motion—In videodisc technology, the controlled movement of the laser from frame to frame at an apparent rate of less than 30 frames per second. Achieved by rescanning each frame x number of times before moving to the next frame.

SMPTE Code—Also known as nondrop or full frame time code, this is a standardized method of addressing a videotape. It was developed by the Society of Motion Picture and Television Engineers, and gives an accurate location of each video frame on a videotape.

Sound Synthesis—The artifical production of speech and sound effects.

Source Media—All media selected for assembly onto a videodisc edit master tape (i.e., 16 mm film, videotape, 35 mm slides, etc.).

Step—To move one frame forward or reverse on a videodisc.

Still Frame—Still material, including photographs, line drawings, pages, and graphics, designed and presented as a single videodisc frame.

Symmetric Digital Video System—A video system which can store and play back compressed digital pictures.

Tactical Geography—The post-production process of "fine tuning" conceptual geography decisions. Includes making decisions about the efficient layout of video elements.

Three-two (3-2) Pulldown—A means of transferring film shot at 24 frames per second (fps) into video (30 fps). The first film frame is actually duplicated on three video fields, and the next film frame is duplicated on two fields.

Touch Screen—An interface usually attached to the front of a display screen which can interpret the intrusion or pressure of an object introduced to the screen.

Transmissive Videodisc—One method by which a laser beam reads data encoded on an optical videodisc. In the case of the transmissive disc, the laser beam passes through the transparent surface of the disc. Largely an obsolete format.

Typeface— A collection of characters having the same general shape or outline.

Vertical Blanking Interval—Twenty-one blanked lines during Fields 1 and 2 on the videodisc, where frame numbers picture stops, chapter stops, closed captions, etc., are encoded.

Video Overlay—The process of keying video from the computer over NTSC video.

White Flag—A code that identifies the starting field in a new film frame.

Window—A portion of a display devoted to a single source of material on a multimedia display screen. A window may occupy a full screen, or it may share the screen display with other windows of information.

References

Alesandrini, K. L. (1984). Pictures and adult learning. *Instructional Science*, *13*, 63–77.

Alessi, S. M., and Trollip, S. R. (1985). *Computer-based instruction: Methods and Development*. Englewood Cliffs, NJ: Prentice-Hall.

Alexander, T. (1985). Artificial intelligence. *Popular Computing, May*, 66–69, 142–145.

American Psychological Association. (1983). *Publication manual of the American Psychological Association* (3rd ed.). Washington, DC: The Association.

Amsterdam, J. (1985). Expert systems. *Popular Computing, May*, 70–72, 150, 153.

Anderton, C. (1988). The MIDI recording studio. *Musician*, Special edition, 22–27, 55.

Anglin, G. J. (1985, January). *Prose-relevant pictures and older learners' recall of written prose*. Paper presented at the Annual Convention of the Association for Educational Communications and Technology, Anaheim, CA. (ERIC Document Reproduction Service No. ED 256 305)

Anglin, G. J. (1986a, January). *Effect of pictures on recall of written prose: How durable are picture effects?* Paper presented at the Annual Convention of the Association for Educational Communications and Technology, Las Vegas, NV. (ERIC Document Reproduction Service No. ED 267 755)

Anglin, G. J. (1986b). Prose-relevant pictures and older learners' recall of written prose. *Educational Communications and Technology Journal, 34*, 131–136.

Anglin, G. J. (1987). Effect of pictures on recall of written prose: How durable are picture effects? *Educational Communications and Technology Journal, 35*, 25–30.

Anglin, G. J., and Kwak, E. (1991, February). *Research on pictures: Knowledge acquisition, visual thinking, and cognitive skill acquisition: A guide to the literature, 1986–1990*. Paper presented at the Annual Convention of the Association for Educational Communications and Technology, Orlando, FL.

Apple Computer, Inc. (1987). *Human interface guidelines: The Apple desktop interface*. Reading, MA: Addison-Wesley Publishing Co.

Arnett, N. (1990). Digital video arrives. *PC Magazine, July*, 152–153.

Arnone, M. P., and Grabowski, B. L. (1991). Effect of variations in learner control on childrens' curiosity and learning from interactive video. In M. R. Simonson and C. Hargrave (Eds.), *Proceedings of the 1991 Convention of the Association for Educational Communications and Technology* (pp. 45–67). Orlando, FL: Association for Educational Communications and Technology.

Arwady, J. W., and Gayeski, D. M. (1989). *Using video: Interactive and linear designs.* Englewood Cliffs, NJ: Educational Technology Publications.

Aspillaga, M. (1991a). Implications of screen design upon learning. *Journal of Educational Technology Systems, 20*(1), 53–58.

Aspillaga, M. (1991b). Screen design: Location of information and its effects on learning. *Journal of Computer-Based Instruction, 18*(3), 89–92.

Barker, P. (1990). Designing interactive learning systems. *Educational and Training Technology International, 27*(2), 125–145.

Beasley, R. E., and Vila, J. A. (1992). The identification of navigation patterns in a multimedia environment: A case study. *Journal of Educational Multimedia and Hypermedia, 1*(2), 209–222.

Bechtel, B. (1989). *CD-ROM and the Macintosh computer.* Apple Computer, Inc. Advanced Technology Group.

Bergman, R. E., and Moore, T. V. (1990). *Managing interactive video/ multimedia projects.* Englewood Cliffs, NJ: Educatonal Technology Publications.

Berry, L. (1991). Visual complexity and pictorial memory: A fifteen year research perspective. In M. R. Simonson and M. Treimer (Eds.), *Proceedings of selected research paper presentations at the 1985 Annual Convention of the Association for Educational Communications and Technology*(pp. 92–102). Ames, IA: Iowa State University Press.

Best, J. W., and Kahn, J. W. (1989). *Research in education* (6th ed.). Englewood Cliffs, NJ: Prentice-Hall.

Black, T. R. (1987). CAL delivery selection criteria and authoring systems. *Journal of Computer-assisted Learning, 3*(4), 204–213.

Blattner, M. M., Sumikawa, D. A., and Greenberg, R. M. (1989). Earcons and icons: Their structure and common design principles. *Human-Computer Interaction, 4,* 11–44.

Bork, A. (1984). Computers in composition instruction. In R. Shostak (Ed.), *Courseware design: Design considerations.* Eugene, OR: ICCE Publications.

Bork, A., and Promicter, N. (1990). Practical techniques useful in authoring technology-based learning material. *Journal of Computer-Based Instruction, 17*(2), 53–60.

Borsook, T. (1991). Harnessing the power of interactivity for instruction. In M. R. Simonson and C. Hargrave (Eds.), *Proceedings of the 1991 Convention of the Association for Educational Communications and Technology* (pp. 103–117). Orlando, FL: Association for Educational Communications and Technology.

Braden, R. (1986). Visuals for interactive video: Images for a new technology. *Educational Technology, 26*(5), 18–23.

Brandon, P. R. (1988). Recent developments in instructional hardware and software. *Educational Technology, 28*(10), 7–12.

Brody, P. J. (1982). Affecting instructional textbooks through pictures. In D. H. Jonassen (Ed.), *The technology of text: Principles for structuring, designing, and displaying text* (pp. 301–316). Englewood Cliffs, NJ: Educational Technology Publications.

Brody, P. J. (1984, April). *Research on and research with interactive video.* Paper presented at the Annual Meeting of the American Educational Research Association, New Orleans, LA. (ERIC Document Reproduction Service No. ED 246 885)

Brooks, L. W., Danserau, D. F., Spurlin, J. E., and Holley, C. D. (1983). Effects of headings on text processing. *Journal of Educational Psychology, 75*, 292–302.

Brozo, W. G., Schmelzer, R. V., and Spires, H. A. (1983). The beneficial effect of chunking on good readers' comprehension of expository prose. *Journal of Reading, 26*, 442–445.

Burger, M. L. (1985, January). *Authoring languages/systems comparisons.* Paper presented at the Annual Conference of the Association for Educational Communications and Technology, Anaheim, CA.

Burns, D., Venit, S., and Hansen, R. (1988). *The electronic publisher.* New York: Brady.

Buxton, W. (1989). Introduction to this special issue on nonspeech audio. *Human-Computer Interaction, 4*, 1–9.

Campbell, J. (1983). *Interactive videodisc design and production workshop guide.* Orem, UT: WICAT, Inc. (ERIC Document Reproduction Service No. ED 244 580)

Canada, K., and Bruska, F. (1991). The technological gender gap: Evidence and recommendations for educators and computer-based instruction designers. *Educational Technology Research and Development, 39*(2), 43–51.

Carrier, C. A., and Jonassen, D. H. (1988). Adapting courseware to accommodate individual differences. In D. H. Jonassen (Ed.), *Instructional designs for microcomputer courseware*. Hillsdale, NJ: Lawrence Erlbaum Associates.

Carrier, C. A., and Sales, G. C. (1987). Pair versus individual work on the acquisition of concepts in a computer-based instructional lesson. *Journal of Computer-Based Instruction, 14*(1), 11–17.

Carver, R. P. (1970). Effect of a "chunked" typography on reading rate and comprehension. *Journal of Applied Psychology, 54,* 288–296.

Clark, M. L., and Romaniuk, E. W. (1989). The effects of groups sizes on achievement and attitude using interactive videodisc courseware. In *Transitions: Proceedings of the AMTEC '89 Conference.* Edmonton, AB: Association for Media and Technology in Education in Canada.

Cockayne, S. (1991). Effects of small group sizes on learning with interactive videodisc. *Educational Technology, 31*(2), 43–45.

Cook, E. K. (1990). The use of Macintosh authoring languages in effective computer-assisted instruction. *Journal of Educational Technology Systems, 18*(2), 109–122.

Cromer, W. (1970). The difference model: A new explanation for some reading difficulties. *Journal of Educational Psychology, 61,* 471–483. Cited by O'Shea, L. J., and Sindelar, P. T. (1983). The effects of segmenting written discourse on the reading comprehension of low- and high-performance readers. *Reading Research Quarterly, 18,* 458–465.

Crowell, P., and Bork, A. (1989). Authoring systems. *Instruction Delivery Systems, 3*(2), 10–15.

Dalton, D. W. (1990). The effects of cooperative learning strategies on achievement and attitudes during interactive video. *Journal of Computer-Based Instruction, 17*(1), 8–16.

Dalton, D. W., and Hannafin, M. J. (1987). Examining the effects of varied computer-based reinforcement on self-esteem and achievement: An exploratory study. *Association for Educational Data Systems Journal, 18*(3), 172–182.

Davies, I. K. (1976). *Objectives in curriculum design.* New York: McGraw-Hill.

Davis, D. B. (1986). Artificial intelligence enters the mainstream. *High Technology, July,* 16–23.

Davis, F. E., Barry, J., and Wiesenberg, M. (1986). *Desktop publishing.* Homewood, IL: Dow Jones-Irwin.

Dean, C. T. (1988). Storyboarding for computer-based training: A technique in transition. *Performance and Instruction, 27*(5), 8–14.

Dear, B. L. (1986). Artificial intelligence techniques: Applications for courseware development. *Educational Technology, July ,* 7–15.

DeBloois, M. L. (1982). *Videodisc/microcomputer courseware design.* Englewood Cliffs, NJ: Educational Technology Publications.

Dede, C. (1990). Knowledge processing: Navigating the sea of information. *Authorware, 3*(1), 17–22.

Devlin, S. (1982). Premastering for an interactive videodisc. *Educational and Industrial Television, 14*(11), 38.

Dick, W., and Carey, L. (1990). *The systematic design of instruction* (3rd ed.). New York: Harper Collins Publishers.

Duchastel, P. C. (1978). Illustrating instructional texts. *Educational Technology, 18*(11), 36–39.

Duchastel, P., and Waller, R. (1979). Pictorial illustration in instructional texts. *Educational Technology, 19*(11), 20–25.

Duchnicky, R. L., and Kolers, P. A. (1983). Readability of text scrolled on visual display terminals as a function of window size. *Human Factors, 25*(6), 683–692.

Dwyer, F. M. (1978). *Strategies for improving visual learning.* State College, PA: Learning Services.

Eckols, S. L., and Rossett, A. (1989). HyperCard for the design, development, and delivery of instruction. *Performance Improvement Quarterly, 2*(4), 2–20.

Felker, D. B., Pickering, F., Charrow, V. R., Holland, V. M., and Redish, J. C. (1981). *Guidelines for document designers.* Washington, DC: American Institutes for Research.

Fleming, M., and Levie, W. H. (1978). *Instructional message design.* Englewood Cliffs, NJ: Educational Technology Publications.

Fleming, M. L. (1987). Displays and communication. In R. M. Gagné (Ed.), *Instructional technology: Foundations* (pp. 223–260). Hillsdale, NJ: Lawrence Erlbaum Associates.

Floyd, S., and Floyd, B. (1982). *Handbook of interactive video.* White Plains, NY: Knowledge Industry Publications, Inc.

Frase, L. T., and Schwartz, B. J. (1979). Typographical cues that facilitate comprehension. *Journal of Educational Psychology, 71*, 197–206.

Frick, T. W. (1988, August). *Non-metric temporal path analysis: A method by which tutorial systems can learn through inquiry.* Paper presented at the 4th Annual International Conference on Systems Research, Cybernetics and Informatics, Baden-Baden, West Germany.

Frick, T. W. (1989). Bayesian adaptation during computer-based tests and computer-guided practice exercises. *Journal of Educational Computing Research*, *5*(1), 89–114.

Frick, T. W. (1990a). A comparison of three decision models for adapting the length of computer-based mastery tests. *Journal of Educational Computing Research*, *6*(4), 479–513.

Frick, T. W. (1990b). Analysis of patterns in time: A method of recording and quantifying temporal relations in education. *American Educational Research Journal*, *27*(1), 180–204.

Frick, T. W. (1991, February). *A comparison of an expert systems approach to computerized adaptive testing and an item response theory model.* Paper presented at the Annual Conference of the Association for Educational Communications and Technology, Orlando, FL.

Galbreath, J. (1992a). The educational buzzword of the 1990's: Multimedia, or is it hypermedia, or interactive multimedia, or ...? *Educational Technology*, *32*(4), 15–19.

Galbreath, J. (1992b). The coming of digital desktop media. *Educational Technology*, *32*(6), 27–37.

Garner, K. H. (1991). 20 rules for arranging text on a screen. In R. B. Frantzreb (Ed.), *Training and development yearbook, 1991 edition* (pp. 4.16–4.18). Englewood Cliffs, NJ: Prentice-Hall.

Gaver, W. W. (1989). The SonicFinder: An interface that uses auditory icons. *Human-Computer Interaction*, *4*, 67–94.

Gay, G. (1986). Interaction of learner control and prior understanding in computer-assisted video instruction. *Journal of Educational Psychology*, *78*, 225–227.

Gayeski, D. (1983). *Corporate and instructional video design and production.* Englewood Cliffs, NJ: Prentice-Hall.

Gayeski, D. (1992). Making sense of multimedia: Introduction to special issue. *Educational Technology*, *32*(5), 9–13.

Geber, B. (1989). Whither interactive videodisc? *Training*, *26*(3), 47–49.

Gillingham, M. G. (1988). Text in computer-based instruction: What the research says. *Journal of Computer-Based Instruction*, *15*(1),1–6.

Glynn, S. M., Britton, B. K., and Tillman, M. H. (1985). Typographical cues in text: Management of the reader's attention. In D. H. Jonassen (Ed.), *The technology of text (volume two): Principles for structuring, designing, and displaying text* (pp. 192–209). Englewood Cliffs, NJ: Educational Technology Publications.

Grabinger, R. S. (1984). CRT text design: Psychological attributes underlying the evaluation of models of CRT text displays. *Journal of Visual Verbal Languaging, 4*(1), 17–39.

Grabinger, R. S. (1985, January). *Relationships among text format variables in computer-generated text.* Paper presented at the Annual Conference of the Association for Educational Communications and Technology, Research and Theory Division, Las Vegas, NV.

Grabinger, R. S. (1989). Screen layout design: Research into the overall appearance of the screen. *Computers in Human Behavior, 5*, 175–183.

Grabinger, R. S. (1992). *Model vs. real screen perceptions: Viewer preferences.* Manuscript submitted for publication.

Grabinger, R. S., and Amedeo, D. (1985). CRT text layout: Prominent layout variables. In M. R. Simonson and M. Treimer (Eds.), *Proceedings of selected research paper presentations at the 1985 Annual Convention of the Association for Educational Communications and Technology.* Ames, IA: Iowa State University Press.

Gregory, M., and Poulton, E. C. (1970). Even versus uneven right-hand margins and the rate of comprehension in reading. *Ergonomics, 13*(4), 427–434.

Grimes, T. (1990). Audio-video correspondence and its role in attention and memory. *Educational Technology Research and Development, 38*(3), 15–26.

Gronlund, N. E. (1985). *Stating objectives for classroom instruction* (3rd ed.). New York: Macmillan.

Gropper, G. L. (1976). A behavioral perspective on media selection. *AV Communication Review, 24*, 157–186.

Hannafin, K. M., and Mitzel, H. E. (1990). CBI authoring tools in post-secondary institutions: A review and critical examination. *Computers and Education, 14*(3), 197–204.

Hannafin, M. J. (1984). Guidelines for determining locus of instructional control in the design of computer-assisted instruction. *Journal of Instructional Development, 7*(3), 6–10.

Hannafin, M. J. (1989). Interaction strategies and emerging instructional technologies: Psychological perspectives. *Canadian Journal of Educational Communication, 18*(3), 167–179.

Hannafin, M. J., and Colamaio, M. E. (1987). The effects of variations in lesson control and practice on learning from interactive video. *Educational Communications and Technology Journal, 35*(4), 203–212.

Hannafin, M. J., Garhart, C., Rieber, L. P., and Phillips, T. L. (1985). Keeping interactive video in perspective: Tentative guidelines and cautions in the design of interactive video. In E. Miller and M. Mosley (Eds.), *Educational media and technology yearbook*. Denver, CO: Libraries Unlimited.

Hannafin, M. J., and Hooper, S. (1989). An integrated framework for CBI screen design and layout. *Computers in Human Behavior, 5,* 155–165.

Hannafin, M. J., and Peck, K. L. (1988). *The design, development, and evaluation of instructional software*. New York: Macmillan.

Hannafin, M. J., and Rieber, L. P. (1989a). Psychological foundations of instructional design for emerging computer-based instructional technologies: Part I. *Educational Technology Research and Development, 37*(2), 91–101.

Hannafin, M. J., and Rieber, L. P. (1989b). Psychological foundations of instructional design for emerging computer-based instructional technologies: Part II. *Educational Technology Research and Development, 37*(2), 102–114.

Hartley, J. (1987). Designing electronic text: The role of print-based research. *Educational Communications and Technology Journal, 35*(1), 3–17.

Hartley, J., and Burnhill, P. (1977). Fifty guidelines for improving instructional text. *Programmed Learning and Educational Technology, 14,* 65–73.

Hartley, J., and Jonassen, D. H. (1985). The role of headings in printed and electronic text. In D. H. Jonassen (Ed.), *The technology of text (volume two): Principles for structuring, designing, and displaying text* (pp. 237–263). Englewood Cliffs, NJ: Educational Technology Publications.

Hartley, J., and Trueman, M. (1983). The effects of headings in text on recall, search and retrieval. *British Journal of Educational Psychology, 53,* 205–214.

Harvey, D. A., and Corbett, J. (1991). Unlimited desktop storage: Optical drives that blow away the competition. *Computer Shopper, 11*(11), 230ff.

Hathaway, M. D. (1984). Variables of computer screen design and how they affect learning. *Educational Technology, 24*(1), 7–11.

Hazari, S. (1992). Multimedia: Is it the right tool for your instructional application? *Journal of Educational Multimedia and Hypermedia, 1*(2), 143–146.

Hazen, M. (1987). Criteria for choosing among instructional software authoring tools. *Journal of Research in Computing in Education, 20*(2), 117–128.

Heath, T. (1981). Alternative videodisc systems. *Videodisc/Videotext, 1*(4), 228–238.

Heines, J. M. (1984). *Screen design strategies for computer-assisted instruction*. Bedford, MA: Digital Press.

Heinich R., Molenda, M., and Russell, J. (1989). *Instructional media and the new technologies of instruction* (3rd ed.). New York: Macmillan.

Helsel, S. (1992). Virtual reality and education. *Educational Technology, 32*(5), 38–42.

Higginbotham-Wheat, N. (1988, November). *Perspectives on implementation of learner control in CBI.* Paper presented at the Annual Meeting of the Mid-South Educational Research Association, Lexington, KY. (ERIC Document Reproduction Service No. ED 305 898)

Higginbotham-Wheat, N. (1990). Learner control: When does it work? In M. R. Simonson and C. Hargrave (Eds.), *Proceedings of the 1990 Convention of the Association for Educational Communications and Technology.* Anaheim, CA: Association for Educational Communications and Technology. (ERIC Document Reproduction Service No. ED 323 930)

Holden, C. (1986). Artificial intelligence techniques: Applications for courseware development. *Educational Technology, July,* 7–15.

Hooper, S., and Hannafin, M. J. (1986). Variables affecting the legibility of computer-generated text. *Journal of Instructional Development, 9*(4), 22–28.

Huber, D. M. (1991). *The MIDI manual.* Carmel, IN: Howard W. Sams and Company.

Huber, D. M., and Runstein, R. E. (1989). *Modern recording techniques* (3rd ed.). Carmel, IN: Howard W. Sams and Company.

Hunka, S. (1989). Design guidelines for CAI authoring systems. *Educational Technology, 29*(11), 12–17.

Isaacs, G. (1987). Text screen design for computer-assisted learning. *British Journal of Educational Technology, 1*(18), 41–51.

Iuppa, N. V. (1984). *A practical guide to interactive video design.* White Plains, NY: Knowledge Industry Publications.

Jesky, R. R., and Berry, L. H. (1991). The effects of pictorial complexity and cognitive style on visual recall memory. In M. R. Simonson and C. Hargrave (Eds.), *Proceedings of the 1991 Convention of the Association for Educational Communications and Technology* (pp. 290-296). Orlando, FL: Association for Educational Communications and Technology.

Johnson, R. T., Johnson, D. W., and Stanne, M. B. (1985). Effects of cooperative, competitive and individualistic goal structures on computer-assisted instruction. *Journal of Educational Psychology, 77*(6), 668–677.

Johnston, S. J. (1990). Multimedia. *Info World, 12*(8), 47–52.

Jonassen, D. H. (Ed.) (1982). *The technology of text: Principles for structuring, designing, and displaying text.* Englewood Cliffs, NJ: Educational Technology Publications.

Jonassen, D. H. (1985a). Interactive lesson designs: A taxonomy. *Educational Technology, 25*(6), 7–17.

Jonassen, D. H. (Ed.) (1985b). *The technology of text (volume two): Principles for structuring, designing, and displaying text.* Englewood Cliffs, NJ: Educational Technology Publications.

Jonassen, D. H. (1988). *Instructional designs for microcomputer courseware.* Hillsdale, NJ: Lawrence Erlbaum Associates.

Jonassen, D. H. (1991). Objectivism versus constructivism: Do we need a new philosophical paradigm? *Educational Technology Research and Development, 39*(3), 5–14.

Jonassen, D. H., and Hannum, W. H. (1991). Analysis of task analysis procedures. In G. J. Anglin (Ed.), *Instructional technology: Past, present, and future* (pp. 170–187). Englewood, CO: Libraries Unlimited.

Justen, J. E., Thomas, M. A., and Waldorp, P. B. (1988). Effects of small group versus individual computer-assisted instruction on student achievement. *Educational Technology, 28*(2), 50–52.

Kang, T. J., and Muter, P. (1989). Reading dynamically displayed text. *Behavior and Information Technology, 8*(1), 33–42.

Katz, L. (1992). Essentially multimedia: An explanation of interactive laserdisc and optical technology. *The Canadian Multi Media Magazine, 1*(1), 18-20.

Katz, L., and Keet, C. (1990). *Innovations in laser and optical disc technology.* Calgary, AB: Alberta Laserdisc Committee.

Kearsley, G. (1988). Authoring considerations for hypertext. *Educational Technology, 28*(11), 21–24.

Keller, J. M. (1983). Motivational design of instruction. In C. M. Reigeluth (Ed.), *Instructional design theories and models: An overview of their current status* (pp. 386–434). Hillsdale, NJ: Lawrence Erlbaum Associates.

Kemp, J. E., and Smellie, D. C. (1989). *Planning, producing and using instructional media* (6th ed.). New York: Harper and Row.

Keniske, F. (1984). 1984 computer-based training guide. *Data Training. March,* 1-21.

Kingsbury, G. G., and Weiss, D. J. (1983). A comparison of IRT-based adaptive mastery testing and a sequential mastery testing procedure. In D. Weiss (Ed.), *New horizons in testing* (pp. 257–283). New York: Academic Press.

Kinzie, M. B., Sullivan, H. J., and Berdel, R. L. (1988). Learner control and achievement in science computer-assisted instruction. *Journal of Educational Psychology, 80*(3), 299–303.

Kleper, M. L. (1987). *The illustrated handbook of desktop publishing and typesetting.* Blue Ridge Summit, PA: Tab Books.

Kolers, P. A., Duchnicky, R. L., and Ferguson, D. C. (1981). Eye movement measurement of readability of C.R.T. displays. *Human Factors, 23*(5), 517–527.

Kruk, R. S., and Muter, P. (1984). Reading of continuous text on video screen. *Human Factors, 26*(3), 339–345.

Lehrman, P. D., and Tully, T. (1991). Catch a wave: Digital audio. *MacUser, 7*(10), 94–103.

Leveridge, L. L., and Lyons, D. S. (1983). Which disc player for education? A comparative evaluation. *Educational and Industrial Television, 15*(7), 50–52.

Levie, W. H. (1987). Research on pictures: A guide to the literature. In D. M. Willows and H. A. Houghton (Eds.), *The psychology of illustration, volume 1* (pp. 1–50). New York: Springer-Verlag.

Levie, W. H., and Lentz, R. (1982). Effects of text illustrations: A review of research. *Educational Communications and Technology Journal, 30*, 195–232.

Levin, J. R. (1981). On functions of pictures in prose. In F. J. Pirozzolo and M. C. Wittrock (Eds.), *Neuropsychological and cognitive processes in reading* (pp. 203–228). New York: Academic Press.

Levin, J. R., Anglin, G. J., and Carney, R. N. (1987). On empirically validating functions of pictures in prose. In D. M. Willows and H. A. Houghton (Eds.), *The psychology of illustration, volume 1* (pp. 51–86). New York: Springer-Verlag.

Levin, J. R., and Lesgold, A. M. (1978). On pictures in prose. *Educational Communications and Technology Journal, 26*, 233–243.

Li, Z. (1990). Transaction shells: A new approach to courseware authoring. *Journal of Research on Computing in Education, 23*(1), 72–86.

Lichty, T. (1989). *Design principles for desktop publishers.* Glenview, IL: Scott, Foresman and Co.

Lockheed Missile and Space Company. (1981). *Human factors review of electric power dispatch control centers: Volume 2: Detailed survey results.* Prepared for Electric Power Research Institute, 3412 Hillview Avenue, Palo Alto, CA 94304. Cited by Shneiderman, B. (1987). *Designing the user interface: Strategies for effective human-computer interaction.* Reading, MA: Addison-Wesley Publishing.

López, C. L. (1990, February). *Personalizing math word problems.* Paper presented at the Annual Meeting of the Association for Educational Communications and Technology, Anaheim, CA.

Lucas, L. (1991). Visually designing the computer-learner interface. *Educational Technology, July,* 56–58.

Lucas, L. (1992). Interactivity: What is it and how do you use it? *Journal of Educational Multimedia and Hypermedia, 1*(1), 7–10.

Luk, HK. (1991, April). *An empirical comparison of an expert systems approach and an IRT approach to computer-based adaptive mastery testing.* Paper presented at the Annual Meeting of the American Educational Research Association, Chicago, IL.

Lynch, P. (1991). *Multimedia: Getting started.* Sunnyvale, CA: PUBLIX Information Products, Inc. for Apple Computer, Inc.

Maddux, C. D. (1992). User-developed computer-assisted instruction: Alternatives in authoring software. *Educational Technology, 32*(4), 7–14.

Mager, R. F., and Pipe, P. (1970). *Analyzing performance problems or 'You really oughta wanna'.* Belmont, CA: Fearon Publishers.

Mann, B. L. (1992). The SSF model: Structuring the functions of the sound attribute. *Canadian Journal of Educational Communication, 21,* 45–65.

Markle, S. M. (1983). *Designs for instructional designers.* (2nd ed.) Champaign, IL: Stipes Publishing.

Mason, J. M., and Kendall, J. R. (1979). Facilitating reading comprehension through text structure manipulation. *The Alberta Journal of Educational Research, 25,* 68–76. Cited by O'Shea, L. J., and Sindelar, P. T. (1983). The effects of segmenting written discourse on the reading comprehension of low- and high-performance readers. *Reading Research Quarterly, 18,* 458–465.

Mattoon, J. S., Klein, J. D., and Thurman, R. A. (1991). Learner control versus computer control in instructional simulation. In M. R. Simonson and C. Hargrave (Eds.), *Proceedings of the 1991 Convention of the Association for Educational Communications and Technology* (pp. 481–498). Orlando, FL: Association for Educational Communications and Technology.

Merrill, M. D. (1983). Component display theory. In C. M. Reigeluth (Ed.), *Instructional design theories and models: An overview of their current status* (pp. 279–333). Hillsdale, NJ: Lawrence Erlbaum Associates.

Merrill, M. D. (1985). Where is the authoring in authoring systems? *Journal of Computer-Based Instruction, 12*(4), 90–96.

Merrill, M. D., and Li, Z. (1989). An instructional design expert system. *Journal of Computer-Based Instruction, 16*(3), 95–101.

Merrill, P. F., and Bunderson, C. V. (1981). Preliminary guidelines for employing graphics in instruction. *Journal of Instructional Development, 4*(4), 2–9.

Miles, J. (1987). *Design for desktop publishing.* San Francisco, CA: Chronicle Books.

Milheim, W. D., and Azbell, J. W. (1988). How past research on learner control can aid in the design of interactive video materials. In M. R. Simonson and J. K. Frederick (Eds.), *Proceedings of the 1988 Convention of the Association for Educational Communications and Technology* (pp. 459–472). New Orleans, LA: Association for Educational Communications and Technology. (ERIC Document Reproduction Service No. ED 295 652)

Miller, D. C. (1987). *Special report: Publishers, libraries and CD-ROM: Implications of digital optical printing.* Report distributed to the registrants of the Optical Publishing and Libraries: Cheers or Tears? Preconference Institute, 1987 Americal Library Association Conference, San Francisco, CA.

Miller, R. (1990). Introduction. In R. Bergman and T. Moore, *Managing interactive video/multimedia projects.* Englewood Cliffs, NJ: Educational Technology Publications.

Misanchuk, E. R. (1989a). *Learner preferences for typeface (font) and leading in print materials.* Saskatoon, SK: Division of Extension and Community Relations, The University of Saskatchewan. (ERIC Document Reproduction Service No. ED 307 854)

Misanchuk, E. R. (1989b). Learner preferences for screen text attributes in a Macintosh microcomputer learning environment. In *Transitions: Proceedings of the AMTEC '89 Conference.* Edmonton, AB: Association for Media and Technology in Education in Canada.

Misanchuk, E. R. (1989c). Learner/user preferences for fonts in microcomputer screen displays. *Canadian Journal of Educational Communication, 18*(3), 193–205.

Misanchuk, E. R. (1990). *Learner/user preferences for leading (vertical spacing) in microcomputer screen displays.* Unpublished manuscript, University of Saskatchewan, Extension Division, Saskatoon, SK.

Misanchuk, E. R. (1992). *Preparing instructional text: Document design using desktop publishing.* Englewood Cliffs, NJ: Educational Technology Publications.

Misanchuk, E. R., and Schwier, R. A. (1991). Interactive media audit trails: Approaches and issues. In M. R. Simonson & C. Hargrave (Eds.), *13th annual proceedings of selected research presentations at the 1991 annual convention of the Association for Educational Communications and Technology* (pp. 499–520). Ames, IA: Research and Theory Division, Association for Educational Communications and Technology.

Misanchuk, E. R., and Schwier, R. A. (1992). Representing interactive multimedia and hypermedia audit trails. *Journal of Educational Multimedia and Hypermedia, 1*(3), 1–18.

Morrison, G. R., Ross, S. M., and O'Dell, J. K. (1988). Text density level as a design variable in instructional displays. *Educational Communications and Technology Journal, 36*(1), 103–115.

Morrison, G. R., Ross, S. M., Schultz, C. W., and O'Dell, J. K. (1989). Learner preferences for varying screen densities using realistic stimulus materials with single and multiple designs. *Educational Technology Research and Development, 37*(3), 53–60.

Muncer, S. J., Gorman, B. S., Gorman, S., and Bibel, D. (1986). Right is wrong: An examination of the effect of right justification on reading. *British Journal of Educational Technology, 17*, 5–10.

Muter, P., Kruk, R. S., Buttigieg, M. A., and Kang, T. J. (1988). Reader-controlled computerized presentation of text. *Human Factors, 30*(4), 473–486.

Nelson, T. (1987). *Computer lib/Dream machines.* Redmond, WA: Microsoft Press.

Noble, K. A. (1989). Good writing: What role for the educator? *British Journal of Educational Technology, 20*, 142–144.

Novick, M. R., and Lewis, C. (1974). *Prescribing test length for criterion-referenced measurement* (Tech. Bull. No. 18). Iowa City, IA: American College Testing Program.

O'Shea, L. J., and Sindelar, P. T. (1983). The effects of segmenting written discourse on the reading comprehension of low- and high-performance readers. *Reading Research Quarterly, 18*, 458–465.

Oringel, R. S. (1989). *Audio control handbook for radio and television broadcasting.* Boston, MA: Focal Press.

Paris, J., and Boss, R. W. (1982). The care and maintenance of videodiscs and players. *Videodisc/Videotext, 2*(1), 38–46.

Park, O. and Seidel, R. J. (1989). A multidisciplinary model for development of intelligent computer-assisted instruction. *Educational Technology Research and Development, 37*(3), 72–80.

Parker, R. C. (1988). *The Aldus guide to basic design* (2nd ed.). Seattle, WA: Aldus Corporation.

Paterson, D. G., and Tinker, M. A. (1940). *How to make type readable*. New York: Harper and Row. Cited by Tinker, M. A. (1965). *Bases for effective reading*. Minneapolis, MN: University of Minnesota Press.

Peeck, J. (1987). The role of illustrations in processing and remembering illustrated text. In D. M. Willows and H. A. Houghton (Eds.), *The psychology of illustration, volume 1* (pp. 115–151). New York: Springer-Verlag.

Phillipo, J. (1989). An educator's guide to interfaces and authoring systems. *Electronic Learning, 8*(4), 42, 44–45.

Pioneer Video. (1984). *Post-production and formatting information*. Montvale, NJ: Pioneer Video, Inc.

Printing layout and design. (1968). Albany, NY: Delmar Publishers.

Publish! (1989). *101 best desktop publishing tips, vol. 2*. San Francisco, CA: PCW Communications.

Quinn, K. (1990). Expert system shells: What to look for. *Reference Services Review, 18*(1), 83–86.

Race, P. (1989). Writing to promote learning. *British Journal of Educational Technology, 20*, 215.

Raskin, R. (1990). Multimedia: The next frontier for business? *PC Magazine, July*, 151–192.

Reinking, D. (1992). Differences between electronic and printed texts: An agenda for research. *Journal of Educational Multimedia and Hypermedia, 1*, 11–24.

Reiser, R., and Gagné, R. (1983). *Selecting media for instruction*. Englewood Cliffs, NJ: Educational Technology Publications.

Reynolds, L. (1982). Display problems for teletext. In D. H. Jonassen (Ed.), *The technology of text: Principles for structuring, designing, and displaying text* (pp. 415–437). Englewood Cliffs, NJ: Educational Technology Publications.

Richards, T. C., and Fukuzawa, J. (1989). A checklist for evaluation of courseware authoring systems. *Educational Technology, 29*(10), 24–29.

Rizzo, J. (1990). Maximum movable megabyte: Erasable optical drives. *MacUser, 6*(11), 102–130.

Rizzo, J. (1991). Multifunction optical storage. *MacUser, 7*(11), 108–114.

Rode, M., and Poirot, J. (1989). Authoring systems—are they used? *Journal of Research on Computing in Education, 22*(2), 191–198.

Romiszowski, A. J. (1986). *Developing auto-instructional materials*. New York: Nichols Publishing.

Ross, S. M. (1984). Matching the lesson to the student: Alternative adaptive designs for individualized learning systems. *Journal of Computer-Based Instruction, 11*(2), 42–48.

Ross, S. M., McCormick, D., and Krisak, N. (1986). Adapting the thematic context of mathematical problems to student interests: Individual versus group-based strategies. *Journal of Educational Research, 79,* 245–252.

Ross, S. M., Morrison, G. R., and O'Dell, J. K. (1988). Obtaining more out of less text in CBI: Effects of varied text density levels as a function of learner characteristics and control strategy. *Educational Communications and Technology Journal, 36*(3), 131–142.

Ross, S., Morrison, G., and O'Dell, J. (1990, February). *Uses and effects of learner control of context and instructional support in computer-based instruction.* Paper presented at the Annual Meeting of the Association of Educational Communications and Technology, Anaheim, CA.

Rossett, A. (1987). *Training needs assessment.* Englewood Cliffs, NJ: Educational Technology Publications.

Sales, G. (1989a). An introduction to videodiscs III: Videodisc hardware. *Computing Teacher, 16*(7), 50–51.

Sales, G. C. (1989b). Repurposing: Authoring tools for videodisc. *Computing Teacher, 16*(9), 12–14.

Salisbury, D. F., Richards, B. F., and Klein, J. D. (1985). Designing practice: A review of prescriptions and recommendations from instructional design theories. *Journal of Instructional Development, 8*(4), 9–19.

Sanders, J. (1988). *The effects of pairing students for work on a graphically-oriented CAI simulation.* Unpublished M. Ed. thesis. Edmonton, AB: University of Alberta.

Santiago, R. S., and Okey, J. R. (1990, February). *Sorting out learner control research: Implications for instructional design and development.* Paper presented as the Annual Conference of the Association for Educational Communications and Technology, Anaheim, CA.

Schallert, D. L. (1980). The role of illustrations in reading comprehension. In R. J. Spiro, B. C. Bruce, and W. F. Brewer (Eds.), *Theoretical issues in reading comprehension: Perspectives from cognitive psychology, linguistics, artificial intelligence, and education* (pp. 503–524). Hillsdale, NJ: Lawrence Erlbaum Associates.

Schloss, P. J., Wisniewski, L. A., and Cartwright, G. P. (1988). The differential effect of learner control and feedback in college students' performance on CAI modules. *Journal of Educational Computing Research, 4*(2), 141–149.

Schwartz, E. (1987). *The educators' handbook to interactive videodisc* (2nd ed.). Washington, DC: Association for Educational Communications and Technology.

Schwier, R. A. (1987). *Interactive video.* Englewood Cliffs, NJ: Educational Technology Publications.

Schwier, R. A. (1991). Current issues in interactive design. In G. J. Anglin (Ed.), *Instructional technology: Past, present, and future.* (pp. 195–201). Englewood, CO: Libraries Unlimited.

Schwier, R. A., and Misanchuk, E. R. (1988). The effect of interaction and perceived need for training on learning from computer-based instruction. *Canadian Journal of Educational Communication, 17*(3), 147–158.

Seiter, C. (1990). Erasable opticals. *Macworld, 7*(3), 152–159.

Seiter, C. (1991). Optical outlook. *Macworld, 8*(6), 139–145.

Semrau, P., and Boyer, A. (1991). Examining educational software from both an aesthetic and cultural perspective. *Journal of Hypermedia and Multimedia Studies, 2*(1), 25–29.

Senese, D. J. (1983). Innovations in educational technology. *Technological Horizons in Education, 11*(1), 98–104.

Shneiderman, B. (1987). *Designing the user interface: Strategies for effective human-computer interaction.* Reading, MA: Addison-Wesley Publishing.

Shuping, M. B. (1991). Assistive and adaptive instructional technologies. In G. J. Anglin (Ed.), *Instructional technology: Past, present, and future* (pp. 292–301). Denver, CO: Libraries Unlimited.

Siegel, E. (1980). *Video discs: The technology, the applications, and the future.* White Plains, NY: Knowledge Industry Publications, Inc.

Sinclair, I. R. (Ed.) (1989). Audio electronics reference book. Oxford: BSP Professional Books.

Smith, S. L., and Mosier, J. N. (1984). *Design guidelines for the user interface for computer-based information systems.* The MITRE Corporation, Bedford, MA 01730, Electronic Systems Division. (Available from the National Technical Information Service, Springfield VA.) Cited by Shneiderman, B. (1987). *Designing the user interface: Strategies for effective human-computer interaction.* Reading, MA: Addison-Wesley Publishing.

Spiegelman, M. (1987). Interior design for documents. *PC World, March,* 178–185.

Steinberg, E. R. (1977). Review of student control in computer-assisted instruction. *Journal of Computer-Based Instruction, 3*(3), 84–90.

Stewart, D. (1991). Interview: Jaron Lanier. *Omni, January,* 45–46, 113–117.

Taylor, T. D., and others. (1987). Interactive video authoring systems. *Optical Information Systems, 7*(4), 282–300.

Tennyson, R. D., Christensen, D. L., and Park, S. (1984). The Minnesota adaptive instructional system: An intelligent CBI system. *Journal of Computer-Based Instruction, 11*(1), 2–13.

Tennyson, R. D., and Park, O. (1984). Computer-based adaptive instructional systems: A review of empirically based models. *Machine-Mediated Learning, 1*(2), 129–153.

Thompson, J. G., and Jorgensen, S. (1989). How interactive is instructional technology? Alternative models for looking at interactions between learners and media. *Educational Technology, 29*(2), 24–26.

3M Corporation. (1981). *Premastering and post-production procedures for Scotch videodiscs.* St. Paul, MN: Optical Recording Project, 3M.

Tinker, M. A. (1955). Prolonged reading tasks in visual research. *Journal of Applied Psychology, 39*, 444–446.

Tinker, M. A. (1963). *Legibility of print.* Ames, IA: Iowa State University Press.

Tinker, M. A. (1965). *Bases for effective reading.* Minneapolis, MN: University of Minnesota Press.

Tinker, M. A., and Paterson, D. G. (1928). Influence of type form on speed of reading. *Journal of Applied Psychology, 12*, 359–368.

Tisdall, B. (1990). Buyer's guide: Optical disk [*sic*] drives. *PC User, 137* (July 18), 74ff.

Tovar, M. (1989). Effects of active vs. passive review strategies on recalling information from an interactive video instructional programme. *Canadian Journal of Educational Communication, 18*(3), 181–192.

Trollip, S. R., and Sales, G. (1986, January). *Readability of computer-generated fill-justified text.* Paper presented at the Annual Convention of the Association for Educational Communications and Technology, Las Vegas, NV.

Troutner, J. (1983). How to produce an interactive video program. *Electronic Learning, 2*(4), 70-75.

Tullis, T. S. (1983). The formatting of alphanumeric displays: A review and analysis. *Human Factors, 25*(6), 657–682.

Twyman, M. (1981). Typography without words. *Visible Language, 15*, 5–12.

Underwood, J. (1989). HyperCard and interactive video. *CALICO Journal, 6*(3), 7–20.

Walker, P. (1990). A lesson in leading. *Aldus Magazine, March/April*, 45–47.

Watkinson, J. (1988). The art of digital audio. London: Focal Press.

Webb, E. J., Campbell, D. T., Schwartz, R. D., and Sechrest, L. (1966). *Unobtrusive measures: Nonreacting research in the social sciences.* Chicago: Rand-McNally.

Webb, N. M. (1985). The role of gender in computer programming learning process. *Journal of Educational Computing Research, 1*(4), 441–457. Cited by Dalton, D. W. (1990). The effects of cooperative learning strategies on achievement and attitudes during interactive video. *Journal of Computer-Based Instruction, 17*(1), 8–16.

Weigand, I. (1985). Videodisc players: Pasts and futures. *Video Manager, 8*(3), 14–15.

Weiss, D. J., and Kingsbury, G. G. (1984). Application of computerized adaptive testing to educational problems. *Journal of Educational Measurement, 21*(4), 361–375.

West, S. (1987). Design for desktop publishing. In The Waite Group (J. Stockford, Ed.), *Desktop publishing bible* (pp. 53–72). Indianapolis, IN: Howard W. Sams.

White, J. V. (1983). *Mastering graphics.* New York: Bowker.

Whiting, J. (1989). An evaluation of some common CAL and CBT authoring styles. *Educational and Training Technology International, 26*(3), 186–200.

Wildman, T. M., and Burton, J. K. (1981). Integrating learning theory with instructional design. *Journal of Instructional Development, 4*(3), 5–14.

Wilson, B. G., and Welsh, J. R. (1986). Small knowledge-based systems in education and training: Something new under the sun. *Educational Technology, 26*(11), 7–13.

Winne, P. H. (1989). Theories of instruction and of intelligence for designing artificially intelligent tutoring systems. *Educational Psychologist, 24*(3), 229–259.

Zachrisson, B. (1965). *Studies in the legibility of printed text.* Stockholm: Almqvist and Wiskell. Cited by Isaacs, G. (1987). Text screen design for computer-assisted learning. *British Journal of Educational Technology, 1*(18), 41–51.

Zollman, D. (1991). What's m-ss-ng? *EBUG, 1*(1), 1–2.

Author Index

Subject Index

learning to use, 251
placement of, 254-255, 254-255
providing keyboard alternatives
for, 250
types of, 251-254

C

Capacitive touch screens, 124
Case study, and audit trails, 292
CD-I (Compact Disc Interactive), 89
CDs, compared with CD-ROMs, 103-105
CD-ROMs
additional readings list, 309-311
amount of data held by, 105
attributes shared with CDs, 104
carrying both CD-ROM and CD
tracks, 107
characteristics of, 105-107
compared with CDs, 103-105
cost-effectiveness of, 105
designing, 104-105
file-naming conventions for
Macintosh, 111-112
file-naming conventions for
MS-DOS, 111
potential for, 110
preparing files for, 110-113
providing random access to
information, 106-107
providing standardized format,
106
quick production time of, 105
slow response time a problem
with, 176-177
sturdy for storage, 106
tips on size and location of
files, 112-113
types of information held by, 106
Chapters on videodiscs, 69-70
Character generators, 54-55
Check cassette, 87
Check disc, 87
Checking and proofing, importance
of, 40
Chunking, 223, 234
Clarity, important in screen
design, 214-215
Cognitive theory, 156, 158
Color

caution advised in use of,
244-246
design specifications for, 167
lack of evidence about
effectiveness of, 244-245
motivating effect of, for
computer games, 244
not recommended, 242, 245
suggestions for increasing
attractiveness of, 245-246
Colored text, not recommended, 242
Columns, for printed material, 279
Command line interfaces, requiring
high memory load, 225
Compact Disc Interactive (CD-I), 89
Compact Disc-Read Only Memory
(CD-ROM). See CD-ROMs
Complementary instruction, 169-171
additional information segments,
170-171
context-sensitive, 171
help segments, 170
remedial segments, 170
Compressed digital video, 88-89
Compression technology, 88-89
Computer vs. Video, design
specifications for, 167
Conceptual geography, 75-78
constructing, 75
Katz's 54,000 Law, 77-78
purpose of, 75
summarized, 78
Confirmation, as a function of
interaction, 12, 14
Consistency, important in screen
design, 213-214
Constant angular velocity (CAV)
videodisc, 42, 46-47
Constant linear velocity (CLV)
videodisc, 42, 48
Constructivist assumptions in
instruction, 159-160
Content
determining placement of material
on the screen, 222-223
options for presenting, 179
segmentation of, aiding learners,
223, 234
Content characteristics, 148-150
calling for use of video, 150